GIA

GIA

Art and Creativity in a New Key

**A BOOK WRITTEN
AND ILLUSTRATED
BY**

JIM MILLER

ISBN: 1542982227
ISBN 13: 9781542982221
Library of Congress Control Number: 2017902038
CreateSpace Independent Publishing Platform
North Charleston, South Carolina

TABLE OF CONTENTS

INTRODUCTION

For a long time now, more than 30 years, I have been studying material from 'the other side'. This is material that has been channeled by a medium named Jane Roberts. Being an artist, I was interested in the fact that both Jane Roberts and her husband, Rob, did visual art. More to the point, there were frequent references in the channeled material to art and creativity, e.g. "Creativity has always been the species' closest connection with its own source, with the nature of its own being. Through creativity the species senses All That Is." The term, All That Is, is the expression used in the channeled material for the first principle, the prime mover.

This book began as an attempt to pass along things I had learned about art and creativity from my studies of the material channeled by Jane Roberts and transcribed by her husband, Rob. During the process of writing this book, I came to realize that there were other things I had learned about art and creativity that had not come from the channeled material. I have been doing visual art since the 1960s and have studied art on the undergraduate and graduate levels. I have also taught art and associated with others, who would be considered artists, for a good many years. As work on the book continued, I came to realize the need to pass along other material, material in addition to the channeled information.

The book now, as written, has many sources. There are times when several sources contribute to the same material. I cannot blame all of it on Seth, the discarnate entity whom Jane Roberts gave voice to in our physical world. The book as written is in a way similar to the things I do in visual art. I try to express clearly what I want to communicate, and at times simply throw paint. That too can be useful and fun at times. To make what I want to pass along more palatable, I weave it in with the warp and woof of a story. It is a fictional account of some people living in Pittsburgh.

In addition to the numerous physical persons appearing in this book, you will meet yet another discarnate entity named Rupert. Much of what Rupert passes along in this book comes from my years studying Seth. Rupert will be the mouthpiece for that teaching from 'the other side'. On the other hand, I would not want the reader to think that all of Rupert's utterances are from Seth. Some of his ideas come from my own experiences and studies.

Jim Miller

One

THE BEGINNING

It had been some months since Gianella Francesco moved into the third floor of the old factory building on an alley in Pittsburgh's Strip District. It was now 2001 with signs of spring starting to show. Soon it would be a year since Gia had moved from her native Italy to Pittsburgh. A cousin, Secula Venturi, had put her up at her place in the South Side of Pittsburgh when she first arrived. Since then, Secula had moved to the Strip District. Gianella had come along and now lived in the building next to Secula's house.

Many things had happened since Gia's arrival in her adopted land.

She had learned about a gift she had, that she had never suspected. She could go into a trance and speak for individuals long dead. She could bring information from the land of the dead into the land of the living. She had been speaking for – channeling – a personality named Rupert from the other side. Her cousin, Secula, was a published author and had written a book from material Gia had channeled from Rupert. The book would soon be published and Secula had promised Gia a good percentage of the royalty from the book.

In the meantime Gia had supported herself tending bar at Metropol, a local hotspot. She was only doing that part time now, one or two days a week. While tending bar she had met a young architect, Bob Stanislawski. She had told him about her interest in art and how she liked to draw buildings. He had hired her to do architectural renderings and work on models for projects he was doing. Business there was picking up. Bob had also expressed a romantic interest in her, but Gia was involved with George Willis, who lived on the first floor of the building she lived in. She had not at all encouraged the romantic overtures of Bob Stanislawski. She was glad she did the work for him in her own space on the third floor of the factory. She did not spend any more time at the office of his architectural firm that necessary. She did not dislike him. She just felt that his interest in her was an unnecessary complication in her life. She actually liked Bob, but encouraged him to pursue his romantic inclinations elsewhere.

On the second floor of the old factory that Gia lived and worked in lived an artist, Wally Bickerstaff. He did illustration work to generate income and paintings which he regularly exhibited. One of those paintings had featured Gia and her cousin, Secula, who lived next door. Wally was in love with Secula and spent most nights at her place. George Willis, on the first floor of the old factory, was involved with Gia and had even proposed to her. She felt that marriage was more than she was ready to deal with just now. She told George that she wanted to get her feet solidly on the ground in this new country before she took that step. She said that she was dealing with as many new experiences as she could handle at present. George seemed to take it in stride and told Gia he understood her situation. He too had a lot on his mind. He contracted his carpentry and building services out, and was setting up a workshop in a part of the first floor of the factory where he lived. He usually had more than enough work to keep him busy.

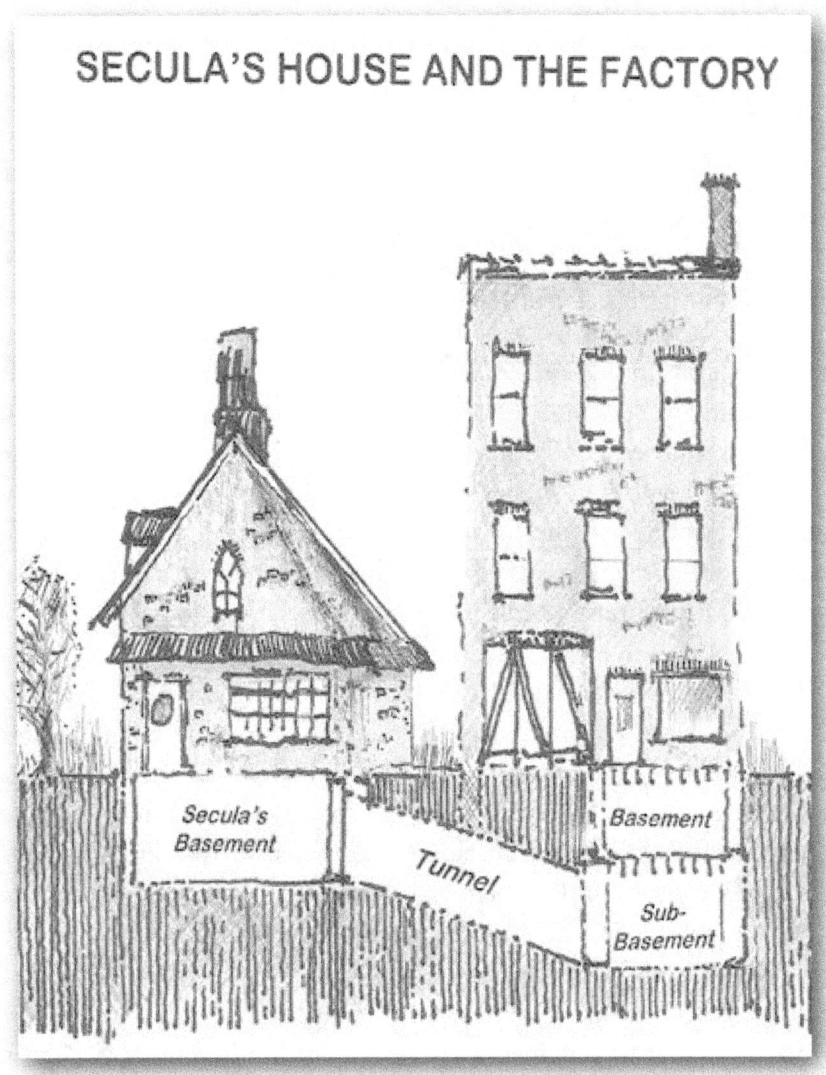

Secula's house, the tunnel, and the place where Gia lives.

George, Gia, and Wally comprised the total population of the old factory building at present. The three of them owned it in common as a limited liability corporation. They had been there less than a year, having moved in during the previous fall. All of them were friends of Secula Venturi, next door. They had become aware of the large, looming, and empty factory building next to her house. When they realized it was for sale, they took advantage of opportunities to go inside and explore the place. What they found inside appealed to them. Even the basement was interesting. What was more interesting was the subbasement below that. Exploration and investigation revealed that the present building had been built upon the foundation of an older factory from the early days of Pittsburgh's history. The ancient steam engine, boiler, tools, and much else remained at that subterranean level telling a story from an early chapter of the city's history. Wally Bickerstaff especially liked the subbasement; he had a penchant for things archaeological. Most interesting of all at that sub basement level was a tunnel. It connected the factory with Secula's house next door. When they first bought the factory, the tunnel had been cemented shut at Secula's basement. During a moving in party, it had been opened.

The factory was not paid for; it was mortgaged. In the year 2000 loans for real estate had been easy to come by. Most months the mortgage had been paid with little strain on the three owners. Gia usually paid off her share of the mortgage with what she made at Metropol. The tips she made there were the significant factor. To say that she was attractive might be something of an understatement. Most guys described her as, 'totally hot'. If there were any anxieties the owners felt regarding the factory, they had to do with code issues. The factory was zoned commercial. Through Ferguson, their lawyer, a variance had been applied for. That was pending. Ownership had been obtained with the help of Louis Venturi, Secula's uncle, once a part of the city government. Gia, Wally, and George had ridden on the magic carpet of connections at City Hall to their present ownership of the fine old factory building.

From uncle Louie's point of view, matters relating to the subbasement – especially the tunnel to Secula's house – could have caused problems. That was in the past now. If their application for a zoning variance came through, they would be in the clear. The tunnel was a feature they all appreciated greatly, especially Wally. Secula often had dinner at her house for the inhabitants of the factory. During the cold winter, Wally had been able to go over to Secula's house without even going outside. He spent a lot of time over there. Secula was not only his girlfriend; she was his artistic muse. He enjoyed drawing her when she was totally naked. Wally was careful not to allow his downstairs neighbor, George Willis, see the drawings of Secula naked. He could tell there was an element of jealousy there, which he did not understand. He did not want to feed the fires of that attraction. Wally had asked Secula about George's fascination with her. She had not told him a lot. What little she did say gave Wally the impression that she knew more than she wanted to talk about. She also gave Wally the impression that she did not want to pursue the thing with George, so Wally decided to leave well enough alone.

When Wally was not worrying about George's fascination with his girlfriend, Secula, he usually got along with George well. He had known George since shortly after he had moved to Pittsburgh. George was a native – from Pittsburgh. Wally was not a native; his origins had been out in the provinces. He had grown up in Jeanette, some 20 miles east of the Burgh. Lately Wally had been talking with George about a project, really a dream of his that he hoped to someday make into a reality. It was late in the afternoon and Wally heard Gia on the steps going to her place on the third floor of the old factory. He had an idea about the project he had been discussing with George, and it involved Gia. He then heard her footsteps on the floor above his head. He could tell she was headed for the bathroom. He waited until he heard the toilet flush upstairs. He heard Gia's footsteps again; he could tell she was out of the bathroom. He went to his refrigerator and grabbed a cold sixpack.

Gia, upstairs, was looking out her favorite window. It was the one in the front that looked in the direction of the river. She heard footsteps coming up the stairs to the third floor. She wasn't expecting anyone just then, but suspected it might be George. The knock she heard at the door didn't sound like George. It was more tentative, a bit more polite. She was glad she hadn't taken her skirt off; she wasn't sure what to expect. She had started to unbutton her blouse, and redid the top two buttons before opening the door. There was Wally Bickerstaff, sixpack in hand and smiling. "Hi Gia – do you have a minute for one of my brilliant ideas?" Gia started smiling too and looked down at the sixpack in Wally's hand. Wally could tell that it had caught her attention. "Well, Gia, maybe a couple minutes; I've been talking with George about something. Maybe he told you about it." Gia, still smiling and saying nothing, signaled to Wally to come in, then turned and walked toward the kitchen area. Wally followed her in, closed the door and couldn't help looking at her butt as he followed her. He had many times thought about painting her naked, but had never brought it up.

Wally put the sixpack on the table and peeled off a can. Gia did that too, then put the remaining four cans in her freezer. She finally said something: "I like beer really cold." Wally was smiling still as he gulped down some beer. It wasn't long before he said something. By that time Gia was sitting too. "Has George ever told you about my idea? I've been talking to him about the buildings close to us here." Gia seemed perplexed shaking her head no. "He never tells me about that." Wally was noticing that at times Gia's speech still recalled that she had come from Italy not too long ago. She could speak in correct English now, when she was being careful; right now she was just being Gia in her own place, being herself.

Wally continued: "Some time ago I was visiting an artist friend who lives in the old brewery on the South Side. It's been converted to living/ working space for artists. I couldn't help thinking that was a great idea, a place where artists could live, work, and exhibit. It's a kind of place where artists can learn from one another – develop a kind of community to keep life going." Gia couldn't help telling Wally that she thought that was a great idea, and Wally continued. "I've been looking at where we are right now. The building on the downtown side of us is bigger than this one, and it's empty. The building in back of us, the one that faces Penn Avenue, it's empty too." Gia was starting to catch on to what Wally was thinking. "You think about a place for artists – this building and the other two. Great idea, but money does not come from heaven." Wally got up and walked to the window, where he could look at the building next door he had referred to. "That's what started me thinking about you, Gia . . . you and your friend, Rupert."

Wally sat back down. Gia got up and went to the window where he had been standing. Looking at the building next door she said: "That one has four floors, more than this one. Rupert . . . Rupert has not spoken through me since Secula and I finished the book. Do you think Rupert can help with your project? Sometimes he is in my dreams and says things to me." Gia got up to get another beer: "You want one, Wally?" Wally was nodding his head as he began talking about Rupert. "Rupert helped all of us when we were getting this building last year. He also seemed willing to help with advice for individuals personally. He often knew things that no one else knew or had a way of knowing." Gia was sitting there deep in thought as she listened to Wally. It was quiet when Wally stopped talking. The refrigerator could be heard humming its monotone song. Gia got up to get some paper and a pen. Coming back to the table, she made notes "Rupert told us that it's a good idea to give projects to our dreams. He says it helps to write them out. We remember better that way. My project for tonight's dream is to get in touch with Rupert; maybe he hears me." "Thanks a lot, Gia. I just want you to know I really appreciate that. You seem quiet today – like you're thinking about something. I hope I didn't intrude at a bad time." "You didn't, Wally; I'm glad you're here."

It was quiet in the kitchen again. They both had a bit of beer. It was a while before Gia spoke again. "If I do see Rupert tonight, I'll ask him about your project. There is something else I want to ask you about. This week I get a letter from Italy; it's about my dad. He was in car accident right before I come to America. Things didn't go right after that. Now I hear it gets worse. My mother thinks he might die. I don't know if she just worries or. . ." There was quiet in the kitchen again. This started Wally thinking about his dad. "My dad died four years ago. I didn't even know he was sick. No one told me, then there was a call from my mother. It was like someone kicked me in the face. Why didn't they tell me? I wish I could have seen him. Are you thinking about going to see your dad?"

"I'm thinking about that Wally. I started to talk to people at work about taking time off." Wally was thoughtful for a bit before he spoke: "Have you told Secula yet?" "No, you know she's out of town right now for a book signing. She's back tomorrow; I'm telling her then. I'm going to ask her if she wants to go. I know she likes Italy. You ever been to Italy, Wally?" Wally did not pause for a second to respond this time: "No, I've always wanted to go there. I have no Italian ancestors that I know of, but I've wanted to go there since I was in grade school. It makes me think about some of the things Rupert told us – about our reincarnational selves. Sometimes – in my dreams – I'm in Italy; it's Italy past tense. I live in a big city like Rome and I'm a painter. People around me, friends I know, are worried about being tortured and burned by the Inquisition." Gia responded: "If Secula and I go . . . do you want to go too?" Wally's eyes lit up at that. "I don't even have a passport right now; do you need one?" Gia said: "I don't know; I'm still an Italian citizen and don't worry about that. Secula might know."

Wally and Gia sat there. They each had another beer. Wally talked about getting in touch with the owners of the two buildings he was interested in. Gia talked about Italy. She told Wally about Venice; it was not too far from the village where she had lived and grown up. "You would love Venice, Wally. It's such a great place to forget the troubles of your life and enjoy good things like art. Before I decided to come to America I wanted to live in Venice. If we go to Italy, we can rent a car, or borrow one from my family. We should visit Venice. Florence and Rome are further away, but we can go there too. I'm anxious for Secula to get home. I want to talk to her about Italy." Wally pondered the issue and responded: "Secula told me that her ancestors came from the same village you lived in before you came to America. I could tell she was interested in Italy by the way she talked about it. I'll bet she'd like to go. I'd like to go too, but I have to figure out a few things. I have to think about the illustration work I'm doing. I have to think about how much it will cost, and that project with the buildings is an issue too. That doesn't even include whether I'll need a passport." Once again Gia and Wally were quiet. Fire trucks blared their horns racing down Smallman Street, just a block away. The refrigerator continued it's very boring song in the background.

Gia got up to get another beer. Wally couldn't help watching her as she bent over getting one can of beer, then another. She didn't ask Wally if he wanted another one this time; she just grabbed one for him. When she sat down, Wally had another issue on his mind. "Gia, for some time I thought about doing a painting of you . . . I never mentioned it because I was afraid it might become an issue with Secula. How do you feel about it? Do you think Secula would get annoyed if I did a painting of you? Wally was glad to notice that Gia was smiling. Without answering him she got up to get some more things out of the refrigerator. It was late afternoon; she was hungry and got out cheese, salami, and crackers to munch on. Wally had been getting hungry too. When Gia sat down again, she started talking after slicing some salami: "a painting we can talk about Wally. I think we should get Secula in on the talk too."

"Have you thought about what I'd wear in the painting? You want me to wear clothes?" Wally brightened up considerably at that question. The thought of Gia not wearing anything was an extremely attractive proposition. He tried not to let on just how excited he was about that prospect. Wally finished the can of beer he had been drinking and opened the can Gia had just given him. He walked to the window again, depositing the empty can in the garbage. Staring at the empty building next door, he struggled to speak. Gia could tell he was struggling to get words out. She knew he was that way at times. "Why does God make us this way, Gia? Wanting so much that we can't have . . . shouldn't have . . . not wanting to hurt people we love. I don't want to make you uncomfortable. Sometimes I think I should just paint – say nothing – I know life is more than that though."

Gia, sensing his frustration, said: "Sit down Wally; life is good. Too many ignorant people try to tell us what life is all about – what we're all about – what God is all about. If they would shut their mouths, the world becomes a much happier place." Wally sat down and was smiling again. Gia continued: "In the village where I grow up, people tell me my mother was the prettiest girl in the village. After she has me and all my brothers and sisters, is not the same with her. As I grow up she tells me that I should be happy with what I am and do the best I can with what I am. She talks of beauty being a blessing. Rupert talks about our human body too. He says our first and most important artwork is our self, our own physical self. So I say okay to a painting. Like my mother, I won't always be young. Someday I may be happy to have a painting of what I am like now. We should talk to Secula about how we do the painting. She is my cousin. I love her and owe her much. Like you I do not want to hurt her or upset her."

Wally considered what Gia said and told her that the painting could be hers if she wanted it, but he would like to exhibit it. Gia started laughing. "I didn't realize I said the painting should belong to me. I be happy with a picture of it." Wally quickly turned to his right looking toward the door. Gia had not been aware of the footsteps on the stairs until she saw Wally looking in that direction. A scraping sound of footsteps was heard on the landing outside the door. Then there was a knock. Gia looked at Wally: "That sounds like George." Gia was on her feet quickly. She covered the 12 feet or so between the table and the door with no waste of time. As the door opened, Wally saw George standing there with a brown paper bag in his hands. George entered with a smile and a brown paper bag containing a bottle of wine. The wine bottle found a place on the table and George found a chair.

Gia

The sound of lead crystal glasses tinkling against one another was heard as Gia pulled three wineglasses out of the cupboard above the sink. "Metropol was getting rid of these; they find a home here. They don't match the other ones, so they throw them out." George laughed and pulled his Swiss Army knife out of his pocket. With the corkscrew he began uncorking the wine. With wineglasses on the table, Gia opened a big can of soup and lit a burner on the stove. As she put the soup into a saucepan, she could hear George pouring wine into the glasses. Gia decided there should be a salad too, and got busy on that project. George, noticing Gia chopping vegetables at the counter, went to the refrigerator and got out salad dressing. Then he got out bowls for soup and salad. Wally not being familiar with the location of things in Gia's kitchen just sat there sipping wine. It wasn't long before he began to fill George in on prior subjects of conversation. "I was telling Gia about my idea for the two buildings next to us, how I want to get them and convert them into artists' space. I asked her if she could talk to Rupert about them. Maybe Rupert knows something we don't. He might be able to tell us if it is a good idea or not. I'm always surprised how Rupert comes through with stuff that none of us has any way of knowing."

George sat down at table and cut off some cheese. Sipping wine he reacted to what Wally was saying. "Being in the contracting business, I realize these are not small issues you're thinking about. We still have bunches of stuff to do before we get this building sorted out. But, I like the idea. Being around creative people makes me feel good. Even though I'm not an artist myself, I do think it's a great idea. I just can't see how it can happen right now." Wally pondered the issue as he sliced some salami. After asking Gia if she needed any help, he began talking again: "that's why I wanted Gia to talk to Rupert. It's a monumental project, and I thought I'd need help and advice on this one."

Things were quiet in the kitchen again. Salad appeared on the table and Gia sat down with Wally and George. Over salad and other munchies,

Wally continued to fill George in. "Maybe Gia told you about her dad being sick . . . maybe worse than sick. She's thinking it might be her last time to see him. She's gonna ask Secula if she wants to go to Italy with her. I'm thinkin' about going too. George, you want to go too?" George exclaimed: "Holy shit - that sounds like beaucoup bucks. Don't get me wrong. I'd like to go. I studied ancient history in college, even though I didn't finish. I'm still very much interested in the Roman Empire . . . the Republic too. There's just so much going on right here in Pittsburgh now. I'm up to my neck with jobs I've agreed to do. This building too - I got more stuff right now than I want to think about." Gia got up to pour soup. "Who all wants soup? Chicken gumbo with egg drop is on. It's an experiment; I put Oriental spices in too." George refilled wineglasses as Gia poured soup.

There was another quiet period as the three in the kitchen had what resembled a meal. Wally was noticing that the sun was going down and was thinking he didn't want to overstay his welcome. He couldn't help commenting that Gia's experimental soup was especially good. He thought about things he wanted to do in his apartment that evening. An awful lot of work still had to be done there to make it livable. He had been avoiding this by spending a lot of time over at Secula's house. Gia's thoughts were on Rupert, hoping he would show up in her dreams that night. But there was always the possibility he might channel through her. That always required someone to write down the things she said for Rupert. When she returned from one of her Rupert trances, she rarely recalled anything that Rupert had said through her. A tape recorder could help with that too, and she had recently bought one. She was having an impulse to get out candles and put some on the table, but she didn't have any on her floor. "Wally, do you have any candles downstairs?" This caught Wally quite by surprise, as he was thinking he should be polite and leave. "By chance, I picked up a bunch of candles at a flea market last week. I really didn't need them, but it seemed like such a good idea at the time." This started George laughing. Wally got up and headed downstairs to retrieve some candles.

As Wally fumbled around in his stash of unnecessary accouterments, upstairs George had located his own stash in a plastic bag in his vest pocket. Wally ambled up the stairs carrying five candles, which he planned to give to Gia as a gift. Among them were two religious candles with markings that he suspected were Catholic. He stood outside the door of Gia's apartment a while. He was trying to decide if he should knock or not. His hand made the decision for him. His left hand reached out and grabbed the doorknob and turned it. Entering the kitchen he detected an odor he hadn't encountered for more than a month. He knew exactly what it was. As he put the candles on the kitchen table and explained to Gia that it was a gift, he noticed George's still smoking pipe in an ashtray there.

Wally also noticed something else that had not been on the table when he left. Gia's tape recorder was there. A professional looking Sony with two microphones attached was in front of her. He couldn't help wondering if Gia was thinking about channeling. Secula had always been present when that happened, but she wasn't here tonight. By this time George was firing up his pipe again. Wally watched him take a heavy toke, then another. Momentarily Wally hesitated as George handed him the pipe. He was thinking about the drywall he wanted to hang downstairs. Wally's left hand reached out and took the pipe as Gia took three candles, lit them and placed them about the room. After several tokes on the pipe, Wally sat quietly looking about the room. His strong resolve about hanging drywall was being replaced by thoughts of Italy – especially Venice. It would be a great opportunity to paint, maybe even paint Gia and Secula – maybe naked. He would have to take some art supplies with him, but probably he could buy things he didn't have once he got there. There was money from his dad's estate settlement still in his bank account. He had been thinking that he must save that. Now it all looked very different. What was money for anyway? Wally's thoughts were interrupted by Gia's voice.

"George, we were talking about going to Italy. Do you know if an American needs a passport to go there?" George passed his pipe to Gia before answering. He seemed to think quite a while, then slowly formulated his thoughts into words. "Aunt Helen . . . Aunt Helen went to Italy a couple years ago. For sure you need a passport; I remember that. You guys should go down to the Federal Building. You too Gia – if you're going to become an American citizen, you should go down there too and find out the lowdown on that stuff. I don't want to say a whole lot, because I never did it myself. I just know you need a passport." Gia sat there looking very thoughtful and watching the candle she had placed on the table. The room lights were not on. Only the three candles provided what light there was in the kitchen. It was almost completely dark out now. Gia began looking at the tape recorder to her left. She pushed it over toward George. "Maybe I channel tonight; I don't know for sure. It feels like Rupert is around tonight. I haven't felt that for a while. If I channel, George, push that button right there." Gia was pointing to the record button on her machine. "I think of something else too. Secula's dad, Dom, maybe he wants to go to Italy with us. We should ask him. Maybe he be offended if we don't ask him. His father came to America from Italy. I know Italy interests him and I don't think he ever goes there."

George and Wally nodded assent. Wally was pondering the possibility of Dom coming along when he noticed Gia spacing out. She was looking very much like she did before she started to channel. Her head was nodding. Her left hand pointed to the record button on the tape recorder. George put his finger on it in case she started to talk for Rupert. *It has been some time.* Wally was not sure if Gia was channeling or not. He did notice that George pushed the record button. Again Gia spoke: *It has been some time since I have been with you.* Wally was noticing Gia's eyes darken. Her face took on a harder, more angular aspect as she continued, still looking at the candle on the table. *I have missed your company these past months. It is good to be back in Pittsburgh again. I realize there are issues you are dealing with , , , issues that you are looking for advice concerning. I can tell these things when you have a strong emotional tendency in a certain direction. Both Gia and Wally are thinking about a trip to Italy. Wally is also thinking about what might be an art colony. The idea and the practice of art may be involved with both the buildings here and the trip to Italy. I realize Secula may be involved in both of these issues. I will say more about them when she returns. Please play the recording you're making when she is among you again. That should be soon. I do not want George to feel left out here. To George my greetings and a reminder: Remember to keep up with the self hypnosis exercises that I suggested to you. They will help you to overcome some of the difficulties you have been facing.*

Gia thinks much about her father lately. They are spiritually connected and are part of the same entity. They have shared lives together in many times and places. From where I am, the probabilities suggest that Gia's father may not be with you long. However, the nature of probabilities are such that it is not wise to make an absolute prediction regarding matters suggested. This is for the reason that human free will is always involved. However, Gia's father at present considers that the useful time of his life has come to an end and is ready to move on. But remember, all this can change; people do reassess things and change direction. At the present though, Gia's trip to Italy might be best for her, her family too. Wally's art could benefit from the trip. Gia too could think of this. The Italian scenery and architecture could be an inspiration. The wealth of works of art there could have a great educational benefit – all this without even mentioning the people there who may contribute to developing one's abilities as an artist.

The city of Venice can be an especially helpful place for those with interests in the arts. In one of my lives I did live there, though it was not exactly as it is now. The multitude of small islands that have been joined together to form the present city were mostly separate then. I was a merchant dealing in glassware in that life. If time permits, other Italian cities could benefit your understanding and practice of the arts. Although most think of the large cities like Florence and Rome, smaller Italian settlements might be visited to afford plentiful and beautiful scenery for painting and sketching. The thought of it all is almost enough to make me want to be physical again. I say almost because I have no real plans to return to physical life. I could do that if it were my choice, but I have spent my time where you are now. I have learned the things I had to learn. Even though I do at times yearn for the kind of life you now have, the present mobility of consciousness I enjoy and my associates here will keep me where I am.

I now speak to the issue that is very much on Wally's mind: that is the project to develop the adjacent buildings into artists' space. I imagine a kind of place or situation where a number of creative types might be able to live, work at their respective arts and crafts, and exhibit the work of their hands. The real benefit that might be enjoyed by those taking part would be what I might call cultural facilitation. I mean by this a kind of fortunate exchange of insights into art. You realize that no one person is able to explore the whole of any one art, let alone the breadth of insights and experiences that can be found in the whole of the field of endeavor referred to as the arts. We might make a rough or crude comparison by saying that no one person is able to explore the whole of your world. When those individuals come together who have explored various parts of your Earth, they are able to share with one another their experiences and understandings of those parts they have explored. A more or less global understanding comes about, can come about, among those taking part in such an exchange. It is this kind of exchange and global understanding that a project such as Wally imagines can bring about. For this reason, you might think about the type of persons who would profit from and contribute to your project. Solitary, hermit-like types may not contribute much to the exchange of experience and thought that cultural facilitation enables.

I now address the issue of funding for your brave adventure. I suggest that you form a nonprofit corporation to own and manage this enterprise. People with the local Cultural Trust will be able to advise you on specifics. Once you have a nonprofit corporation formed, you might apply for Federal tax-exempt status. That can help you in several ways. One big plus here is that donors who might help to fund your project can deduct such gifts from their taxes. One item here that is not to be forgotten relates to your articles of incorporation for your nonprofit. If you hope to get tax exempt status, you must have a disbursement clause in your articles. Any lawyer you deal with should advise you on this issue.

A lawyer who is not aware of this issue should not be dealt with. Now, as to where money is to come from . . . I have two individuals to suggest. One of them you met last year when you were purchasing your building. That was Donnie Diangelo's father. He is quite well off and nearly retired. He has been thinking to use some of his money for a good purpose. In addition, he is a lawyer; that too could be helpful. Work to convince him that yours is a worthy project. Also, I think of Secula in this regard. Royalty from her latest book that she wrote for me will be coming soon. Gia too will be in receipt of some of that since she did the channeling.

I think I have said enough tonight. I leave you with fond regards and best wishes for your projects and adventures. But on second thought, maybe big brother should say a few words. When I do this I have concerns that you may think I'm meddling in your lives. On the other hand, there are times when I feel I have a responsibility to pass on a bit of good advice. This is on a subject that I did bring up to you last year. As you know, one of my favorite expressions is: "Repetitio est mater studiorum." I do repeat things at times when I feel there is a need. You will recall that means repetition is the mother of studies.

George and Wally looked at one another; they were both wondering what this might be about. Then they looked down at the wineglasses on the table and the stuff in the ashtray. Gia, speaking and observing for Rupert, was taking this in. *Yes, that is my concern. I did, in the past, speak to you about the way temporary coping strategies can become permanent habits. Though I don't expect you to be teetotalers and practice total abstinence with regard to mind altering substances, I want to remind you that temporary expedients can become permanent arrangements. I should note that the marijuana you smoke is a natural substance. You could do a lot worse in your choice of recreational drugs. Stick with the natural things and you should be better off. I have no intention of making this a long harangue. I only feel that a bit of good advice here and there can be helpful in keeping you on the right side of health and happiness. During the course of many lives on your good Earth, I have seen the sad results when things get out of hand. Also, I do not want to pretend that*

I have never myself in those lives gone astray in the use of alcohol and what you would consider drugs. One life in particular I recall in what was a place you now call Turkey. I did much damage to myself and to those around me. It was damage that could have been avoided had I been more moderate. With that thought I'll leave you, and please recall to play the tape you're making for Secula. I expect she will be with you tomorrow.

Gia's eyes closed and her hands could be seen feeling the surface of the table they sat at. At first George and Wally just looked at one another; their attention then went to Gia. Her eyes were opening again. She breathed what might have been a sigh of relief. Then she spoke as herself: "Don't know what Rupert talks about. I remember some pictures. One picture shows a place that might be Turkey. Another shows Rupert talking with people who seem to advise him. Maybe they tell him things to tell us. In another picture I see the buildings next to us here. Then I see my father; he does not look well. It makes me want to go to Italy to see him." Wally spoke up. "I hope we can talk Secula into going." George reached out and turned off the recorder. Then he put it on rewind. George began speaking: "you want to hear this Gia; Rupert said things about your father . . . and about Italy. He thinks you should go. Rupert thinks Venice is a good place." Gia started to smile. Italy was on her mind. Wally politely excused himself and was on his way downstairs. George talked with Gia as she put things away. It wasn't long until they heard the sound of Wally's portable drill downstairs. He was hanging drywall.

Two

Secula

It was the next morning. Gia was in the kitchen putting together what she could find for breakfast for herself and George, who had spent the night. Both of them wanted to listen to the tape of the channeling session of the night before, when Gia had channeled Rupert. Gia's recording machine was now on the counter. On it Gia was speaking for Rupert. For the most part, it was material she was hearing for the first time. She was trying to juggle the breakfast cooking with listening to the tape. George was putting silverware and paper napkins on the table as he listened too. Gia noticed that the fried potatoes had been on the burner too long already. She really wanted to sit down and listen to the tape when she was not worrying about burning the potatoes, eggs, and bacon. She asked George to pour some orange juice as the tape recorder stopped suddenly. It had come to the end of the first side and the automatic-off kicked in.

Although Rupert's discourse had been interesting, Gia was glad for the silence. She could pay attention to getting breakfast on the table and hear the tape later. George was quiet – not in a chattering mood that morning. City sounds from a distance now and then made their way into the kitchen. All of a sudden Gia and George looked at one another as they heard

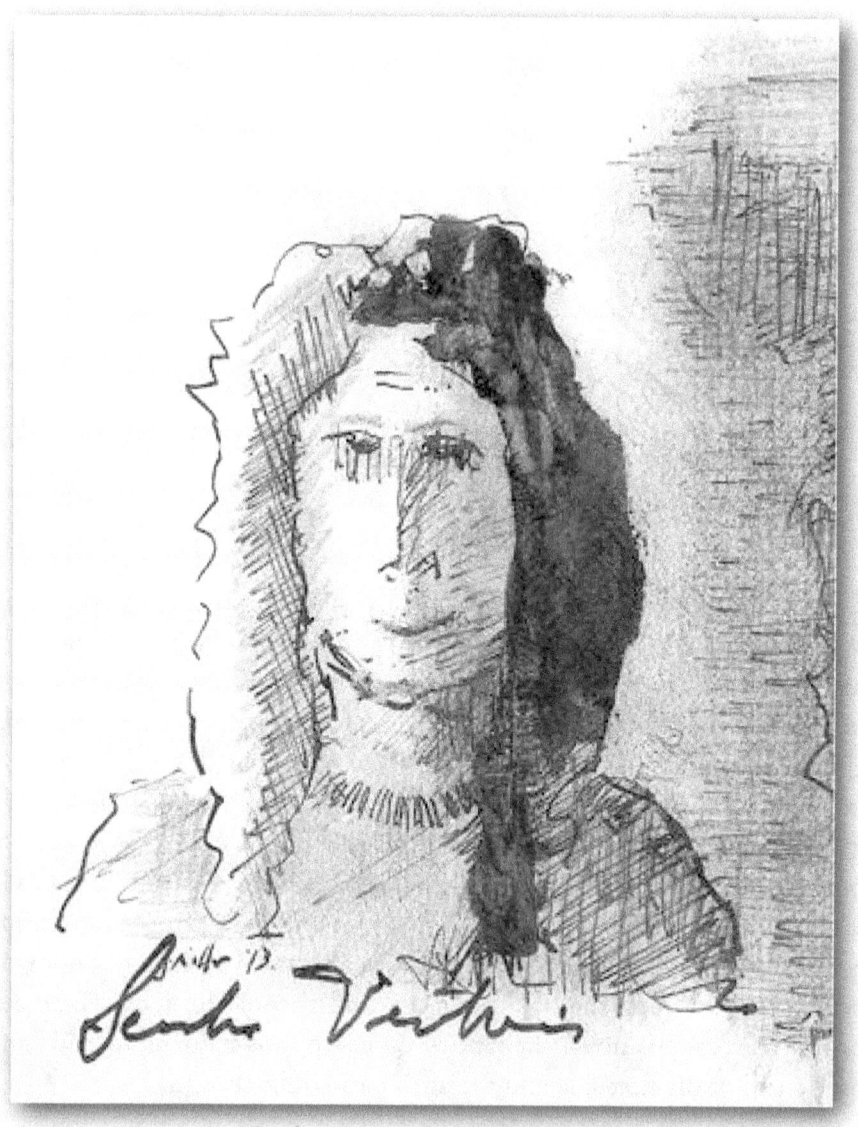

Secula Venturi, who lives next door.

sounds coming from downstairs, from Wally's place. It sounded like Secula had just come in the door downstairs. They knew Secula would be coming back today, but weren't expecting her so early. Downstairs Wally had not been expecting her so early either.

Wally's cell phone had awakened him just about 7:30, about 20 minutes ago now. It was Secula. She had gotten in during the night and wanted to come over. Wally invited her for breakfast. He was rummaging through his refrigerator when Secula came in without knocking; he had unlocked the door. Wally was coming to the gradual realization that inviting Secula for breakfast had been a bad idea. The nursery rhyme Old Mother Hubbard was going through his head when his cell phone rang for the second time that morning. He recognized George's voice, who told him he was upstairs. "Did I hear Secula come in?" Wally hesitated, unsure of what to say next, when he heard George's voice again: "Do you two want to come up for breakfast?" Wally saw an instant solution as to how he was going to get breakfast for Secula. ". . . absolutely, we'll be right up." Upstairs, George was surprised that Wally had responded so quickly, then just hung up.

Downstairs Wally was pondering how to explain things to Secula when she spoke up. "Was that Gia?" Wally just said: "not exactly, but we are invited for breakfast." As Secula and Wally made their way up the stairs, George was explaining to Gia that he had invited them for breakfast. He immediately sensed that Gia was not prepared for breakfast guests and offered to cook for the guests. Gia disappeared to get some clothes on and George opened the door. Amidst a barrage of crossfire chatter, Wally and Secula entered Gia's world and immediately smelled good things cooking. Secula was noticing the onions and garlic that had been cooked with the potatoes when Gia walked back into the kitchen area with clothes on. More chatter ensued, and George insisted that Gia sit down and eat with Wally and Secula.

At the stove George was working on getting more potatoes, bacon, and eggs in edible condition when he recalled Wally and Secula should have some orange juice. He made his way to the refrigerator as he listened to Wally tell Secula that Gia had channeled Rupert last night. George was a bit concerned that Gia had channeled in Secula's absence as was Gia. Both were relieved to see Secula's reaction. "I'm so glad that Rupert manages to have a life of his own without me. Being a ghostwriter for a ghost was something approaching a frightening experience." There was laughter in the kitchen as George chopped up another potato. He was trying to slice it very thin when he heard Wally ask Secula if she wanted to hear the Rupert tape. "Of course, I'd love to hear it." As George put sliced potatoes into the sizzling skillet, he could hear the tape recorder rewind.

Gia was enjoying scrambled eggs and bacon as she listened to her own voice channel a little man from a non-physical world. It was much nicer listening to him this time. She was not preoccupied with burning the potatoes. Then Rupert started talking about her father. She started to experience much emotional pain as she realized that her father may soon be making a journey to the nonphysical world Rupert lived in. The thought of living in a world that her father no longer inhabited especially distressed her. Somewhere deep inside her a deep resolve was forming to go to Italy – and soon. Although she would like her friends with her, she was thinking that she would go even if Wally and Secula didn't come along. George was another issue. Although she wished he would come, his absence would give her a certain freedom that she looked forward to.

George was always more than nice to Gia. He was very conscious of the fact that the guys around her were usually more than willing to make total fools of themselves to ingratiate themselves with her. Other then the element of the competition, George did really like her. He realized that any normal guy would. In addition to her alluring physical characteristics, she was actually a nice person. He knew from experience that many women with her level of appeal were much less than nice people. They took advantage of their charms to get what they wanted without much care or concern about whom they hurt. Gia was not that way.

Gia did appreciate George's solicitous and fawning care for her, but she did have a dimension that did not fit neatly into his somewhat conventional, middle-class agenda. She was none too anxious to get into a marriage where she would be little more than an adjunct to a man's life projects. Her time in America – short as it was – had taught her that she had projects of her own that were important for her to work on. The small world she had lived in during her life in Italy had not allowed her to see how she might develop as a woman on her own.

Secula had been talking about events that had transpired during her book signing tour, but had become quiet. The tape had rewound and Gia was starting up the recording of last night's session when she had channeled Rupert. As Gia, Secula, and Wally sat quietly listening to Gia channel Rupert, George fussed at the stove with breakfast. It wasn't long before food was on the table. Secula's habits as a writer were evident even as she ate. As they all listened to Rupert's discourse during breakfast, Secula quietly made notes on her paper napkin. Parts of Rupert's commentary caught her attention. They were things she didn't want to allow to slip into oblivion. Once breakfast and the Rupert recording were finished, Secula expressed her great interest in going to Italy. There was some banter about passports, then Secula brought up another item from the book tour she had just come back from. "One of the places I stopped on my tour was Johnstown, in southern Cambria County. I met several people there who filled me in on a haunted house in Cambria County. One of those people lived in the place. I was invited to come up there this weekend. The house is very big and I was told I could bring up to five people along. They were interested in the things I said about Rupert. They thought Rupert might be able to give some advice about the ghost, or ghosts, who haunt the place. I told them I couldn't guarantee anything, but the place fascinated me from what I heard. Do any of you guys want to come up this weekend? It's not in Johnstown, but a bit north of that."

This was followed by silence as everyone just sat there looking at one another. George was the first to speak up. "I may not be able to do the thing to Italy right now, but a weekend away really sounds good. I'd be able to get my head out of some of the stuff that's giving me grief right now." For

Wally, the idea of George and Secula traveling together alone didn't sound good to him. Gia hadn't said anything yet, so he didn't know if she would be along. Although Wally wasn't wild about the trip, he was even less keen on the idea of George and Secula traveling together. It wasn't long before he came out with: "yeah, why not?" At that point, attention seemed to shift to Gia. Secula, noticing that Gia was trying to make her mind up about the weekend, spoke up: "it might be a good chance for us to talk about the trip to Italy. We could have strategy sessions and talk about things we should take along and preparations we should take care of before we go." Then followed another period of silence. It seemed that some amount of mental telepathy was taking place during this silent interval. It was as though they were talking to one another without words in some subvocal manner.

Gia seemed to be playing a mental game of chess. She did want to go away for the weekend, but there were things she wanted to get done at home. On the good side, she was not scheduled to work at the bar this weekend. Then another thought came bumping into her mind. She was recalling what Rupert had said about Donnie Diangelo's father. He had a lot of money that he wanted to do something useful with. He might help finance the nonprofit artists' space venture. In addition, he was an attorney. That could prove useful in setting up a nonprofit corporation and buying the two adjacent buildings. Just then another thought came bouncing into Gia's mind. Did she really want to go to a place where there was a ghost? She recalled the ghost who had been in Secula's garage, Peter. Peter was not dangerous or harmful, but a ghost of any kind is scary. With Rupert's help they managed to get Peter out of Secula's garage and help him get on with his nonphysical life elsewhere. The thought of helping someone – even a nonphysical someone – had an appeal for Gia. It made her feel like her life had some kind of meaning. These and other thoughts were going back and forth in her mind when she just started talking and broke the silence.

"Let's invite Donnie Diangelo to come with us to the haunted house. He's had us up to his dad's island on the River twice last year; that was fun. We can talk to him about his dad, about what Rupert tells us about his dad. From what Secula says, that's not too many people." Eyes opened up. It was obvious that Gia was interested in the trip, and a whole new prospect opened up with the mention of Donnie Diangelo. It was Wally's project – the idea of the artist space thing. Wally especially liked the idea and spoke up. "George, you know Donnie better than any of us. Do you want to invite him up for the weekend?" George sat there pondering the matter. "Secula, you okay with this? You are the one who got the invite. Are you okay with Donnie coming?" Secula obviously thought it was a good idea. "Okay with it? Yeah, thanks to Gia for thinking of it. It's a first-class good idea." Wally was sitting there with very conflicted thoughts. He was happy that Donnie would be there. It could help get his project off the ground, and he liked Donnie. On the other side was Secula's enthusiasm about having Donnie along. Tinges of jealousy were erupting again. Did Secula have ulterior motives for inviting Donnie? It was quiet again and Wally broke the silence.

"Secula, you said you could bring five people. Does that mean five people beside yourself? I'm thinking about your sister, Susan. She's good friends with Donnie. She might be offended if we don't ask her." Another period of silence followed. Secula rummage through her purse. Out came her cell phone and some slips of paper. Gia got up to clear the table as Secula dialed a number. George went over to the sink to help with dishes; he could hear Secula. "Is it too late to call? I can call back later." Another period of quiet followed before Secula spoke again. "You said I could bring five people. Is that five beside myself?" Indistinct conversation followed. Before Secula said so long, George heard her say: "we will bring some food. Is there anything special we can bring?" George became distracted as Gia brought over more dishes. Secula said so long. Wally inquired what was happening.

"I can even bring more people than Susan if I want. I think that is enough though. Six people is a bunch. Are we all going in one car? My

BMW is available if we want to go in one car." Gia had been listening and provided a bit of good advice: "before we think about six people in one car, maybe we should ask Donnie and Susan if they want to go." There were some snickers and laughter.

It was late Friday afternoon. The rendezvous place was the factory building where Gia, Wally, and George lived. As it turned out, Susan and Donnie were going too. Susan was bringing her yellow VW beetle and her sister Secula her silver BMW. It was a case of two Italian girls with two German cars. The cars were parked in the alley in front of the old factory. Last-minute packing and decisions about what to bring were going on. Secula was standing in the alley beside her car and talking on her cell phone. She was in touch with the people in Cambria County at the house they were headed for. "We're about ready to leave here. Is there anything you want us to bring along?" George could overhear her talking as he stuffed a bottle of tequila into the trunk of her BMW. He could hear Secula respond on the phone: "okay, we'll stop in the Strip and get some fresh vegetables to bring along. The trip may take us a couple of hours, but hopefully we'll get there before nine."

The little caravan of two German cars stopped in the Strip District on Smallman Street to pick up vegetables, fresh bread, sausage, and some exotic types of tea. Once on the road again, the two cars were up over Polish Hill and headed out of the city. Just before the Squirrel Hill tunnel, traffic was nearly at a standstill. It being Friday, evening traffic was very heavy. In the front seat of Secula's car, Gia passed along some interesting information. "Last night Rupert shows up in a dream. He knows about the . . . should I say ghost?" Wally in the backseat turned around and saw Susan's car behind them. Susan, Donnie, and George were back there. Wally was wishing they were in Secula's car to hear this.

Gia continued: "Rupert is aware of that spirit or ghost in the house we go to. It is another case of a person who hasn't been convinced that they are dead. She continues to haunt a house she used to live in. It is a woman who died having her seventh child. Always she wanted to be an artist. Her husband kept her pregnant all the time, and she was so busy with kids that she rarely had time to do the art she wanted to do. She believes her life is not complete there. She has not done the art she wanted to do. The people, the houses, and the wooded hillsides of the country she lived in always made her want to paint them. She haunts that place because she believes she hasn't finished her work there and doesn't believe she is dead."

By the time Gia finished talking about the things Rupert told her in the dream, they were emerging from the east end of the Squirrel Hill Tunnel. Wally was talking about making contact with this spiritual presence, the ghost. He had thoughts about encouraging her to listen to her teachers so she could move on to another life. He was suggesting that in that other life she may be able to do the painting she had wanted to do. As an artist, he realized how important it is for a person to create in concrete physical materials the things one dreams of.

Secula, at the wheel, had a need to comment: "we don't know if any teachers came to this woman's spirit yet. Also, we could talk to her about what Rupert said about our first and most important artwork being our own physical presence – our physical self. While I'm thinking about that, I recall that she had six children. We could talk to her and explain that those children are a form of artwork." Gia was sitting there quietly taking all this in. "This makes me think of what Rupert says about families of consciousness, or psychic families. One of them is the Borledim. For them the family, their children, are the artwork. Their creative work goes mostly into raising good, healthy kids. But maybe this lady is part of another of those psychic families, the one that is composed mostly of artists of one kind or another – the Sumari."

There was a sudden jerking of the wheel as Secula realized someone was cutting her off. A screeching of tires followed. Wally quickly looked behind. Susan had been aware enough to hit the brakes before she almost bashed into Secula's car. Some swearing followed directed at the fellow in the blue Toyota that had nearly caused a very unpleasant disruption of their trip. By this time the journey was nearly at Monroeville and they were coming on to Route 22 East. Traffic had thinned out a bit. Wally was getting bored and was making faces at the people in Susan's car behind them. George was back there giving him the finger; Wally turned around, ignoring George. He started to talk to Secula: "Secula, I know you are the only one who can see Rupert, but has he been talking to you so you can see him since you finished that book for him?" Secula was being more careful with her driving since the incident with the blue Toyota. She was in no hurry to answer. Gia seemed interested in this too. She turned to her left, waiting for an answer from Secula. They were almost at the Route 66 turn off for Delmont. Once past that intersection, Secula seemed more at ease and began to talk. "Only in my dreams have I seen Rupert since last year when we finished the book. It's always a surprise when I see him. I mean, it's just like seeing you and Gia here, but he always wears this long overcoat, and he's so short." Wally was interested: "I remember Rupert helped us with Peter, the ghost in your garage. I'm thinking maybe he'll show up to help with this ghostly artist at the haunted house." Secula thought a bit, then commented: "I really hope he does. We sure aren't professional ghostbusters. If he doesn't appear so I can talk with him, we will have to rely on Gia to channel him. There is no guarantee that any of that will happen. We'll feel pretty stupid if we can't get in touch with him somehow."

They were about a mile out of the New Alexandria when Wally brought up the subject of the painting he had talked to Gia about. He was getting bored again and wanted to break things up a bit. "Secula, I was talking to Gia about something that I hope won't be a sensitive subject." This somewhat took Secula by surprise. "Gee, Wally, you bring that up like you're going to tell me you got her pregnant." Both Gia and Wally started laughing. Gia especially found it amusing. Wally laughed with a kind of nervous laughter that indicated he was a bit uncomfortable with the subject. "No,

Secula, that's not the issue. I got to talking with Gia about doing a painting of her. I've been thinking about that for a while and finally got to talking about it. The reason I'm bringing it up is . . . I'm wondering if it will bother you if I do that."

Again, Secula was in no hurry to answer. This time too, Gia was curious what her cousin's response might be. Secula was paying attention to traffic as an impressively-large 18 wheeler was passing her. With that hulking piece of machinery on its way down the road, it was obvious Secula was thinking about Wally's question. She did finally get out an answer: "In a way I wish you wouldn't even ask me. I don't like you to feel that you – either of you – have to ask my permission to do things." At that point she was interrupted by Wally. It was obvious that Gia was wanting to say something too, but it was Wally who spoke. "Secula, this isn't a matter of asking your permission. Both Gia and I are very fond of you and don't want to be doing anything that might make you unhappy. If doing the painting would cause you any grief, we just wouldn't do it." Gia expressed concurrence with what Wally had said. Secula started talking again: "Both of you are big, grown-up people. I think I know both of you well enough and trust you so that I won't be thinking you are doing sleazy stuff behind my back."

Secula's response seemed to calm Wally's concerns. They were quiet as they paid attention to the vista of Chestnut Ridge spread out before them. Wally commented: "That's the last of the ridges as you go westward toward Pittsburgh. After we go over that, we'll go over Laurel Ridge; it's a bit higher." Gia seemed curious about the ridges, so Wally continued. "The biggest of the ridges is the Allegheny itself. It's the top of the Allegheny Front, the eastward face of the Allegheny Plateau. We'll get close to that, but from what Secula told me, were not going that far."

It was obvious that their journey was taking them to some higher ground. Pittsburgh in elevation was somewhere around 700 feet above sea level. Going over Laurel Ridge, a sign there had told them they were over 2200 feet. Gia had never seen this territory before, except from the airplane she had come from Italy on. It looked very different from this point of view; she was fascinated by all this and started talking. "The hills make me think of Italy. I don't call them mountains. In Italy where I live we are not so far from the Alps. We have some real mountains there. I've been wondering if you two are still thinking about going to Italy with me." Wally had been looking out the back window watching Susan's yellow Volkswagen. He was concerned whether it would be able to keep up with them on some of the hills they had been climbing. He noticed that Secula had been watching it in her mirror too. Gia's question about Italy got his mind off of Susan's VW.

Wally first started talking about Susan's car commenting that, so far, it had been able to keep up with the BMW they were in. He then started to talk and think about Italy. "When dad died I inherited some money. I had been thinking I should save it for something special. Not long ago I realized that the trip to Italy would be about as special as an event could be, and I should spend some money on that trip." He could tell that made Gia happy and continued. "I've never been out of this country I was born in. I often thought that an important part of my education has been sadly neglected – I mean by not traveling." Secula, still keeping Susan's car in her mirror's view, added: "that's so true Wally. I've learned things by going places that I'd never be able to learn just staying home. The people you meet, the different attitudes you find in other cultures are things that no book or lecture can teach you. It's especially true for you as an artist, Wally."

Secula explained she was looking for a turnoff. "We're going to get off of Route 22 up here, and I want to pay attention to what I'm doing. The road should take us through the county seat. It won't be too far from there to where we're going." Gia caught the expression, county seat, there were some things she didn't understand. Wally in the backseat, realizing Secula was busy driving, started talking about county government, townships, and other matters relating to local government. Gia's Italian background hadn't prepared her for a system more akin to England than Italy. In the midst of Wally's discourse on local government, his cell phone rang. "Yeah George, what's happening?" George, in Susan's car, was getting in touch. Wally didn't say much; he just listened, saying finally: "okay, later." Wally then addressed Secula: "they want to make a bathroom stop in this town, Ebensburg." Secula muttered, "Yeah" and went back to watching the road. Gia said: "Does he say where they want to stop?" Wally got out: "No, he just said to find a place that has parking." Secula mumbled something about a pain in the ass with reference to George.

They were able to find parking space along the main street. Susan's car pulled in behind them. George got out and shuffled into a restaurant two doors down. No one in Secula's car needed to use facilities at the restaurant, but they all got out to stretch. It was close to eight in the evening, but not dark yet. Secula and Wally decided to find the courthouse to show Gia. Turning the corner at High and Center Streets, it came into sight. As they walked on, Gia commented that the town didn't seem like much of a place for a county seat. Wally commented that some county seats were even smaller. Secula added: "when the county seat was chosen, three places were considered. One is now a ghost town and the other is almost one." She went on to talk about the remainder of the trip as they headed back to the car. "About 4 or 5 miles out of this place we go through a little college town. When we get there I have to be careful about where I'm going. I'll be turning onto roads I've never been on. From that point it's only about 2 miles."

Coming back to the car they could see everyone was back in Susan's car and ready to go. Secula talked briefly to Susan, filling her in on details of the remainder of the trip. The road through town went downhill and there was a lake at the bottom of the hill and a kind of Y in the road. Secula went left. She was watching Susan's car in her mirror to make sure she followed. In not too many miles they went past a convent of cloistered nuns. Then came the small town with the college. Wally was somewhat interested in local history and talked about the school and the town. Gia listened with waning enthusiasm. The history of the town and the school were much connected with the Catholic Church. Gia's experiences in Italy and this country with that Church caused her to have a distinct aversion to that group. In Italy a priest she worked for had gotten her pregnant, then abandoned her. She lost her job and also the baby. In this country a priest had accused her of being in league with the devil when he heard about the channeling thing. Although she had grown up in the Catholic Church in the village where she was born, recent experiences had left a very bad feeling toward that institution.

Wally was summing up his discourse about local history. "The priest who founded this place, Gallitzin, built a house that's still in town. The house dates from the 1830s and it's just a bit south of here. There are stories that place is haunted too. Maybe we could check it out while we're around here." Gia expressed a distinct aversion to anything having to do with the Catholic Church. This became especially apparent when Wally commented that the house was still used for Church purposes. Wally then began talking about Charlie Schwab, who had grown up in the little village. He had become a well-known wheeler and dealer in the steel industry and dealt with the likes of J. Pierpont Morgan, Andrew Carnegie, and H.C. Frick. He had financed the building of the convent of cloistered nuns they had gone past, since his sister was a member of the order. However, the great depression had erased most of his holdings. His palatial mansion was now occupied by the Franciscans who ran the college. Wally was still talking about Charlie Schwab when Secula pulled into the house that had been the object of their quest.

Three

An Old House

Darkness was setting in as the two cars pulled into the driveway of the old three-story brick house. A young couple stood on the back porch waiting to greet their visitors. Gia, still in the car, was registering a lot of interest in the house itself. She had not been expecting anything of the proportions or style of the once grand old edifice they had just encountered. She was thinking that she would like to draw the place in better light. As she looked over the house from Secula's car, it was obvious that it needed some attention, and that it had seen better days. Nevertheless, even in its present state it was an edifice that commanded respect. Wally and Secula were getting out of the car to meet their hosts. Gia still sat there for a bit studying the house. Its placement on the hillside gave it a prominence in accord with the dignity of its Victorian-style. There were no other buildings close to it. That fact helped set it off as a unique artifact of a bygone era.

Secula was calling to Gia. She was on the back porch with the young couple who lived there. It somewhat disturbed Gia's reverie about the old house. Gia slowly pulled herself out of Secula's car. Standing beside it, she smoothed out her shirt tail over the jeans she was wearing. Not knowing

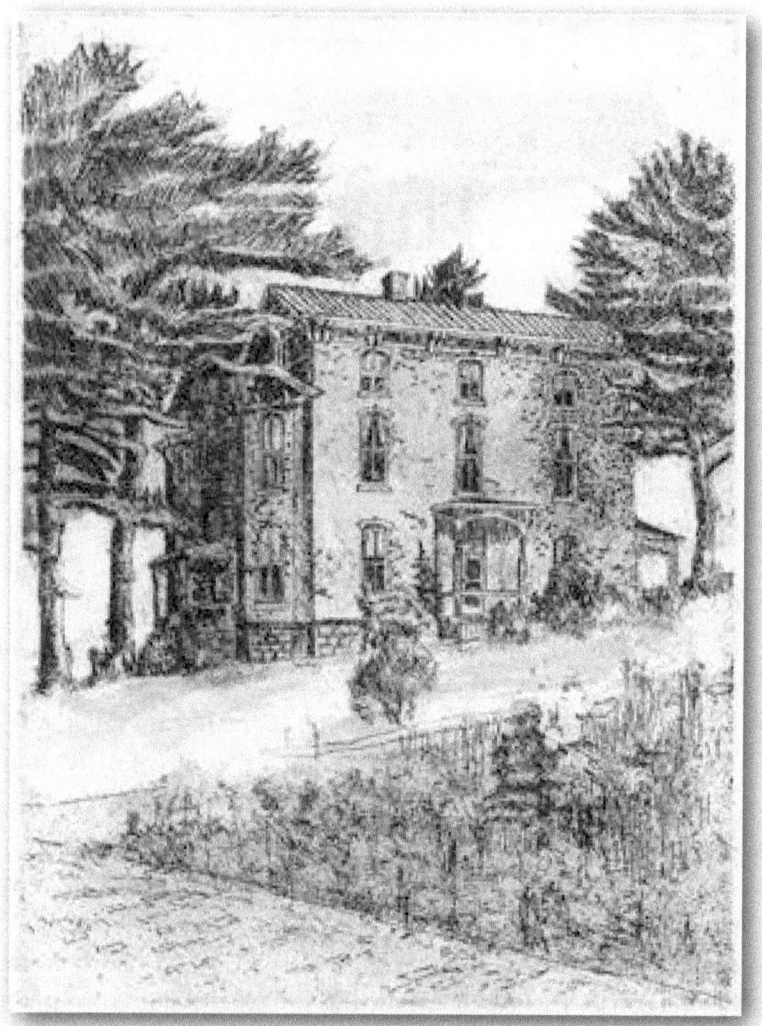

The haunted house that Gia and her friends visited.

what to expect, she approached the group on the back porch with a wide-eyed kind of anticipation. Wally was now also on the porch, carrying a few food items that he had unloaded from the car. The people in Susan's VW were just getting out of it. Observing their behavior, Gia was guessing they might have done a joint during the latter part of the trip. They hadn't seemed that way when they stopped in Ebensburg. Walking up on the porch, Gia was introduced to Shane and Twyla McKenzie. Twyla was explaining that her mother had loved to dance and named her for Twyla Tharp. Neither were locals; they had come from upstate New York. Shane was an English professor at the college they had come past. Twyla had been investing most of her energy lately in the house they had recently purchased and moved into. She was describing her attempts to re-plaster some of the old walls and ceilings that had been lathed with wooden stripping. In the midst of that, Susan, George, and Donnie stumbled up onto the porch.

The three new arrivals on the porch were giggling self-consciously when Shane McKenzie cast a knowing glance in their direction. He started to smile and talk to them: "You guys must've been doing some dynamite stuff." This got George really laughing. Gia was standing there wishing the people in the Volkswagen had put off their potfest until later – all to no avail. George whipped out a plastic baggie from his vest. "This is totally mind wrecking shit; do you guys have any papers?" Everyone was laughing as eight people filed into the kitchen. A kind of assembly line formed at the kitchen table as rolling papers were laid out in a row. Along came someone with a bag, and cannabis was sprinkled onto the papers. Those with skillful hands rolled nice, tight joints and placed about 10 of them in the middle of the kitchen table.

Others were bringing in things from the cars out back. Fresh vegetables from The Strip District were deposited on the kitchen counter. George plunked a big bottle of tequila on the table. Twyla found a gallon of Gallo red wine in the refrigerator and that too found a place on the table. Secula brought in a big hunk of Jarlsberg cheese. Clothes and other personal items from the cars landed in the hall just beyond the kitchen. A cooler full of other food items found its way into the kitchen by way of Donnie Diangelo. After putting on a Rimsky-Korsakov CD, Shane McKenzie fired up one of the joints. Twyla was explaining that the big beef roast was not quite ready yet when everyone in the kitchen became aware of a thumping sound upstairs. It sounded like footsteps. Twyla and Shane knew exactly what was going on. The new arrivals just looked at one another. Wally finally got out the question: "Is that the ghost?"

Twyla and Shane stood there looking at one another. Twyla started talking about the cheese casserole with broccoli, then interrupted herself. "I was hoping it wouldn't start so soon, but yeah; that's our spiritual house-guest. Wally was curious whether anyone had ever seen it. Shane had been toking on the joint and passed it to Wally. "Sort of . . . just sort of . . . mostly we just hear it. Every now and then we see some kind of a smoky-looking form that doesn't have well defined boundaries." Wally wondered if it ever spoke. Twyla had just pulled the big beef roast out of the old Chambers oven and stabbed it with a meat thermometer.

As she watched the dial on the meat thermometer rise, Twyla tried to answer Wally's question. "It talks now and then. It sounds like a mother talking to her children. We've tried to ask it questions, but it never answers us. It doesn't seem at all harmful. It's just – to use a word – spooky. Having a ghost in the house is hard to get used to – even if it is not harmful." Gia seemed anxious to change the subject: " . . . not ready to deal with a ghost on an empty stomach . . . you mind if I make a salad?" Laughter followed. The joint made its rounds again. Gia was slicing tomatoes when it came to her. After a couple healthy tokes on the joint, Gia grabbed one of the wineglasses Twyla had put on the table. She was pouring some of the Gallo red into it when Twyla asked her if she wanted some red peppers for the salad. Gia couldn't help smiling, and out came: *Grazie mille,* Twyla." She then realized that Twyla didn't know Italian. Laughing she said: "Thanks a million." Twyla started laughing herself as Gia handed her the joint.

It wasn't long until Twyla pulled out the beef roast again and stabbed it with the meat thermometer once more. As she stood there watching the dial on the thermometer, the others gathered around and watched too. Wally couldn't help commenting: "This stuff is all so mysterious. What's the temperature we're looking for here?" Twyla hesitated a bit before she responded: "I think about 150° is well done. The thing is just inching up past 146." In the silence that followed, the spiritual houseguest on the upper floor was again heard bumping around. Shane felt the need to comment: "There's an old English litany that has the line: 'From ghoulies, and ghosties, and three headed beasties, and things that go bump in the night – deliver us O Lord.'" A lot of laughter followed that. Twyla waited until the laughter quieted down, then got out: "We're hitting 151." George, seeming to be in agreement, chimed in: "It smells great; it must be done." Although the house had a dining room, it seemed to be the right thing to eat there in the kitchen. The kitchen table easily had room for eight people.

As they sat down to eat, Susan asked if they wanted Donnie to say a blessing. "Donnie had minor orders in the seminary; he put up with all that stuff. He might as well put it to some good use." The scraping of chairs quieted down as they all found a chair and sat down to eat. In a profound silence that followed, a cat that had been hiding in the dining room showed itself. Donnie spoke first: "I was in the seminary, but I've put a good, healthy distance between myself and the Catholic Church. If anyone objects to me doing a blessing, I won't do it." Donnie looked around. Everyone was quiet. "Okay, but I'm going to do it in Latin. It seems less offensive that way. Catholic stuff always seems so freighted with repression. Here goes . . . *Benedic, Domine, nos et haec tua dona, quae de tua largitate sumus sumpturi, per Christum, Dominum nostrum. Amen*". There was a mumbling of amens around the table. As Shane was slicing the roast, he asked Donnie: "You don't have anything to do with the Church anymore?" Donnie was shaking his head. "Absolutely nothing – it gets me in a bad mood talking about it. I'd rather just enjoy a good meal."

The casserole came out of the oven too. Gia's salad was enhanced with a pomegranate vinaigrette dressing that Twyla had put together. Some cooked turnips garnished with parsley made their rounds. The clinking of lead crystal was heard as the gallon jug of wine was passed around the table. When the jug got to Shane, he hesitated and started talking. "Have you ever noticed how creative types manage to mess up their lives with so much excessive indulgence in mind altering substances?" George immediately became self-conscious. He had just filled his wine glass with the tequila he had brought in from the car. In response to Shane he said: "Yo, dude, don't think creative types have a corner on that market. I may be a carpenter – a contractor for sure, but I've done more than my share of damage in that direction." A lot of laughter followed.

Shane talked absentmindedly as he watched red wine slowly pour into his glass. "Have you ever noticed how many carpenters can make really respectable drawings of the things they are thinking about making? That's really not what I'm thinking about though. I was thinking about, if I have to admit it, myself. Then come the kids in classes I teach. I'm thinking about the creative writing classes. Some kids show up in those classes that . . . and I really have a hard time admitting this . . . I actually envy. Some of them have an ability to put words together . . . put words together in a way that the words actually make music when they bounce off one another. I'm always so glad to see this. On the other hand, they – the kids who write this really good stuff – are the ones I worry about. I see so many of them really fuck up their lives with drugs, booze . . . ."

There was a big, dark pool of silence that followed. People ate, drank, stared out into space and thought. Gia had not said much for a while. As she sprinkled salt on a slice of roast beef, she started to talk. "Rupert says something about the way we do too much of the mind altering stuff. Rupert is the little invisible guy I channel. Sometimes I see him in my dreams. Secula is the only one who ever sees him – alive in our world. Anyhow, Rupert talks about the need to make adjustments. He says we use this stuff too much . . . too much wine, and all that stuff. We use it because it is easier than making the adjustments we should make." Gia went on to comment that the adjustments are important because they help us get our lives into a better state, a state in which we won't be feeling so much pain. "When we don't feel so much pain, we don't have to take the stuff to kill the pain."

George was firing up another joint. "This stuff is getting too serious. Another good way you can fuck up your life is by being too serious all the time." There seemed to be a consensus that George had a good point. Twyla found some chocolate chip cookies, and brought some chocolate ice cream from the freezer. George passed around the joint. Shane made his way into the front room. It was still early spring and not too warm for a fire in the fireplace. People ambled around as he got a fire going in the fireplace of what was a very comfortable old parlor. He commented on the room as he tinkered with the fire: "Some of the furniture was already here when we moved in. We bought the carpet, used, and some of the stuffed chairs from an antique dealer.

It does help the room. There were some very old photos in the attic. They're the ones on the walls." This prompted Wally to ask a question. "Do you think the ghost shows up in any of the pictures? It's likely that she might have lived here one time."

"That's a really good question." That was Shane's comment. Gia had sunk into one of the big old stuffed chairs. Wally was paying attention to her because she was starting to look the way she looked when she channeled. She had that faraway look and was just staring into the fire, or past it. Secula walked into the room and Wally tapped her on the shoulder. Secula looked at him and he pointed to Gia. Secula just stood there saying nothing, looking at Gia. Then she did a 180° turn and headed for her car. It wasn't long before Secula come back into the room carrying her battery-powered recorder.

The others had come into the old parlor in the meantime, but there was still room left. There was a chair close to Gia where Secula and her recorder found a place. She wanted to be close to Gia in case she channeled. Secula wondered if Wally had said something to the others in her absence, something about Gia. Gia didn't seem at all bothered that most were looking at her. Secula put the recorder on the floor beside her. She placed it so she could push the record button if Gia started talking. Shane's fire made occasional cracking sounds. The old pine logs had knots that made noise when they got really hot. No one was speaking and the wind could be heard outside blowing through the valley. There was a sense that something was about to happen. Secula, Wally, Susan, Donnie, and George had an idea what might take place. Shane and Twyla had no idea what to expect.

There was an old grandfather's clock in the hall that could be heard ticking the minutes. Gia seemed oblivious to whatever was going on. Several times she opened her mouth as though starting to speak. The influence of the tequila and marijuana on George was still a potent factor; he couldn't resist the urge to speak. "Gia, are you trying to channel?" Finally Gia said something, and it came out very quickly: *Please be quiet. Circumstances are not the best right now for me to speak through Gianella. Your questioning does not help matters. Later on, if things improve, I'll indicate so and tell you that questions are acceptable.* Another period of silence followed. The old clock in the hall struck a single chime. It did that on the half hours. No one in the room was sure what half hour it was. It could have been 10:30 or 11:30. No one really cared.

Finally, the ticking of the clock, the wind blowing up through the valley, and the crackling of the fire were interrupted by Rupert. Gia was the one sitting there making sounds, but it was Rupert who spoke. *I think of Shane's question. I think of things he said about creative people misusing drugs and alcohol. But before I direct myself to those thoughts, I know you all have another matter on your minds.* Secula leaned over to her right to turn the recorder on. Rupert, using Gia's perceptual apparatus, was watching Secula do this and was momentarily quiet. He then continued: *Tonight I do hope to speak of, and perhaps to, the unwelcome houseguest who has been making the lives of our good hosts less than happy. You are correct when you perceive that spiritual presence not to be harmful. In fact, most presences that people might call ghosts are not at all harmful. The unfortunate media productions catering to sensationalism are largely responsible for the aura of evil that people associate with spiritual presences. In reality there is little to fear from them, but their presence can be annoying and frightening.*

The particular no-longer-physical individual I speak of did at one time live in this very house. The family portrait that hangs to my right includes her, her husband, and their six children. She was at one time known as Milberg McGuire, though people who knew her called her Millie. McGuire may not have been her name when she married. She was a lady who died without having realized a long cherished dream. She had a very strong artistic bent. Her duties as a wife and mother kept her from ever realizing her artistic goals. Her abiding presence here has much to do with the artistic part of her not having been realized. She considered her obligations toward her children to be of prime importance and sacrificed her art. She died while giving birth to what would've been her seventh child; it died soon after. With the help of her teachers I hope to effect a meeting here tonight. I hope to show her that she is intruding upon the lives of our hosts. More importantly for her, I hope to show her that she prejudices her own situation by not listening to her teachers and moving on. This moving on will be better for her and for all concerned.

Earlier I had said that I would let you know when you could ask questions. Gianella is in a more stable trance state now, so you may ask questions. It was George who asked. "Rupert, can you tell us when the lady lived here? I'm talking about the ghost." *Specific numerical quantities don't pertain as much in the world where I live, but I can try to give you a rough answer. By the year 1910 the lady was surely no longer living. I can say that her death took place some few years before that date. In the year 1900 she was certainly alive. She was not quite 40 years old when she died. She may have been born around 1870, or a bit before that. Hers was really an unrealized life. She gave life to others and was a good mother, but her own life was, in a sense, not really lived.*

I now want to say more on a subject that Shane introduced among you. That people of a creative bent do tend to abuse mind altering substances is not something I have to prove or document. Those among you who have been around creative types have observed this to be a fact. I have a number of things to say about this. The first and overarching issue I bring up involves creativity misapplied – or applied only to what is considered art. As a beginning to address this issue, I bring up something Gianella recalled that I had passed along to you last year. I did in the past speak to six of you here about the necessity of making adjustments. I said this with reference to your lives. We spoke of how persons tend to use and abuse mind altering substances when their lives are not in good order. They are those times when pain, misery, frustration, and misunderstanding abound. There is a tendency to tune this static out by using chemical means. This applies to people in general and not only creative types.

When your lives are out of order, what is implied is that an adjustment or adjustments need to be made to make things right again. Instead of making the adjustments implied by the troubles in your lives, some try to kill the pain with substances introduced into the body. What I am working up to here is the role of creativity in making these adjustments. I can point to a kind of miseducation in the areas of creative endeavor. What I will mention is more pronounced to the degree that more academic training has been received in a subject. Whether a person is trained as a visual artist, musician, writer, filmmaker, or what have you, often the training they receive teaches them that their creativity only applies to their art music etc.; this is a big mistake. That creativity can be all-important as applied to the adjustments that need to be made in your lives. Often artistic types live in human wastelands not realizing that if their creativity were applied to the adjustments needed in their lives, things could be much better. The pain that occasions the use of mind altering substances would go away.

One more area we can talk about relating to the tendency to overuse chemical alteration in creative types is perception. When I say perception I do not mean only visual perception. This relates to people in all branches of the arts. We can almost define an artist as a person who has on the one hand a unique insight into [perception of] the world they live in. On the other hand they also have the ability to express that insight/perception in some medium. Creative *types are often ones who perceive much more than their contemporaries. Because of this expanded perceptual ability, creative types are the ones who realize, understand, perceive the discrepancy between the world as it is, and the world as it could be. They see how the world could be changed to institute a better world. Yet they still live in and experience the world as it is. The perception of this dissonance brings about much angst in creative types. This angst is yet another prompting agent for the use of chemical erasers. One good suggestion here is that artists continue to show to their contemporaries those dissonances that they are so well aware of. Artists have done this in the past. Their art can be a wakeup call to their contemporaries. Awareness is always a first step toward change. Filmmakers especially have a medium well suited to prompt this kind of awakening.*

I do not want to bore you, but some of these things are matters you should be aware of. You should be aware that there are other issues in this discussion of the abuse of substances you introduce into your bodies. We might speak about the feelings of the people we call artists. There was an American artist and writer, Robert Motherwell, who spoke about the task of the artist. He was known to say: "The task of the artist is to express the felt nature of reality." I am always a bit suspicious of types who like to bandy the word reality about, and you should be too. But in this case he makes a good point. For artists, their stock in trade happens to be their feelings. We might compare the situation of many artists to a person having a hearing aid that is turned up too high. Often for artists, the feelings come full blast. Those feelings are in no way attenuated and hit with the impact of a hurricane.

Many who live under the impact of this deluge of feelings implied here find it impossible to endure this continuing barrage. Thus comes about the recourse to substances that might lessen this impact. I offer here only the advice that artists in the past seemed instinctively to understand. Artists must continually allow these feelings to go through them so as to propel them to produce the works in their chosen media. In this way the storms of feeling do not cripple them into inactivity. The feelings blow through them like a spring

43

storm. They take with them the strong currents of life's impulses and engender in creations that we call artwork.

If these feelings stop with the artist, they most often only produce monstrous results. They should be allowed to move along and instigate the production of those works that the artist him/herself will experience and be encouraged by. Not only that artist, but those who are allowed to experience the work the artist has created will be given a gift. When we speak of gifts, it should be mentioned that the artist is given a gift that is not for him/herself alone. If this gift is not shared, it putrefies and sickens the one to whom it has been given. Once it is shared, it is like the feelings the artist experiences. When it is passed along it enriches the giver and the receiver.

You may not immediately understand the import of what I have said. It may happen that the truth of my words will only be borne out in your lives, in your experience. Other matters should be passed along. The social context artists live in is one more very potent factor that can cause dismay . . . . Suddenly the old grandfather's clock in the hall began to chime. There was extreme quiet in the room as all counted the chimes. When the old clock stopped and silence reigned once again, all realized that it was 12 midnight. The silence felt good, and it was some time until Gia began talking as Rupert once more.

We have come . . . we have come to the bewitching hour once again. I sometimes forget that I am talking to people . . . talking to people who do take time seriously. In my life as I usually experience it, time is usually not a fact, or factor, that concerns me. I want to give you all a break here. Get up and move about; eat if you are hungry. When you have had some moments to refresh yourselves, I hope we can meet again. When you are taking a break, I hope to be in touch with Milberg, the spiritual houseguest here. I will also be in touch with her teachers. They are all here tonight, though not present to us as a group yet. Sometime after we reconvene here in this room, I shall try to effect a bringing together of all in the house here tonight. This should include Milberg, her teachers, myself, and all of you. Please inform Gianella of all this as she is usually not able to consciously retain all that she says in trance. If we do get this meeting to take place, you should be able to see Milberg in the doorway of this room that leads out into the hall. She will probably be a shadowy, or smoky form and not very distinct. I shall be to her right – your left – out in the hall. Only Secula will be able to see me. Milberg's teachers will be to her left out in the hall – to your right. None of you here will be able to see them.

The people in the room were left just looking at one another. Secula got up and held Gia's shoulder, rocking her back and forth. It was not long until she was also conscious and present in the room as were the others. Slowly people got up and gravitated toward the kitchen. At first things were very quiet. Out in the kitchen most seemed a bit stunned at the prospect of a ghost appearing in their midst. There were little bits of conversation and then a dawning awareness that a spring storm was moving in. George was filling in Gia about the pending visit of Milberg. The rumble of thunder was heard in the distance. It didn't take long to realize it was getting closer. Some moved out to the back porch. Gia was standing on the edge of the porch looking toward the West. The storm seemed to be coming from that direction. She was aware of a man standing behind her, too close. She didn't have to look to know it was Shane. His wife was still in the kitchen. Gia couldn't tell if she were imagining it, but it felt like an erect penis rubbing against her left butt cheek. In some situations she might have been turned on by this; this time she was just annoyed. She stepped down about 8 inches onto the walk beside the porch. She reeled around giving Shane a glance telling him to back off. Secula had been taking all this in. Her writer's instinct usually took note of interesting goings-on. George and Wally stood looking at the night sky oblivious of what had transpired. Donnie and Susan were still in the kitchen with Twyla.

A sudden and bright strike of lightning to the South caught everyone's attention. Wally started to count. He hadn't gotten to four yet when the booming clap of thunder arrived. He knew this was close, and started to talk: "I don't know if this will interfere with Rupert's project here tonight. Maybe we shouldn't be in a big hurry to go back into the parlor." Looking over at Gia, she seemed to concur with his suggestion to go slowly with the meeting with Milberg. Gia moved back onto the porch, since the sprinkles were starting. She kept a good distance from Shane, who was now avoiding her glance. The rain got heavier. Twyla, Donnie, and Susan came out onto the porch too. In five minutes it was a downpour. Thunder, lightning, and rain were all around. Shane couldn't resist reciting the lines from Macbeth with the witches: "Where shall we three meet again . . . thunder, lightning, or in rain?" George came in with: "When the hurly-burly's done, when the battle's lost and won." Donnie was about to say something when a huge strike lit up all of the southern sky. The very ground shook with the thunder that followed so closely. The rain was now coming down in bucketsfull, a giant cosmic orgasm. No one dared speak in the presence of such a grand show put on by Mother Nature.

Four

A Country Weekend

The rain was finally starting to subside. Some spring peepers could be heard coming from the hollow down below the old house. A bit of a chill had set in after the rain and most were now in the kitchen. Gia was recalling what she had been told about Rupert wanting to continue the session. She usually had good instincts about what was going on around her, both physical and otherwise. Without saying anything to anyone, she walked directly into the old front parlor and took the chair she had been in previously. First Wally and Secula, then the others, were aware that Gia had gone back into the parlor. Conversations quieted down; all filed into the parlor and placed themselves were they had been previously. Donnie moved his chair a bit so he could see the doorway. He was recalling what Rupert had said about Milberg's appearing.

Shane fussed with the fire a bit, adding another log. Gia, realizing she was the center of attention, put her head back in the old chair and stared at the ceiling. There was little noise in the room except for the fire. The others tried to remain quiet, hoping Gia would begin to channel again. The old clock in the hall did a single chime. The people in the room realized it was 12:30. Gia seemed to be still in a relatively conscious state. Secula moved her tape recorder a bit closer to her, keeping an eye on her cousin Gia. Five minutes later, the silence was getting oppressive. Secula noticed George wiggle in his chair; she hoped he could keep quiet. It was Donnie who first noticed Gia's mouth starting to move. He looked over at Secula, getting her attention. Secula reached down toward her recorder. There were some mumbled sounds coming from Gia. She was starting to speak.

I thank you. I thank you for assembling once again here in this fine old parlor. I also thank you for taking your time to meet me once again. The atmospheric disturbances with the storm could have caused some difficulties for me getting in touch with Gia to talk through her while the storm was abroad. While you were taking a break I have been busy. If all goes as planned, you should meet Milberg this evening, or this morning. Her teachers will be here too, but it is unlikely that you will be able to see or hear them. Secula is the only one who will be able to see me, but you should be able to hear me with Gia's help as you do now. Secula got up out of her chair and peered out into the hall. Some in the room could see her smile as she waved to Rupert. From Gia came Rupert's words again: *Good to see you again Secula. You are about to have another presence among the group here. Sitting down again would be appropriate.* Secula sat again, looking toward Gia.

Shane was fussing with the fire again when it happened. He was facing the fireplace on the outside wall, and had no idea what the others were experiencing. There was complete silence in the room and all were staring at the doorway that went into the hall. Shane's fire tending activities were very suddenly interrupted by a rather shrill and scolding female voice. It was not a voice he recognized as belonging to anyone in the room. Reeling around quickly, he saw the shadowy, smoky, form that Rupert had predicted would appear in the doorway. Up to this point, he had seen Gia's channeling activities as some sort of carnival sideshow. Right now he was faced with something he could not easily dismiss. The form in the doorway then began to address him. "Sit down; there are things I have to say to you and everyone here." Shane wanted to respond, but his voice failed him. He meekly took his seat. Milberg continued: "this is my house and you have no business here. My children will be home shortly and I have no desire for them to see unbidden guests in my house." Shane was stammering, unable to formulate a response. It was Gia who spoke next, channeling Rupert: *Milberg McGuire, this is no longer your house and these people are not unbidden guests. The only unbidden guest here is you. Among the people present are ones who do truly own this house.*

To all in the room it was apparent that Milberg was in a state of great consternation. Waving her hands she spoke: "My name has not been McGuire since I married a man." Rupert interrupted her using Gia's voice, now strong and booming. *Milberg, you are no longer married. In fact, you are dead as far as the earth you knew here is concerned. Your refusal to listen to your teachers has caused much grief to Shane and Twyla present here in this room tonight. I tell and command you to look to your left to those who will help you understand these things if you will only listen.* Milberg was seen turning to her left. It was quiet in the room again. Those present assumed she was listening to her teachers. The quiet did not last long.

Again Milberg seemed to be perturbed. She was not liking what she was being told. She began addressing no one in particular; she just seemed to have a need to speak. "I have no wish to pass on to somewhere else. I have not done what I wanted to do here. I raised children here. I did a good job of that. I wanted to paint the beautiful wooded hills, the houses people lived in, and the people of these hills I wanted to paint. I was always too busy to do that. This is where I want to do that and not somewhere else. I would sometimes find a little time to paint. I realized that I would have to spend much time to teach myself the craft of a painter. That time was taken by the children and the chores around here. I am proud of what I did, but there is much more I want to do."

As she stood there collecting her thoughts, it seemed she wanted to say more, but Rupert would not let her. Again, Rupert began speaking through

Gia: *Milberg, it is time someone told you a few necessary and important facts. The place you're in now – this house – is not in the same environment that you left close to 100 years ago now. All of the people you knew are gone. Only one of your children remains in this world, and in a very poor mental state. The hills have changed much. Lumbering and development have taken their toll. Many of the houses now are things you would not recognize. In short, this may not be a world you would want to live in to paint pictures. You must, to make yourself and the people who live in this house happy, do as you are told. You must move on. I can tell you for certain that as long as you continue as you are, you will never realize your dream of doing art.*

Again Milberg was quiet. It is likely she was thinking. The fire cracked and sputtered. Wind could be heard blowing up the hollow. Finally she spoke: "If I do as you say, move on, can I again be on the Earth at a time when it was beautiful as I remember it?" *At times a yes or no answer is not a possibility, Milberg. Answers to some questions can only come about when other conditions are fulfilled. Once you have accepted the instructions of your teachers, and only then, other possibilities for a new life on earth for you can begin to be explored. You may be shown places and times that you may find even more beautiful and interesting than the world you knew when you were physical. Also, there may be people with whom you were associated in other lives – friends, relatives, lovers – that you may want to be associated with in your new life. There are many possibilities that your teachers can show you. What's more – something important to you as an artist – you may want to be born the son or daughter of an artist, or be born into a family of artists. This is one of the best ways to learn your craft of painting.*

Milberg was stewing around as if she wanted to ask a question. Rupert was taking note of this and became quiet. "I hear you say that I may come back as the son or daughter of an artist. Does this mean that I do not have to be a woman in some other life I may take on?" *To be sure, Milberg. You may choose the role of a man in your new life if that is your wish. Truth to tell, it may be easier for you in that situation to carry out your strong desire to do your painting. In the great cycle of births and deaths that one experiences, one must be both male and female. Both roles must be experienced.* Milberg had much more on her mind and interrupted Rupert with the question. "Could I come as a male person into the world I knew and loved here? You are right. A man might more easily do art without the worry of children to raise and care for." Rupert seemed thoughtful, and an answer was not forthcoming immediately. When he did respond, the words were weighed carefully.

I can see that your desire to come back to this locale is very strong, Milberg. Once you have allowed your teachers to show you other possibilities for another physical life, that may not be so. However, if becoming aware of other possibilities you still want to return here to this locality, you must know this. You must return into the physical world in the same manner that all come into it. You will come in the form of an infant born by a woman. Now, the arrangements for this must be made with some woman while she is in the dream state, at night while she sleeps. If a willing mother can be found, you may – I say may – be able to come back here. Contrary to what many think, these matters are arranged beforehand. It is not a chance affair.

Rupert could tell that Milberg was taking all this in. He had the impression that she had a question, or questions. He was glad that she was starting to consider these matters, but he had concerns about others present. Once more, through Gia, he started to speak. *I sense that you may have matters to discuss Milberg. I too have something to say, but do proceed with what you may be considering.* Milberg could see that the ball was again in her court. Usually not slow with a response, she again spoke: "You present me with many things to consider. The thoughts of these things bring up many questions. You speak of a woman who must give birth to me as an infant. This brings up to me the consideration of not just one person but a family. Is only one woman consulted, or other members of her family? Having come from the Maguire family, I may once again want to be associated with those people. This makes me also want to know how many lives a person must go through in this cycle you talk about. One more matter I cannot help considering is this: if a person does have a choice in the life one is born into, why are some people's lives so wretched and miserable? Why would one choose such?"

If a person had a direct channel into Rupert's consciousness at that point, they would see he was quite impressed by Milberg's response. *Milberg, you have been blessed with no ordinary mentality. I will not say brain power, because your brain rotted years ago in the cemetery at Loretto. It was the cemetery that your ancestor, Michael McGuire, donated to the church there for burial purposes. The mind – consciousness – continues past physical death, which is the state we find you in. Your fine ability to understand things is part of the problem of your not moving on. Your unwillingness to accept what your teachers tell you comes from your ability to question. One less endowed than yourself would have docilely and obediently simply done what she was told. I want you to know there are answers to your questions. I also want you to know there are others here I must take into consideration. Some here are still physical beings. They live the kind of lives that we one time did live. That means they require sleep at night. I have taxed them over much already. Some have traveled miles to get here. Now, we must call an end to this tonight. I invite you and all here to join together on the morrow. When dark has settled in tomorrow, I hope we shall meet again.*

Milberg voiced a quaint goodbye: "may your travels be blessed until we meet again." After saying that, she was no longer seen in the doorway. Rupert then spoke: *I think I speak for Milberg's teachers when I say: so long to all and may the Good Spirits be with you until we meet again.* At that point Gia tossed her head back into the big chair. Her mouth came open and she seemed to heave a sigh. Secula especially was taking note of this and got up and walked over to her cousin. As she stood there looking down at her, she could tell the Gia had come quickly out of trance. "Gia, it looks like you are back with us. I don't know if you recall any of the things you said for Rupert. Let me know and I can fill you in." Gia didn't say anything. She just got up and walked over to the fire. She picked up the poker and moved one of the logs a bit. Only after that she spoke: "No, Secula, it is mostly a blur. I am tired, but tell me what I should know." Others in the room were getting up and milling about as Secula filled Gia in on Milberg's appearance. Secula related how Milberg had appeared in the doorway, things that had transpired, and Rupert's request that all should meet on the next night.

As before, the kitchen was the place where all eventually regrouped. Twyla was inquiring among her guests what kind of sleeping arrangements that each would require. She was finding out who would be sharing rooms, who might want a room of their own, etc. As it turned out, the six people who came from Pittsburgh only needed three rooms. Twyla seemed happy about that. She was explaining that, although rooms on the third floor were available, there was a good bit of water damage up there from leaking roofs. She said that the second floor could easily accommodate all those in the house. George insisted on firing up another joint from those still left on the kitchen table. Some stayed in the kitchen and had a good night smoke with George. Others started carrying things upstairs and bringing in a few more items from the cars out back. Sometime around 2:00 AM the house was quiet. There were no ghostly bumpings in the night. Milberg allowed all to take advantage of a quiet night in the country and get a good sleep. Not all went to sleep immediately. On the second floor some of the beds had the old open springs under a heavy mattress. If a person had remained on the first floor, they might have heard the rhythmic squeaking of the old-fashioned springs coming from a few of the rooms upstairs.

Gia was guessing it was sometime between 7:30 and 8:00 o'clock when she got awake. The big old bed that she and George had shared for the night had a comfortable feel to it, especially with the heavy quilts over the linen sheets. George was still asleep. He had been rather horny when he went to bed, crawling in beside Gia. She had been less enthusiastic in that direction, but it had felt good anyhow. Part of her less than excited attitude toward George had been because of Milberg. Gia couldn't help wondering if Milberg were watching them. She was wondering if ghosts got envious. She couldn't imagine ghosts having sex, and wondered if they still wanted to do the things they had done while physical. She thought about getting Secula to ask Rupert about that if she went into trance that night. She thought about getting George awake, but thought better of it. She slid out from between the sheets quietly, and stood beside the bed for some seconds. Being totally naked, the room felt chilly to her. She started getting clothes on.

Panties came first. Gia then thought about just a sweatshirt and no bra, but there was something about Shane's attitude toward her that made her want to put on a bra. It felt good pulling on her old faded jeans. They were an old pair that Secula had given her shortly after she moved to Pittsburgh. She was pulling on a 'Pitt' sweatshirt over her head when she heard crows outside. George got the sweatshirt during his school days. He hadn't worn it much and gave it to Gia; she liked it. She thought the noncommittal gray went well with the faded blue jeans. Socks and sneakers completed the ensemble. She grabbed a sweater that she had brought with her from Italy just in case. Quietly she went out into the hall and closed the door. The hall had an old runner that gave the impression of days gone by. The old stairs creaked as she made her way to the first floor. Pausing in the front vestibule, she looked outside a bit. In some ways it reminded her of Italy, and in some ways it did not. That got her thinking about her dad. She didn't want to spend too much time on a sad thought and quickly spun around heading for the kitchen.

Walking down the hall toward the kitchen, she made a quiet resolve to get to Italy as soon as it was possible. She didn't want her dad to die without seeing him. Walking into the kitchen a totally different sensation greeted her. The smells of bacon, eggs, and potatoes on the old Chambers stove made her brighten up. Secula asked if she wanted coffee. Twyla opened the cupboard and grabbed a cup and saucer for Gia, putting it on the table. Secula poured coffee for her without even waiting for an answer. Gia just said, "*Grazie*". Picking up the cup, Gia walked out onto the back porch. She wanted to stand and stare for a while as she enjoyed some black coffee. Her eyes were on the hillside that sloped up toward the South. Catching her attention were a few small pine trees. Crows could be heard overhead. Closer to the ground were smaller birds, making the pleasant chirping sounds they make in springtime. She was looking for the nice yellowish green grass of spring. Over to her left she spotted a nice patch of it on the hillside. Gia was thinking about how it would feel walking through it barefoot when the screen door opened. "Gia, do you want to have breakfast with Twyla and me?"

Inside on the kitchen table Gia found a plate with fried eggs, bacon, and fried potatoes. Twyla asked her if she wanted orange juice. Gia thought a second and said: "please". Breakfast proceeded with just the three of them. Twyla had made extra in case more showed up. Twyla was curious if anyone had heard the ghost, Milberg, during the night. "I had such a different feeling about her, since we saw her and heard her talk. I didn't hear her last night. Did either of you hear her?" Gia and Secula looked at one another. Both shook their heads indicating a negative on that question. Gia was glad for the quiet during breakfast. It seemed all were digesting the experiences of the previous night along with their food. Gia was just finishing her breakfast and got up to pour herself more coffee. This time she wanted some milk in it. She spied a small pitcher of milk on the table and was pouring some into her coffee when footsteps were heard on the stairs.

Next in the kitchen was Wally Bickerstaff. Twyla got up and moved over to the stove. "How hungry are you Wally?" She lifted lids from pans on the stove to show Wally the menu. After getting a plate for him, she showed him the microwave and asked if he wanted coffee. There was a bit of shuffling about and it wasn't long before Wally too was seated. Wally was asked if he had heard Milberg: "No, not at all. Did anyone else?" A few mumbled no's were heard. Once Wally had sampled some of the breakfast items, he started talking amidst sips of coffee. "Right after I got up I was looking out my window down into the little valley below the house. I thought I could see some old stone ruins down there. I'm thinking about going down there with a sketchbook when the sun comes up a bit more." Twyla had something to add: "Once upon a time there was an old mill down there turned by water power, or so I'm told." That caught Gia's interest too: "Tell me if you go down there Wally. I might want to do some drawing too."

Wally brightened up at the prospect of Gia going drawing with him. He was explaining to Gia where he had seen the ruins when footsteps were heard on the stairs. Things became quiet in the kitchen again as people there anticipated new arrivals. Twyla headed over to the stove, getting ready to show the new arrivals the menu. As Donnie and Susan came into the kitchen, Twyla asked them if they wanted coffee. Some shuffling about followed, accompanied by conversation and the clinking of china. Wally was interested in talking to Donnie about his project with the buildings in the Strip District. He signaled to Donnie to sit by him. Donnie and Susan both joined Wally on his side of the table. Wally had been encouraged by Rupert's comments presenting Donnie's father as a potential source of funding for his project. He was hoping that Donnie could put him in touch with his father. He let Donnie get a good start on his breakfast before he brought up the project. "Donnie, I don't think I've told you about a project I've had in mind for some time . . . ."

Wally was surprised that Donnie seemed very interested in the project himself. "You know, Wally, I'm working with an architect now. In a couple years I may want to start out on my own and will want some good loft space myself for architecture work. This is a good time to hit dad up for what you're thinking about. He retired recently and is looking for worthy projects to invest in. His background as a lawyer would probably be helpful to you when dealing with the city about zoning issues. He knows a lot of people at City Hall." Wally was more than happy to hear all that. He came back to Donnie with: "I've not been in either of those buildings yet.

I hope to do that this summer, and maybe you'd like to come along." Susan had been listening and suggested: "Donnie, why don't you ask your dad to come along too. That might get things started." Wally and Donnie both like the sound of that.

Gia had been listening from the other side of the table. She wanted to know if Wally was still interested in the trip to Italy. As it turned out he was. "Yeah, Gia, I think I'm going downtown this week to find out about visa and all that. Secula is coming. You want to come along too?" "Yeah, I have to do some things down there too. I'm still Italian citizen and want to find out more about being a citizen here. You know what day you and Secula doing that?" There was some conversation going on between Wally and Secula as Shane appeared in the kitchen doorway and made his way to the stove. He seemed to be in a rather evasive mood that morning. Gia maintained an awareness of his presence as she listened to Secula and Wally talk about going downtown. It wasn't long before Thursday was decided upon for that excursion, and Gia said that day worked for her too. By that time Shane was quietly sitting sipping coffee and chewing bacon. Sometime during Shane's second cup of coffee he started to become verbal again. "That ghost thing really has me freaked out. I never thought it was the kind of thing you could engage in conversation." Comments followed as others volunteered their reactions to Milberg. Twyla was talking about how glad she was that Rupert had started to convince Milberg to move on when George appeared in the doorway.

It was a bit after 11:00 as Wally headed out – sketchbook in hand – for the ruins. He had told Gia where he was going and she told him she'd be down in 10 minutes or so. Wally was just sketching in the rough outlines of what was left of the old mill when Gia arrived. Neither said a thing. Wally was seated beside the stream on the side opposite the ruins. He was surprised how close Gia sat down beside him. He didn't mind it at all; he was just surprised. There was ample vegetation behind them so that no one from the house could see them. Wally didn't want to make Gia

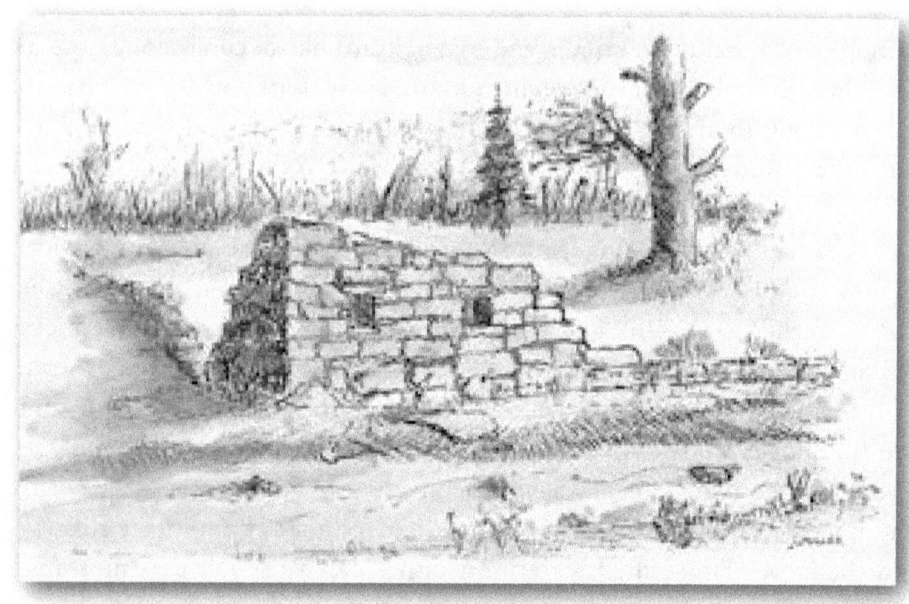

The ruins of the old mill that Wally and Gia drew.

self-conscious by looking at her beginning efforts to block in the foundation of the old mill. She was glad he didn't. Wally whistled now and then. When he wasn't whistling he could hear Gia hum the funny little Italian song she sang when she was happy. It was probably 15 minutes before anything was said. It was Gia who spoke. "So many times, Wally, I wish I study art. Since I am a little kid I draw. I have no training. I just draw." Wally was wondering if he should say something. He had always felt a sexual tension when he was around Gia. He was first aware of her when she started tending bar at the place where he went in the Strip District. All the guys there thought it was their lucky day when she started working there.

Wally got involved with her cousin, Secula, and had since then tried not to think of Gia.

Wally's efforts were of no avail. Any time Gia was anywhere within sight, he could feel the thing happening. "How do you feel about it Gia? I mean the old mill." Part of Wally knew he was not talking about the crumbling old stone walls on the other side of the stream. Wally was becoming aware that this was the first time Gia was also feeling what he felt when the two of them were anywhere together. "It's a good feeling, Wally, really good." After that they continued to draw in quiet for nearly 15 minutes. Gia got up then and walked upstream a bit. "I want to see it from up here a little bit." Wally was really relieved when she walked back down and sat beside him again. "Wally, you went to school to study art. Maybe you could tell me some stuff you learn." Wally was watching Gia draw lines along the stream with her No. 4 pencil. "Some people will try to tell you that you must never erase; just commit your pencil to the paper and draw. I think that is a big mistake. For me the eraser is one of the most important drawing instruments – like your No. 4 pencil. I use my finger the same way, to smudge things. What you are doing now is the best teaching – just draw. Keep doing it. It is like the exercise you get at the gym, or by going running. You have to just make yourself keep doing it."

"Something that helps is looking at drawings of artists you think a lot of. I like to look at books of Rembrandt's drawings and graphic work. Oriental artists keep me going too. Just look at the stuff you admire. It'll keep you going." The sun had moved a bit in the sky since they started. Gia noted how the shadows had changed. That started Wally talking about value. "There is something you should learn to focus on. In America we call it value. It has nothing to do with money." That caught Gia's attention; she was all ears. "Your talking about shadows got me thinking about value. It's really all about how much light is or is not reflected from a surface. It's what the light meter of a camera registers. The light meter does not have to think about it, but you do. Whatever you look at and draw, notice how much or how little light is reflected in every part of the scene before you. A good way to talk about this is to refer to a black-and-white photograph." Wally could tell the Gia was a bit perplexed. He thought she might want to ask a question and became quiet." "Yeah, Wally, I can see what you talk about, but everything I see has color. The color often makes it hard for me to see what's light and what's dark." Wally looked at Gia and smiled.

"That's why I talked about a black-and-white photo, Gia. Some artists even wear dark glasses to filter out the color; that helps them see only the differences in value. It's just one of those areas where you have to train yourself if you want to become good at drawing. Doing black-and-white photography is another method you might use to train yourself to see the differences in value – the various shades of light and dark."

"That's the kind of stuff I hoped you could tell me, Wally. Maybe you have some more things to say that can help me draw better." Wally was working on drawing the stones of the ruin across the stream and didn't say anything for a while. The sun moved slowly across the sky and the bit of remaining morning chill was burnt off by *sol invictus*. The hint of rain that presented itself earlier was now totally gone. Good smells of the moist earth rose up from the ground beside the stream. The birds seemed pleased with it all and accompanied Wally as he began speaking again. "I don't know if you've ever heard the term negative space, Gia. It's another way of looking at things or seeing things that you should be aware of." Wally was quiet, giving Gia an opening to say something if she wanted to. "I never hear of that, Wally." Wally listened to the birds briefly before he started talking again.

"When I think about negative space, the first thing that comes to mind is a bicycle wheel or an old-time wagon wheel – something with spokes. Instead of thinking about the spokes or the round wheel, focus on the shapes created by the things that are actually there. Focus on the shapes where nothing is, those pie-shaped empty spaces that the spokes and round wheel create. Draw those spaces instead of drawing what you see as physical objects. This gives you a totally different viewpoint. It will help you structure any visual field that you look at." Gia was staring at the ruins across the creek and trying to apply what Wally said to what she was looking at. "Again, Wally, I see so much stuff over there. Can you talk about negative space in what we're looking at?" "Look at those two window openings. Don't draw the stones around them. Draw the empty spaces created by the stones – the shape where nothing is. Look at that vee shaped opening on the downstream side. Maybe there was a door there once upon a time. Again, don't draw the stones, draw that opening. Draw that space where nothing is – negative space."

Five

MILBERG, ETC.

The sun was getting higher in the sky. The warmth of the fiery orb felt good. Gia and Wally continued to quietly draw the ruins. The brook between them and the ancient stones made pleasant babbling sounds as the water made its way to lower elevations. Wally had been there longer than Gia and was beginning to get saturated with the visual field in front of him. His mind was going in a couple different directions. Gia was one of those directions. Breakfast had been some hours ago, and thoughts of food were coming into his mind. He also had images of the shadowy figure of Milberg coming into his awareness. No one had said anything for about 10 minutes and Wally felt like saying something. "Do you think Milberg will show up again tonight – for that matter, Rupert?" This somewhat broke Gia's spell, her intense concentration on drawing. "Umm, Wally, there are no guarantees there. I just hope I can do my part. You don't know what it's like for me. I do this less than a year, and never know if . . . if I can do it again."

This gave Wally pause to think a bit. Most of the actual structure of his drawing had been finished. He was just working on shading – issues of value. He did eventually say something: "I can't help wondering what it's like for you, Gia, when you're doing that channeling thing. Last night, with Milberg, how did you handle that?" "I can't say I handle much of anything. This morning after breakfast I listen to the tape Secula made. I am amazed, amazed. Rupert provides the energy and the – I think the word is ideas. I just let it go through me. I'm not aware of a whole lot. Every now and then I can remember struggling with trying to speak an idea that Rupert gives me. You mentioned Milberg. I don't recall her at all. I am first introduced to her with Secula's tape this morning. How surprised I am listening to it when my voice gets loud and I command her to listen to her teachers."

"Do any of the things you say come into your mind before you channel for Rupert?" "No, my mind is empty. I am usually just a bit fearful, because I'm afraid I can't do this again." Wally was noticing that Gia might be close to being finished with her drawing. He then recalled another bit of advice for her about drawing. "You asked me for advice about drawing, Gia. There is something else that was helpful for me when I was just learning." He didn't go on. He wanted to see if she had any response. She did. "Please, Wally, tell me." Wally felt better that she was still interested. "This is about symbols. This story begins when people are little – just little kids. When kids are little and starting to draw, they usually develop a symbol system. Symbol system is an impressive term for what kids do naturally. Developmental psychologists have things to say about it, but for our purposes, just remember. You, and most kids you knew, on their own came to a more or less standard way of portraying the various things and people in their world. By the time kids enter first grade, they often have the beginnings of a symbol system figured out."

Gia had a question: "Maybe I know what you talk about, Wally. I remember me, my sisters, my brothers and how we all draw pictures. When I get older I remember my nieces and nephews, the pictures they draw. Most kids figure out a way to draw a house, a person, the sun, a car, a lot of things they know. These pictures don't look exactly like what they draw, but enough is there to tell you what they draw." Wally was surprised how

Gia caught on quickly. "That's what I'm talking about, Gia. But notice how the symbols are used. Always the same symbol is used for different things. If a kid draws a house, no matter what house the kid looks at, it is the same house that is drawn. It is the same with people, cars, and most things that kids draw. They have a standard symbol for a tree, a horse, a dog. There is nothing wrong with this. It's just the way kids learn things."

Gia again had a question: "Wally, do you tell me this because you think I still use symbol system like kid?" Wally started smiling and looked at Gia. "No, Gia, the answer is no. I might see a little bit of it in the stones you draw, but you have come far past the drawing kids do. I mention it as one thing you have to become aware of to become good at what you do, draw. Everything you look at is unique and different. No stone is like another. I'm just reminding you to be aware of a symbol system. Once you become aware of it, you can begin to concentrate on the individual differences of every object you look at – even stones." Gia again intervened: "How about bricks?" Wally started laughing: "I wish you hadn't brought that one up." Wally looked up and down the little stream as he mused over Gia's question. His drawing was finished. "I'm not going to deal with bricks today; they are made to look like one another, aren't they? I just think it's funny how kids struggle to develop a symbol system. Then as they get older, they have to then struggle to get rid of it. They have to get rid of it so their drawing looks respectable, realistic. A lot of grown-up people still use their symbol system when they draw. If you look at the drawings of our primitive ancestors on cave walls, you can often see a symbol system working. I'm not saying there is anything wrong with that. It's just something you should be aware of if you want your drawing to be taken seriously by contemporaries.

Wally was listening to the babbling brook as Gia finished her drawing. It was after noon by the time Gia and Wally scrambled back up the hillside toward the house. Wally had made it to the top of a rather sharp declivity just below the road. He was within sight of the house. He stood there waiting for Gia as she clawed her way up the bank. When she got close enough, Wally held out a hand to pull her up. She seemed glad for the extra help on the last three feet. It may be that neither of them planned what happened next. When Gia got up to where Wally stood, he grabbed her, putting his arms around her. They stood there with their arms around one another. Neither of them was aware that Secula was on the front porch watching them. She had been sitting on a porch chair reading, her head barely visible above the porch railing.

Down below the road, Gia and Wally seemed reluctant to break up something that felt to both of them very good. Wally was starting to get a very firm erection, and Gia was beginning to feel it. As they looked into one another's eyes, they were both thinking that this might not be the best idea – at least not where they were standing. They became disentangled and scurried up to the house. Secula on the porch was relieved when the railing hid them from view. She quietly slipped into the house, and neither of them had been aware that she was watching. Once in the front hall, she peered into the front room with the fireplace. Memories of last night's session with Milberg came flooding in. Sunlight was pouring into the room. She felt it inviting and went in. There was a lot of light to read by. The chair she had been in last night sat empty. She settled into the comfy old chair, noticing particles of suspended dust in the air made visible by the bright sun. With her book in her left hand, she sat there thinking.

Secula sat there thinking about the expression: "To do or not to do." Should she confront her cousin, Gia, about her and Wally together? Should she confront Wally, the man she had slept with last night? Should she confront the both of them together? Should she just wait until more evidence might show up? It may have been a momentary, innocent dalliance. She had done things like that herself, a spur of the moment impulse. She found herself in these quandaries often, questioning whether or not to act on some information, in some situation. This was a circumstance where she had no really strong feeling to make a move one way or another. She was starting to hear voices in the kitchen. She could hear Twyla, Wally, and Gia out there. Hardly noticing what she was doing, she got up. Book in hand she made her way to the kitchen.

There were hotdogs and sauerkraut on the stove. Potato salad and buns were on the table. Gia and Wally were already sitting down eating. Polite hellos were exchanged. Secula found a plate and poured herself some coffee after getting a hot dog. With the potato salad it was much like a picnic. Secula noticed that Wally seemed evasive. Gia seemed apologetic, though she didn't know that Secula had watched her and Wally embrace. Gia was describing the ruins they had been drawing down along the creek when Susan and Donnie came in. Twyla pointed out what was available for lunch and asked them how their walk had been. Donnie talked about a little place called Bradley Junction that they had walked to. Susan talked about the roadbed of an old railway they had walked on for part of the way, then asked where Shane and George were. Twyla talked about errands Shane wanted to take care of: "he asked George to come along; George wanted to see some new territory."

It wasn't long until conversation went to the coming evening with Rupert and Milberg. Secula was concerned about what time things might happen: "I don't recall Rupert saying a specific time to meet, any ideas about what time to get together?" There wasn't much by way of response until Twyla contributed: "It should be dark by nine o'clock. That would leave enough time in case anyone wants to go out for dinner. George and Shane were talking about that." There were questions about where to go to find a restaurant. "Shane was talking about a place in Ebensburg. We could all go. Let me know who all wants to go and I'll make sure they have room for us." It became clear that everyone felt like going out for dinner. Wally remarked: "That gets Twyla out of the kitchen." Some laughter followed. Twyla then tried to get Gia to talk about channeling. She was very curious how the whole thing worked and what it was like for Gia to do that. Gia didn't answer immediately. She sipped her coffee a bit, then noticed that everyone at the table was looking at her. "Twyla, don't be insulted by this. I just don't want to talk about it. Maybe after I've done it longer it won't bother me." Twyla was genuinely surprised. "I'm not insulted. I just can't understand how it would bother you. It seems like such a wonderful gift." Silence followed until Gia contributed some explanation: "It is a wonderful gift. I'm glad I can do things to help people. It does make me feel useful. But I feel like a freak. I just want to be a normal person and be happy. Maybe I'll get used to it as time goes on. I've only done this for not even a year now."

Twyla was apologizing for saying something that bothered Gia and telling her how grateful she was for trying to help them with Milberg. In the midst of this Shane and George came across the back porch and into the kitchen. "Man, am I glad I took George along. He helped me with three issues at the hardware that I didn't have a clue how to deal with. One involved a leaking toilet on the third floor." Before he had a chance to continue, Twyla was directing him and George to the hotdogs on the stove. She got more potato salad out of the refrigerator. "And how about that part for the washer?" "We had to order one. Shettig says it'll be in on Thursday." Shane and George were contentedly munching on hotdogs when plans for dinner were finalized. Twyla had put in a call to Ebensburg and announced: "they have room for all of us. They said to show up some-time after 5:30."

A welcome spring rain blew in during the middle of that afternoon. Those who had talked about going for a walk were glad they hadn't done that. Shortly after 5:00 Secula's BMW and a van that Shane drove pulled out with all eight aboard. Dinner was preceded by a tour around uptown Ebensburg, the County Seat. All seemed to enjoy the little park that sat beside a formidable looking old jail. While sitting on the grass there, most realized they were getting hungry. A place called the Noon-Collins Inn was next on the agenda. Dinner awaited. The old stone inn had once been a stopping place on the Philadelphia to Pittsburgh Pike; dinner was good, if not exotic. By 8:00 that evening all were back in Shane and Twyla's excessively large old house.

Gia had no idea when or if Rupert would show up. She thought it would be best to be ready and made her way to the front room, planting herself solidly in one of the big old chairs. The clock in the hall chimed 8:30 shortly after she set down. She just wanted to sit there and be quiet. She had gone past Secula in the kitchen before going to the front room. Secula had decided not to bring up the issue of Gia and Wally embracing earlier that day. When Secula noticed Gia heading for the front room, she went upstairs to get her notepad and recorder. A bit later she walked into the front room where Gia was seated. When Gia saw her cousin, she understood Secula was getting ready for a Rupert session. Secula seemed to understand that Gia wanted to be quiet and said nothing. Smiling at her cousin, she just sat down. This was the first time Secula actually felt like talking to Gia about the episode earlier with Wally. Since they were waiting for Rupert, she did not do that. Secula felt that bringing it up might disturb her cousin and make it difficult or impossible to have a session. They just sat there.

There were noises in the house. Muffled sounds and voices could be heard upstairs. People came and went in the kitchen as Gia and Secula quietly sat there. It was not long until Secula noticed that her cousin was beginning to space out. She usually got that way before she started channeling. Just in case, Secula pushed the record button on her machine and got up and went through the house telling people that something was about to happen. When Secula came back into the front room, Gia was still quiet; she turned off her recorder and waited. Shane and Twyla drifted in. Secula indicated to them to be quiet. George appeared followed by Wally. Gia was starting to babble in Italian and Susan and Donnie came down the stairs and quietly made their way into the front room. Although Secula couldn't understand what Gia was saying, she pushed the record button.

People just sat there, listening. No one really understood Italian. The old grandfather's clock in the hall began banging out 9:00 o'clock. Maybe that made the change, maybe not. Whatever the case, it did get Gia to become silent. After the 9:00 o'clock bells, there was maybe a whole minute of silence. No one said a thing. Then there was speaking again. Gia commenced talking in English. *I greet my friends one more time. I thank you for showing up. Milberg is busy with her teachers right now. I am hopeful she and they will join us too. Until then I shall proceed to take care of a bit of unfinished business. I had been speaking to you about the challenges one faces when trying to live the life of a creative artist. Shane had introduced the subject with his question about creative types and substance abuse.*

I mentioned a number of challenges that creative types face. These might tempt them to fall back on the temporary expedients of drugs, alcohol, and the other avenues of escape. Although I briefly mentioned the social context of the artist, I did not get to say what I had in mind. I shall say something in that regard tonight. If Milberg should show up, we will shift to matters pertaining to our discussions with her.

Those blessed with a creative bent often do not realize how different is the outlook of their contemporaries not similarly gifted. It would be very helpful to creative types to be temporarily transplanted into the psyche of an individual of a more practical disposition. They would soon see that there is a very different outlook there. Instead of seeing a world that admits of much creative change, the more practical ones see a world fixed in place. In their minds, one should accept the world as it is and not be given to dreaming of a new world order where the state of everything and everyone can be changed for the better. That brief excursion into the consciousness of so many of your contemporaries was only to give you better insight into the real world you do live in. Creative types often begin to feel at variance, at odds with, their fellow human beings because they sense their worldview differs so greatly. Because of this, the creative ones often do not get along well in social situations, business enterprises, and in so many of the common adventures that humans are involved in. The upshot of this is often a feeling of isolation and rejection.

This sense of aloneness and apartness can and does lead to the use of the temporary expedients we mentioned. Helpful here can be an attitude shift that allows the creative person to accept those not so blessed as themselves. I might make a comparison here to people blessed with high intelligence as it is judged in your society. Often high IQ individuals have a very difficult time dealing with people not similarly blessed. They feel that everyone should be able to understand things as they do. There seems to be a blind spot in their intelligence that does not allow them to understand that, in truth, you are not all born equal. The greater number of their contemporaries are simply not able to comprehend the world as they do. This often leads to misunderstandings, isolation, and disagreements. Their case is similar to those with strong creative abilities. And, at times, high creative ability and high IQ are combined in the same individual. These especially will do well to heed what I say. What I say is this; do not fall into the habit of judging harshly those unable to see and understand the world as you do. Often their gifts allow them to do things that you are incapable of or unwilling to do. You will be a happier person if you can accept your contemporaries as they are and not assume that they are capable of the insights you have been blessed with.

Since Milberg has not as yet appeared among us, I shall continue with my comments on social context. Your society generally does not hold art and artists in high regard. More fortunate are the creative types whose work has practical application. Architects come first to mind here. Filmmakers come to mind too. An artist might be tolerated if his or her works sell. In general, artists are looked down on in your society as dissolute, disorganized, immoral, and- add what adjectives you will. It must be admitted, artists have done their share to encourage those attitudes. Such was not always the case. There were times when art and artists were held in high esteem. Your contemporary culture has respect and admiration for science and matters related to it. The practical application of science to technology is what commands respect and attention in your world.

It might be said that technology is your art, the art of the present day. Don't be surprised that many of your contemporaries will not look with high regard upon your work. If your art can be convertible to money, it might find respect and acceptance. Money, science, and technology are things your society holds in high regard. Despite the fact that the educational processes in your culture downplay the arts, here and there are still to be found individuals capable of seeing worth in art that has nothing to do with money. Be kind to those people when you find them.

This somewhat gloomy appraisal of the arts in the society you are a part of is not an attempt to discourage you. It is to wake you up to the realities of your times. It is also given by way of explanation. You might look at this as one more factor why creative types often look to the escape routes offered by chemical means. Often the young artist has hopes that his or her works will be a viable means of support. So often this proves not to be true. Wallowing in sadness and misery is no solution. I offer some advice that I hope you'll take to heart. In addition to training yourselves in the skills of your chosen art, it is a very good idea to work on developing backup skills that can provide income when your art does not. Do not look down upon the humble skills of a carpenter, plumber, electrician, and all the trades that normally can find employment. Teachers are in demand . . . .

Rupert had become silent. All eyes in the room were now fixed on the doorway to the front hall. It was the doorway in which Milberg had appeared the previous night. There was a shadowy presence there. As the clock ticked, that shadowy presence got somewhat more distinct. It never got to the point where the image in the doorway was as clear and definite as the other individuals in the room. Nevertheless, those individuals in the room could see and understand that they were seeing another presence like themselves. Milberg was again among them. Secula rose from her chair and looked out into the hall to Milberg's right. She was looking for Rupert. She began to wave, evidence that Rupert was indeed there in the hall – but still able to speak through Gia. Then a shrill voice was heard in the room, emanating from the presence known as Milberg McGuire. "Young lady, please sit down. I wish to speak to this group assembled here."

Secula quietly sat down and awaited Milberg's words. "Perhaps I owe an apology to some here. It has come to my attention that this is no longer my house, and I have rudely insulted its true owners. Please hold my apology in consideration. One day, when your condition is as mine, you may understand my situation and think more kindly of me. To the others here present, I ask that you might not consider my rudeness with such harshness. To the one who calls himself Rupert and stands beside me, I extend greetings and ask a question. Might you gratify me with answers to questions asked when we last met?" Gia moved back and forth in her chair a bit. She looked squarely at Milberg and began to talk, in Italian. Her cousin, Secula, began waving to her, then spoke: "*Italiano, Italiano* – say it in English." Gia quickly became quiet and sat there appearing to be regrouping. She rubbed her hands over the armrests of the big old chair and seemed to struggle to utter words in English. *Gia speaks well for me, but there are times when she forgets she has come to a new land. I greet you Milberg McGuire and will try to answer some of your questions.*

You did ask me how many lives a person must live. That is another question to which I am not able to give you a specific answer. The answer to that question depends very much upon the individual involved. Physical lives are meant to be learning experiences. If we learn the lessons quickly, we have fewer lives. If we do not learn these lessons quickly, more lives will be required until we learn what physical life is to teach us. Rupert sensed that Milberg was wanting to ask a question; Gia became silent. "You say that our lives are <u>meant to be</u> learning experiences. Where does this <u>meaning</u> come from?" Rupert became somewhat jovial. A laugh could be heard coming from Gia – then words. *The answer to that question could take several of your lifetimes for me to answer. Religious persons like to use the word, God, to answer that question. That is a kind of short circuit thinking, but better than no answer at all. Just remember that what you call God is not apart from who and what you are. You are a part of what is called God.*

Again, Milberg was wanting to ask a question. Rupert could sense this and remained quiet. "You, Rupert, speak to me of the things we are to learn in the processes of our earthly lives. Might I be so bold as to ask what it is that we are to learn?" Gia could be seen smiling when hearing this question. There was a quick response from Rupert. *You have a talent for asking difficult questions, Milberg. If I could answer that question for you with a few easy words, there would be no purpose for your earthly lives. I am risking an accusation of short circuit thinking myself here, but I will give you what might be one simple and easy answer, not the answer, but an answer.*

Point One: all of you are to learn that you have a share in the creation of the physical reality you experience. What is called God is usually blamed for the creation of yourselves and your world. You are to learn that you are co-creators in this physical experience. Your first and most important product while physical is your physical body, yourself. The world about you is also part of a joint creation. You and the people of your world create that world with your common beliefs. Your beliefs are key here. You might think of your physical universe as a construction of beliefs. You might think of your own body as a belief construction. When you want yourself and/or your world to change, it is the beliefs about yourself and/or your world that must change. I am not saying that what you call God is not involved in this. I am saying that each of you is given a great part in this creation. You must learn to come to the point of being conscious co-creators of your world. I mean this in no abstract theoretical or philosophical sense. You must learn to the point of deliberately constructing with your beliefs – you and your world. Perhaps you now see that creativity involves much more than putting paint on a surface. You are all involved in the creation of yourselves and your world.

Point Two: a very important matter to be learned about this creation is as follows: the present is your point of power. The present is where you exercise the greatest leverage in the exercise of your power of creation. You create you and your world now. Those with degrees in psychiatry will try to tell you that events from the dim dark past have influenced your present life and impede you from being happy. I tell you that if their thinking had any merit, they would not as a group have the highest suicide rate in your country. Exercise your power of belief in the present; believe in the things you want. Also, do not acquire the habit of looking only to a future where you will be able to carry out your life's dreams. You will only be putting off the creation of the world you want. Your present is where past and future intersect. It is where you exercise influence over all those dimensions of time that seem to influence your lives. These are two important points, Milberg. They must be learned in the conduct of your life, not in the dim caverns of your mind. What I have left unsaid here could take volumes to explain. This is only a slight beginning.

Milberg seemed attentive to the things Rupert said, but interrupted him often with questions. She was annoyed with things Rupert said about what we call God. She also couldn't understand how it is that we create ourselves on a daily basis in the world of our experience. Rupert countered questions like that by explaining much of that creative activity takes place in states when our usual conscious focus is asleep. In the dream state we visit the world where much of the creative activity takes place. Rupert spoke of different frameworks of activity. One of those frameworks is the conscious state of our daily experience. The other framework is one we visit when in less than conscious states. Maybe in our daydreams we take a few steps into that world. Surely in our dreams at night we go there. In these visits we meet with other individuals and entities. We make arrangements with them there for projects we will be involved in together in the physical world. We meet those who will become important in our lives, ones with whom we will share major events of our lives. They might be marriage partners, business partners, lovers, or best friends. We meet there the spirits of those who will come into our lives as our children. We do the creative work there that keeps our bodies healthy and keeps our lives on a good track.

Rupert's discourse went on into the night. He mentioned that the division of ourselves into the different realms, or frameworks, is not necessary. Things can be structured differently so that much more of who and what we are might be accessible to us. It is possible that we can take a more conscious part in creating ourselves and our worlds. What must change are our beliefs. Once we come to believe that these changes can take place, they can come about. We create the world we believe in, according to Rupert. One of the obstacles to us making these changes is the belief climate we live in, the attitudes of the society around us. We must rise above the small, yesterday thinking of our contemporaries; this enables us to move on to a better world, a world in which we have access to who and what we really are. Rupert explained that within not too many years these changes will begin to take place. The conditions for these changes are upon our world now and only need to be realized. He explained that the teaching he was passing along will help this come about. Rupert then went on to encourage Milberg to listen to her teachers and move on to better things in her life. Sometime after the old clock in the hall banged out one solitary chime, it was noticed that the image of Milberg in the doorway became gradually less distinct. It got to the point where she was almost transparent. The hall stairway with its banisters could be seen through her. Rupert noted that Milberg was leaving the gathering. He told Twyla and Shane that it was unlikely she would continue her residence in their house.

Six

BACK TO PITTSBURGH

S unday was a less than memorable day. Some went into the little town by the college and looked around. Gia spent time in the morning listening to the tape Secula had made of the previous night's session with Milberg. She felt a kind of relief hearing Rupert's words about Milberg not returning to bother Shane and Twyla. It made her think that the trip there had been worthwhile. She had a need to feel useful and do good things. Milberg could move on and Shane and Twyla wouldn't be bothered by her any longer. After lunch Gia spent some time out in the yard doing a drawing of the big old house they were staying in that weekend. Some time out of the city had been good for Gia. Change always did her good. Having grown up in a small village, Pittsburgh did weigh on her at times.

Gia was, despite that, anxious to get back to Pittsburgh. On Thursday she would be going downtown with Secula and Wally to take care of bureaucratic matters relating to the trip to Italy. She would also be inquiring about becoming a US citizen. Her concerns about her father were the large, looming issues behind this trip to the land of her birth. She also looked forward to seeing the rest of her family again. Though not all of them still lived at home, they were not so far away that she couldn't see them. She looked forward to walking in the little streets of her village again. There were so many memories there and people she knew. Her thoughts started to go to the far end of the village against the mountain. The church was there. She did not want to think about that end of the village. She had worked at the church there. She did office work and took care of many things. She even cooked for the priest at times. When she started working there the priest was old; she had known him since she was a child. After some years he died. A young priest took his place. She got along well with him – too well. He told her he would leave the priesthood and marry her. She became pregnant. She thought he would be happy. He was enraged; he denied fathering the child. Soon she lost her job; she was dismissed. Soon after that she miscarried. She was brokenhearted, jobless, and living at home.

This had been the prelude to her coming to America. Then she had just wanted to forget it all and begin anew. Now she had been in America long enough to see it all in perspective. Rupert had helped her see things differently. Her cousin, Secula, had helped her get a new start. George had shown up. Even though she liked her life and her new country, she wanted to go back to Italy to visit. Especially she wanted to see her father. She didn't want him to die before she got back home. She had a strong intuition that he would not be too much longer in this world. Rupert had told her that she and her father were members of the same entity. To her, this had meant that they were close in this world and probably had shared time together in other dimensions of existence. Whether those other dimensions had been physical or nonphysical ones, she was not sure. It all made her curious as to whether she had lived in other lands during different times. Had she lived during the plague years? Had she lived in the dark shadowy times before history began to record the panorama of human events? What had she thought about then? Who had she know? How did her present father fit into those scenes?

These mental excursions were interrupted by her cousin, Secula. "Gia, we're going to be leaving for Pittsburgh in about an hour. I just wanted you to know in case you didn't have your stuff ready yet. I thought you might want to say so long to Twyla and Shane too. They are down in the kitchen now. Twyla is getting sandwiches and soup ready for us before we leave." "I do want to say something to Twyla. Shane I am not too anxious to talk to." Secula was quietly juggling ideas in her head, ideas about things she wanted to say. "I noticed Shane getting a bit too friendly with you during the lightning storm on the back porch." Secula paused a bit before saying what else was on her mind. "I think maybe you would like Wally to be friendly with you that way." This took Gia very much by surprise. "Why you say that, Secula?" Secula was fumbling her way through this. She wasn't sure just how much or how little to say. "When you and Wally were coming up the hill from drawing yesterday, I was on the front porch reading." A look came over Gia's face telling Secula that she now knew why Secula had spoken about her and Wally together.

"Since I come to this country, Secula, you do so much for me. If you are not here, things would not turn out so good for me." Gia was not paying so much attention to English grammar now. She was a bit upset. "I like Wally, but don't want you to think I'm trying to take him from you. That's not what I do." Secula wanted her cousin to know that she wasn't upset with her. "I didn't bring this up to make you feel bad, Gia. There is something I wanted to say about you and Wally. Rupert talked to me one time last year about feelings I was having for George. He explained that we had been together in lives in the past. Rupert said that was the reason I was feeling jealous about you and George together. I never told Wally about this; don't tell him. The reason I bring this up has to do with Rupert. I'm thinking we should ask him about you and Wally. Maybe there are things that he knows, things that we don't know. It's possible that you and Wally shared lives together, lives in other times that are hidden from us now."

Gia was quiet for a bit. She seemed to be thinking about things. Finally she spoke: "That's . . . that's a lot to think about, Secula. Do you ever see Rupert to ask him about these things?" "Most of the time, Gia, since you've come, I only see him when you channel. When he knows that something is on my mind, he'll show up in my dreams or get in touch some way." Again, Gia seemed to be thinking about all this. She looked away for a bit, out the window, then looked back at Secula. "Do you think you could ask Rupert about this the next time you have a chance? Rupert always has a way of making things better. He knows the things the rest of us never think of." This time it was Secula who was quiet for a bit. Then she responded: "You can be sure I'll bring it up with Rupert if I have a chance. Right now I'm getting hungry. You want to go down to the kitchen to get something to eat?"

In the kitchen things were rather subdued. People there were aware that a departure would soon be taking place. There seemed to be mixed feelings about this. Twyla invited the Pittsburgh people to come again. Donnie Diangelo responded by talking about his family's island on the Allegheny River. "The place there is about the size of a motel. We still have boats there: the rowboat, speedboat, and the old Chris-Craft. I always like to have visitors when I go out to the island. I'll let you know next time I go. It's big enough that no one gets in one another's way." There followed comments from the other Pittsburgh people about their experiences on the island. Twyla and Shane seemed genuinely interested. Talk about Donnie's Island broke up the somber mood of the gathering in the kitchen. The cat came out of its hiding place in the dining room and joined the visitors for a change. People began bringing down luggage to the back porch after they had something to eat. Sometime around 5:30 Secula opened the trunk of her car and began putting things aboard. This seemed to be a definite breakpoint, but George insisted on firing up a joint on the back porch and passing it around. This somewhat delayed the exit scene.

It was close to 6:00 and the trip was still an event of the future. A third joint was making the rounds. Shane was thinking he should apologize to Gia for events on the porch during the storm. He had sat down close to her on the porch floor, and was thinking how to begin the conversation.

Before he had a chance to do that, Gia got up and went into the kitchen. That left Shane sitting there thinking about composing a letter to her, which he would send to her in Pittsburgh. In the kitchen a big jug of red wine came out from the fridge. Gia found a glass and poured herself some. She and Twyla were talking about the big old house they were in. Then Gia told Twyla about the factory she lived in and her efforts to make it livable. Secula came into the kitchen, intending to move people in the direction of the cars. That didn't happen. Twyla began to talk about everyone staying for another night. George fired up another joint and found his bottle of tequila in the refrigerator. Wally made the rounds asking everyone if they absolutely had to wake up in Pittsburgh the next morning. Around 6:30 the luggage on the porch began to move back into the house. Secula and Susan had refrained from drinking up to that point since they had planned to drive. Once they noticed people carrying their belongings back into the house, there was a rethinking of that agenda. Twyla had made a trip to the basement to find a jug of homemade wine she had brought from upstate New York. Secula, upon seeing Twyla emerge from the basement with the gallon jug of wine looked at her sister, Susan. They both started smiling and found a couple wine glasses. Several people made phone calls to re-schedule Monday a bit.

It turned out to be the best evening of the weekend. The dining room had not been used since the Pittsburgh people arrived. Lights were on in there and people drifted in from the kitchen. Secula, observing from the kitchen, watched Gia and Shane have some serious conversation in there. Gia sat in an old rocker as Shane stood and seemed to be explaining or apologizing. Secula could guess what it was about. Twyla seemed somewhat concerned about it, and Secula dropped a few hints to her as to what might be going on. George wandered in with a joint and passed it around. There was an old vintage couch in there that Susan and Donnie made use of. The dining room became the place to be for the evening and Twyla brought in some munchies, putting them on the table.

With the arrival of marijuana and more people, Shane and Gia's serious discussion was quickly replaced by laughter and just foolin' around. Shane got out his guitar. Wally unpacked an old Hohner harmonica in the key of C he had brought with him. Something resembling music accompanied the wafting of marijuana smoke through the room. Now and then people sang. Secula noticed Gia, still in the rocker, was starting to space out. Just in case, she unpacked her tape recorder. Others in the room began to notice that Gia was getting that faraway look in her eyes. Wally was talking to Secula when he noticed Gia's mouth beginning to move. He pointed this out to Secula and to others in the room. Secula turned on her recorder.

I am glad . . . I am glad to see you having a good time. I do not want to spoil your fun. I won't be here long this evening, or this night. I come as the result of a question asked by Gia – the lady who speaks for me – and Secula Venturi. There was a question whether two of you here, Gia and Wally, might have been associated in a life or lives in some other dimension of time and space. I am able to answer that for you in the affirmative. Wally may not have considered the possibility, but I know Gia and Secula were curious about that. You might think about Italy. It was the time of the Renaissance. Your names then were not Gia and Wally. Lorenzo and Lucia worked as names for you then. You were sister and brother. Despite that close blood relationship, there was a strong physical attraction between the two of you then. People around you noticed this. Especially your parents cautioned you that this fascination was wrong and must not be followed.

Causing much grief for your parents, as teenagers you ran away together. You had been living with your family in Rome, but made your way out into the countryside where it was hoped you would not be recognized. You spent some very enjoyable summer nights together in an olive grove by a village not far north of Rome. You worked to establish yourselves in that small village and marry. You lived into your 20s in that village as a married couple. However, Lorenzo – Wally wanted to be a painter. The impulse for this brought the two of you back into the city, Rome. Economic matters became a crucial issue. It was discovered that the earnings of an unknown painter could not support the both of you. After struggling together for some time, you separated. Your lives continued in that city and you did maintain contact but lived separately. Eventually the both of you reestablish contact with your family, discovering that your mother had passed away. There is more to tell you about those lives, but not now. I want to point out that the probabilities point to another life together for the two of you in what you would think of as the future. I think it would be in the country you now live in, on the West Coast. I do not tell you these things to cause friction with others you know and care about – quite the opposite. I only say these things to give both of you better insight into your life situations. That can be helpful to anyone trying to navigate a course through life. Although I could say more, I will say good night now. I enjoyed the company of your pleasant gathering. One final comment relates to Milberg. Having been in touch with her teachers, I was told that the likelihood of her causing any more disturbance here is very slight. I truly enjoyed your pleasant gathering, and now say good night with whatever blessing I am able to bestow upon this house and those assembled here.

Secula looked over at Gia in the rocker. She was shaking her head; it seemed to mean that she was coming out of trance quickly. Gia heaved a sigh saying, "I'm back." A number of the people in the room welcomed her back. Secula told her about the tape of Rupert and briefly recounted items about the lives in Italy. Wally filled Gia in on a few more details of their Italian lives. He also recalled some of his dreams: "often I've had dreams of living in a big city in Italy. In those dreams I was a painter, and many of my friends were also. The time was hundreds of years in the past. There was a girl who kept showing up in those dreams. This makes me wonder if it was that earlier version of Gia named Lucia. It also makes me think just how wonderful and mysterious life really is."

After Rupert's exit, the evening continued to sometime around 11:00. Shane was concerned about an early class he had in the morning and headed upstairs. Gia helped Twyla put some of the munchies back that had been on the dining room table. As Gia was carrying crackers and ham salad into the kitchen, Twyla was filling her in on details of the earlier life in Italy. The warm summer nights in the olive grove captured her imagination. The others slowly made their way upstairs. A few lingered on the back porch watching the stars. When Gia came into the kitchen next morning, Shane was sitting at the table going through class notes. He quickly got up to get coffee for her. Handing it to her, he smiled. Gia smiled back saying, "I'm glad we talked last night. It makes things better. What are you doing in class this morning?" Shane was talking about William Blake as others drifted into the kitchen. "After Blake's death his wife was asked what he talked about. She informed the questioner that she didn't talk much with Mr. Blake, commenting that Mr. Blake was mostly in heaven." Secula helped Twyla get some pancakes cooking; others got plates out and set the table.

At sometime between 9:00 and 9:30 that morning the two-car caravan got on the road. As Secula drove, Wally was talking about William Blake. "I wish we could have stayed longer to listen to Shane; Blake was such an unusual character. He was an experimental printmaker, a poet, and many speak of him as a mystic." Just approaching Loretto, Wally's cell phone rang and interrupted his musings on Blake. "Hi mom, how are things in Jeannette?" Gia and Secula noticed Wally was quiet for quite a while; then he spoke again: "maybe we can stop in. We're on the road right now. I'll get back to you." Wally was quiet for quite a while after he said so long. Gia and Secula were expecting some explanation. Wally just sat there quietly thinking how best to bring this up. A couple miles out of Ebensburg Wally finally got something out of his mouth. "Okay you two, this is just a wild brainstorm, but I want to run it past you. Mom is having a really bad day. My aunt just died. Is there any chance we could stop in at Jeannette on the way to Pittsburgh? I don't have any idea what your schedules are like today." Wally's two friends in the car had heard the end of his conversation with his mother and were not surprised by the request. Secula was the first to say something: "I don't want to spend a whole lot of time there, but I wouldn't mind meeting your mother. Can we limit it to a two-hour visit?" Wally commented that it might not be that long. Gia was up for it and gave Wally the go-ahead. She wanted to know where Jeannette was. Wally began describing it as being not too many miles south of the road to Pittsburgh and got back on his cell phone. After calling his mother, he called George, riding in Susan's car. "We'll turn off at Route 66 and go south and see you guys later in Pittsburgh."

As they rode along, Secula was curious how much Wally had told his mother about her and asked him about that. "She knows you're a very important person in my life. I call her often. Since dad died and my sister moved out, she's all alone. I've been talking to her about you since last year. I've mentioned Gia too, but not as much. I remember telling mom about Gia when we moved into the factory building. I've never told her about the channeling thing. I never saw any point to bringing it up." Just then a big coal truck went past silencing all conversation. Stopping at the light in New Alexandria, Wally became talkative again. "It'll just be a few miles to the Rt. 66 turn off. Keep your eyes peeled for signs for 66; we will be going south on that." Having said that, Wally got on his cell phone again and called George in Susan's car behind them, letting him know they would be cutting off shortly. After the call his thoughts turned to his mother again. "When I was a little kid, mom used to draw and paint. It was one of the things that got me interested in art. We used to draw together sometimes. It seemed to make her happy and feel good about herself. Since she's gotten older, she doesn't do that anymore. If I can, I'd like to try to get her to do that again. If you two want to, you could help by talking about art. We could even bring up the trip to Italy."

Secula had heard Wally talk about his family often, but that was a subject Gia knew next to nothing about. Just as Secula was turning off to go south on 66, Gia began asking Wally what it was like for him growing up in Jeannette. "It never seemed like I lived in Jeannette. We lived on Maple Avenue. It was a nice suburban neighborhood. Kids I knew lived

Gia

in Jeannette; it was not the same there. Jeannette is a gritty old mill town built around the glass industry. A lot of that had shut down and things there were not so good anymore. Dad was an engineer at Elliott Company. That wasn't part of the glass industry thing. In a way I lucked out. My Jeannette friends seem to have a lot rougher life." Wally was quiet for a bit; he was looking for another turnoff. Once that was made he continued to talk. "My sister was about two years younger. Most of the time, I was really glad she was around. She reminds me of my mother a lot. She went to nursing school in Pittsburgh then got a job in Morgantown. Sad to say, I don't see her much anymore." There were a few more turnoffs, then Wally began talking about the kids in his neighborhood. As they drove up Maple Avenue, he pointed out some of their houses.

Maple Avenue looked like a good place to grow up. A person could imagine it being far from a population center if they were not aware that it sat between Jeannette and Greensburg. Houses were on a hillside and not built too close together. The oldest ones looked to date from the 1930s. Newer houses predominated, likely dating from the 50s and 60s. An abundance of trees and green stuff said something about the people there caring about natural surroundings. Wally pointed out a tree he had fallen out of it in third grade, breaking his arm. Just after that he told Secula to pull into the next driveway. The house had an attached garage and the big garage door was open. Wally's mother stood in the garage waving. Although the garage had been built for two cars, only one was visible, a metallic gray mid-90s Cadillac. Wally made a comment that his dad always liked Cadillacs; he appreciated the combination of good engineering and style. Wally's mother, Bernice, was quite impressed with Wally's two Italian friends. She invited everyone to stay for lunch before they even got into the house.

It was a rather informal meeting, and then Bernice invited everyone to come in through the garage. A door toward the back of the garage led quickly into the kitchen after going across a landing for the basement stairs. Gia was taking note of a spacious, well accoutered kitchen as she imagined

Wally growing up there. Wally was being told there would be a funeral on Wednesday that he was expected to attend. Bernice grabbed bottles of beer, wine, and pop out of the refrigerator as she talked. Plunking them down on the table, she began talking about a very unfortunate auto accident in which her sister had been killed instantly just days ago. "Your uncle Billy is still in intensive care. They were in the state of Indiana when it happened. My sister's body should arrive in Greensburg today . . . ." Bernice went on at length about her sister's demise until the three from Pittsburgh began to look at one another and consider some strategy to get her mind off of that sad event.

Gia noticed a framed drawing hanging to her right. It was a drawing of an old house in a rural setting. It was tolerably well done. It demonstrated an appreciation of the old building if not an academically-trained hand. It was signed, 'Bernice 1979'. Gia started talking about the drawing, hoping to distract Bernice. "You must like that place. The drawing shows that you care about the old house." Wally took the subject up before his mother had a chance. "Mom grew up there. It was on an old farm out by Latrobe. I went there when I was a kid, but it's gone now. Do you still think about that place, mom?" Bernice looked at the drawing a bit before saying anything. When she started talking, it seemed difficult for her to get the words out. "So much . . . so much is gone now. Mother, dad, now my sister is gone. My two younger brothers are still alive." Secula asked if Bernice had done other drawings of the house. "No, but I've been thinking about it lately. My brother gave me a copy of a photo he had; it's one I never saw before." Wally brought in another drawing that had been hanging in the dining room. "Mom did this one too." Bernice started talking before Wally could continue. "That was our horse. We had that when I was growing up." The framed drawing was passed around for everyone to look at. This one was really good, surprising for a person with no academic training.

Secula started talking about her sister, Susan. "My sister does physical therapy – works as a therapist. She often talks about art as therapy, or art therapy. Although she's a trained physical therapist, she sometimes does art therapy with people. She never studied that; she just does it instinctively. She always liked to draw since she was a kid. She says that doing art stuff has often helped her personally to deal with things in her life." This seemed to catch Bernice's attention. "Working with someone like that might help me get to doing art again. Since Ed died, there's a lot of money available here, but not much motivation to do anything. I'd be happy to pay someone like your sister. It would be nice to have someone to draw with. Wally and I used to draw together when he was growing up." Mentioning Wally directed Bernice's attention to her son. "Wally, why don't you just stay here for the funeral? Your sister is coming in tomorrow; she'd like to see you. Now, don't start talking about having nothing to wear. A lot of your dad's suits are still here and they would fit you." This caught Wally totally by surprise. He was working on the illustration project for the History and Landmarks Foundation; he could use that as an excuse. One real issue of concern was getting back to Pittsburgh. "When Secula and Gia take off, I'll be stranded here. How will I get back?" Bernice had that one covered: "Westmoreland Transit still runs in to Pittsburgh. Better than that, I can still drive, you know. I've never seen that factory you moved into. I can drive you in on Thursday morning."

Wally was thinking that he had stopped in to help his mother out, and this might be the best way to do that. He wanted to show Gia and Secula the rest of the house. When they were upstairs, he asked Secula about her sister. "Did you make up that stuff about Susan and art therapy?" Secula got something of an offended look on her face. "No, that's for real." They started going through some of Wally's father's suits. They were doing that when Bernice came upstairs. "I put something together for lunch. It's nothing elaborate, just frozen things, and I made a salad from fresh vegetables. Lunch was a rather anti-climactic affair. Wally talked with Gia and Secula about Thursday. Plans were still on for the trip downtown to look into passports, visas, etc. That would be an afternoon trip now. By 1:30 Secula and Gia were backing out of the driveway onto Maple Avenue. Wally and his mother were in the garage waving.

Once on the road again, Gia had a chance to say a few things to Secula. "You think Wally's directions get you to the Pittsburgh road okay?" Secula nodded. "If we just keep going north, we'll run into it." This seemed to satisfy Gia; she had more questions. "This thing Rupert says about Wally and me – you okay with this?" Secula was in the passing lane and the BMW was approaching 75 miles an hour. She slowed down and shifted over a lane before saying anything. "Since I met Rupert, the world looks like a whole different place. I've come to realize it's a lot more complicated and wonderful place than I could have made up in one of my books." To answer your question, I'm just glad that it helps you make some sense of what goes on with you and Wally."

Once up on Rt. 22 again, Gia's questions continued. "I'm thinking about Bernice. You think someone should put her in contact with Susan about the art therapy thing?" Secula smiled a bit. "I know I'll be talking to her about it to see if she's interested. I know she does things mostly around the Bergh, and Jeanette is a bit out of the way; we'll see. Gia was still thinking about this: "She can drive. She has that big car. She could come into Pittsburgh." Secula commented that she hadn't thought about that. Once past Murrysville and Monroeville, traffic was heavier. Noticing this, Gia let Secula drive uninterrupted and asked no more questions.

Pulling into the alley they lived on, Gia asked Secula if she could sit on her back porch when they got in. "I like my apartment, but I miss the back porch." "Gia, you know you can. I told you before you moved out of my place that you could use the back porch anytime you want. I know you like to sit on the swing and look out into the backyard." Arriving at Secula's place, Gia got out and opened the big garage doors. Once Secula pulled in, she left them open; they still had unpacking to do. Gia brought her things in and left them on Secula's porch before she sat on the swing. She had no real agenda just then, just a need to sit for a bit. After Secula brought her things into the house from her car, she joined Gia on the back porch. Coming out of the kitchen door, she was carrying a half empty wine bottle and two glasses. "I didn't have anything to drink at Bernice's place since I was driving; I brought a glass for you too."

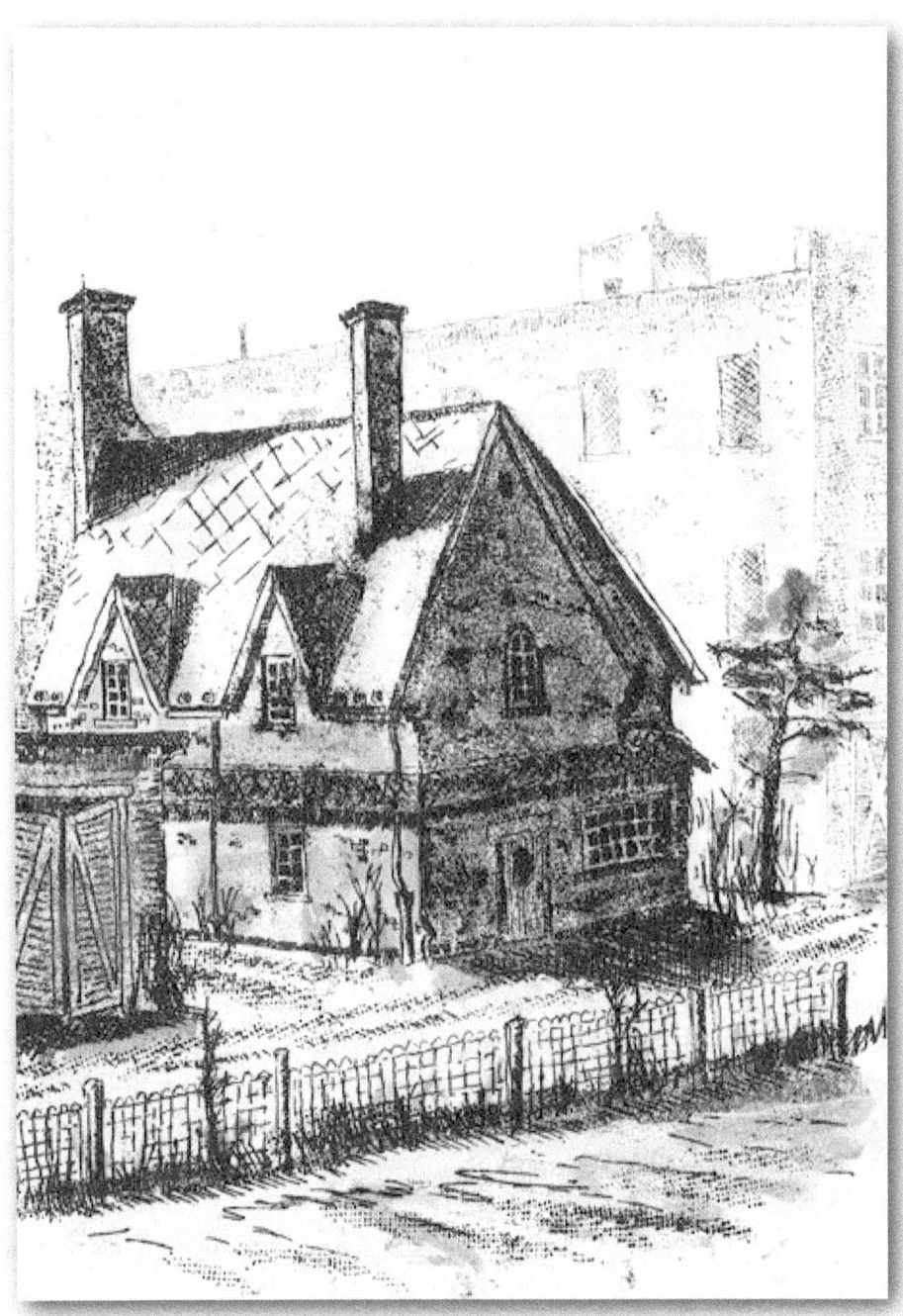

Secula's house between her garage and Gia's building.

Perching birds chirped on the fence at the end of the backyard. Gia watched Secula's yellow daffodils sway in the breeze. The rusty chains on Secula's swing sang a repetitive song as Gia and Secula sipped wine and went back and forth on the old wooden swing. Gia was thinking it almost seemed like being a kid again. She mentioned that to Secula; she just smiled. Gia spoke again: "maybe Secula, maybe we'll need the recorder. It feels like Rupert is around. I'm not sure yet, but maybe." It wasn't long until Secula disappeared into the house. She soon had strung an extension cord onto the porch and brought the recorder out. They just sat there for a while. The sound of Secula's cell phone on the kitchen table was heard ringing. She went in. "Hi Susan, where are you?" Susan had left Donnie and George off, done a bit of shopping, and wanted to know if it was okay to stop in. She had been in the Strip and, being close, thought about a visit. "Yeah Susan, Gia and I are on the back porch. We'll be glad to see you."

On the porch, Gia had heard bits of the conversation. She did know that Susan had called but not a whole lot more. When the screen door opened and Secula reappeared, she was expecting Secula to say something. She didn't say anything right away. Secula sat there with one of her mental juggling acts going on. On the one hand, Gia had said that she might start to channel. Susan might arrive; would that interfere? She had told Susan to stop in. She could have told her it wasn't a good time. She didn't do that. Secula was thinking that she shouldn't try to control everything when Gia started talking. "It sounds like Susan calls." Secula, now on the swing, was nodding her head. "She did. She was shopping in the Strip and is going to stop in. She should be here pretty soon." Gia said: "good, I like Susan." Gia was thinking about the first time she had met Susan at the airport last year. It was a good memory. She also thought about Dom, Susan's and Secula's father. He had met her at the airport too.

"I was thinking about your dad, Dom. Do you think he'd like to go to Italy with us?" Secula nodded her head again. "Dad would like to go along. I've no doubt about that. What I also have no doubt about is that mother will raise high holy hell about him going, and she will not go herself." "What's wrong with your mother?" This time Secula didn't hesitate to answer. "It's a serious case of religion and the damage done. I had to deal with it when I lived there; I just feel sorry for my dad who still has to put up with it." Gia seemed to understand and said nothing. The two of them sat there on the swing a while quietly until they heard a car pulling into the driveway. There was no doubt it was Susan's VW. The very characteristic sound of a 60s beetle announced her arrival.

The sound of the beetle got Secula musing about her sister and her car. She made enough money to buy something a lot newer, but still she kept the old relic. She even worked on it, doing things she was able to. Secula wondered if Susan's mechanical ability was related to her ability as a physical therapist. There was something about her ability to get hold of anything and make it work. Her abilities seemed to bridge the gap between nonliving mechanical things and the world of conscious physical organisms. Secula smiled as her sister stepped up onto the porch. Gia got up, went into the kitchen and got a wine glass for Susan. She didn't bother to ask if she wanted any. She just poured some wine for her and handed it to her. "Thanks Gia, you're my favorite cousin."

Susan didn't sit on the swing. She sat on the porch floor, leaning on the corner porch post toward the driveway. To her right she spied Secula's recorder with the wire going into the kitchen. She was wondering if she had interrupted something when Gia spoke up. "Maybe I channel for Rupert this afternoon – not sure yet." Gia had noticed her paying attention to the recorder. Secula started to tell Susan what she had told Bernice earlier, about Susan doing art therapy. Secula became quiet then. She was watching Gia; she seemed no longer physically present. Gia's lips were starting to form syllables. Secula reached down and pushed the record button on her machine. Neither Secula nor Susan said anything.

I am here . . . I am here because I have things to say. I will not take a lot of your time this afternoon. I was paying attention to your concerns about art therapy. Susan does have a gift. She belongs to that family of consciousness that works with healing. It is named Tumold. She also has abilities in the visual arts. There are connections there, connections with or between the healing arts and visual arts. It is sad that in your culture much of what is called art education damages people's abilities to actually do art. The rational bias in your culture looks down upon those whose visual expressions are not in strict lockstep with rational visual logic. People must be allowed to be free from this kind of thinking. Once they have cut themselves free from this domineering attitude to do art that looks like a machine did it, their visual expressions can have healing qualities. People are not photographic machines. Cameras can do better work. People should stick to what people can do.

Once people free themselves from the logic of the machine, they will be able and allowed to do art that is truly therapeutic. Art can be therapeutic in a number of ways: some works of art are therapeutic in themselves. The experience of viewing them can trigger healing mechanisms in the human system. Your world needs more of these. People free from the domination of rational logic are able to do these healing artworks. It is unfortunate that your culture names some people who do these things as being mad.

There is another sense or manner in which art can be therapeutic. This manner is the one in which people are allowed to do art themselves, art not constrained by the chains of visual logic. This is art that does not have to conform to the rules of perspective, design, the dictates of the art market, and photographic exactitude. Your culture silences people from expressing their very deep feelings in words. Unless these feelings are expressed somehow, people become sick – sick mentally and/or physically. Art is a way for these people to express their feelings so that they might remain whole.

There are many more things to say here. I have only tried to say a few. Wally's mother, Bernice, could profit from the ministrations of a person like

Susan. I think Susan understands that art does not have to conform to the principles of photographic precision. People are not machines, but they do have things to say. By allowing people to say and speak the messages from deep inside, they can become whole.

Seven

New Horizons

It had been some weeks since the trip to Cambria County and the visit with Shane and Twyla. Rupert had spoken several times since that through Gia. He spoke about art therapy again. He spoke about how it can be helpful to mental health professionals. The context was comments about people who had suffered severe trauma. Rupert mentioned that some of these people are not able to express verbally the deep-seated issues that bother them. He advised giving these people art materials and suggested they use them to express the issues they cannot express verbally. He mentioned Carl Jung in this regard, and the usefulness of this kind of therapy in working with children, who may not be able to describe their inner problems verbally.

Rupert spoke another time, about a week later. That time he talked about the need to actually do art, interacting with the materials of expression, rather than talking or thinking about it. He began by quoting a discussion between the French poet, Stephane Mallarme, and the French painter, Edgar Dégas. Dégas, the painter, had been trying his hand at poetry. He was working with Mallarme, the poet, who encouraged his efforts. One day Mallarme and Dégas came upon one another in the street.

Mallarme was curious how his friend was progressing with his poetry. He quickly pursued the subject. "Dégas, how is your poetry coming along?" It would seem that Dégas had not written much since he had last seen Mallarme. Not wanting to appear remiss he quickly commented: "Oh, Mallarme, I have ideas, so many ideas." Mallarme was quick to respond to that: "poems are made with words, Dégas, not ideas." Rupert used this as an entry point for what he wanted to say about doing art. He went to great pains to make the point that a person must interact with their chosen medium, whether it be words, paint, musical notes, etc. Just to think about these things is not enough. There must be interaction, physical interaction, with the elements of the medium for the magic of creativity to happen.

Gia was going over notes that Secula had made of that session. She was musing on these thoughts when a knock came at the door of her third-floor apartment. She suspected it was Wally. She thought she had heard his door downstairs. "Hi, Gia, can I come in?" Gia didn't have to be at work for several hours and was glad to see Wally. They had been downtown to see about passports and visas for Secula and Wally. She was wondering if there was any word on that. *"Que se diche, Wally?"* Wally mumbled some Italian as he came in the door. It was mostly unintelligible and Gia quickly flipped into English. "Do you and Secula hear anything about visas?" Wally was still in mumbling mode, but did manage to get out: "I talked with them about it. It's not come through yet, but the news is good. They tell me that they're coming through pretty quick right now. We shouldn't have to wait long. It could be next week." That made Gia feel good. She went to the refrigerator, getting out a bottle of wine. There was a tinkling of lead crystal glasses. Wally was watching with a smile. Gia poured wine into a glass and put it on the kitchen table in front of Wally. Wally sat down there. Gia was still standing, with a full wine glass in her hand. Wally raised his glass to her saying: "To the trip to Italy."

Gia sat down too, just opposite Wally at the rectangular table. They were sitting at the long sides of the table, facing one another and not far apart. Gia spoke: "When you and Secula get visas, how soon do you want to make the trip?" Wally looked to his left, out the window above the sink. He was looking at mostly sky. There were a few vapor trails from jets being distorted by the upper wind currents. Finally he looked back at Gia. There was a moment there when the two of them almost got lost looking into one another's eyes. Wally was grabbing the edge of the table when Gia looked away, taking another sip of wine. For both of them, there was a conflict thing going on. They both felt a sense of loyalty to Secula. She had helped Gia get established in America, and they were cousins. Secula was Wally's girlfriend, lover, and muse. He had a difficult time even thinking about being disloyal to her. But there was Gia, here now and appealing as ever. Wally was starting to get a headache brought on by the conflict when Gia spoke. "Wally, you still thinking about the trip to Italy? If you and Secula get visas, when you want to go?" Wally was glad for the distraction. It got his mind off of the conflict between his feelings about the girl he was with now and the girl he had slept with last night. "I think it should be on the first flight we can get that can take the three of us to Italy."

"Okay Wally; I'm glad now. I'm getting hungry too. It's lunchtime – you hungry?" Wally was nodding in the affirmative. "Big-time – yeah, hungry a lot." Gia was also thinking about her cousin, Secula. "You think Secula wants to have lunch with us?" Wally pondered the issue, again looking out the window. "She and her dad, Dom, are going out for lunch today. They'll probably talk about the trip to Italy. I know Secula wants Dom to go, but I don't think it's going to happen." Gia got up to pull some stuff out of the refrigerator. "You up for chopping vegetables, Wally?" Wally said, "Yeah," very quickly. It wasn't long before the sound of bubbling pasta filled the kitchen. Pasta sauce with mushrooms simmered slowly contributing its aroma. Wally was sitting again, thinking about finding some silverware when Gia plunked an old glass ashtray down on the table cloth in front of him.

Wally sat there staring at the ashtray. There was a bit of pot, papers, and matches. Wally really wanted to get high with Gia. But there was that conflict again. If he got high alone with Gia, he didn't know if he could stop himself from coming on to her. As Wally sat there wrestling with his conflicting feelings, Gia's hand grabbed the ashtray. Over at the counter she rolled a nice, well packed joint. Wally watched her fire it up and take a couple tokes. She handed it to him. Wally was sipping wine. A bit of wine in his system always made his sense of smell more acute. Before he took a toke, he noticed the smell of marijuana was now part of the olfactory medley in the kitchen. Salad was on the table. A balsamic vinaigrette dressing contributed to the medley. Wally took a big, deep toke.

It had been some time since Wally took his first toke. He had no idea how long it had been. It didn't matter. He couldn't keep his eyes off of Gia as she moved around in the kitchen. The seams of her panties under her tight black skirt especially caught his attention. This caught and kept his attention. There could have been an earthquake and he wouldn't have been distracted. Wally was totally fixated on Gia's ass. This was why he didn't want to get high with her alone. He didn't know if he could control himself. Gia was high too. She was thinking it had been a while since Wally said anything. She wasn't sure how long. She knew that getting high changed her sense of time. She just threw a few well-spaced words at Wally. "What you think about, Wally?" Wally's head bobbed up and down. His internal censor was now totally off-duty. Any socially-induced shoulds and oughts were totally inoperative. The words came marching out like well-trained little soldiers, totally oblivious of consequences. "I'm thinking you got the most gorgeous ass in the universe, Gia." He just sat there, stupidly staring at her. Gia couldn't help laughing. Wally couldn't help laughing either. Wally got a big smile on his face. Gia did too. Wally sipped some wine and Gia talked: "the last guy that says that to me got me pregnant. He said it in Italian, and he is a priest."

Wally's head rose, and he looked at Gia with big, open eyes. He was obviously surprised, maybe shocked. "Gia, you got a kid?" "No, I got a miscarriage; also lost a job. When we go to Italy, don't say anything about this to my family. They don't know anything about it. Secula knows." Wally just sat there trying to digest all this. Gia rolled another joint. Wally was sitting there thinking that Gia had been sleeping with his friend, George. For some reason, the thought of having sex with Gia didn't have anything to do with George. His friendship with George didn't stand in the way of that at all. He was just wondering if Gia was on birth control. "Gia, you on birth control?" Gia looked out the kitchen window and smiled. She had a good idea now what Wally was thinking about. She was thinking about the same thing. She had another toke on the joint. Her feelings of loyalty to her cousin Secula were fading into the background.

Wally noticed that Gia was staring out the kitchen window. From his point of view, seated at the kitchen table, mostly sky was visible. He also knew that from Gia's vantage point, standing, she could see one of the buildings he had come to talk to her about. He had almost forgotten why he had come up to see Gia. He wanted to go over and stand beside her, where he could comment on the building she was looking at. He still had a very firm erection; he knew he would be embarrassed if he got up and Gia saw this. "Gia, do you have any paper I can draw on?" Wally was still struggling with thoughts of loyalty to Secula. His idea was to draw a view of the building he and Gia were in – a drawing that would include the building next door and the building just to the south of it. He had come up to talk with Gia about these. It had finally occurred to him that was the reason he had come up here and that talking to Gia about the buildings might get his mind off of trying to get her clothes off.

The request for paper drew Gia out of her marijuana-induced reverie. Instead of getting paper, she said, "Yeah, I'm on birth control." Wally now sensed that they were both on the same wavelength. Instead of his erection going away, it started to get firmer. "Oh, you wanted paper, didn't you? You need pen too?" Wally was groping into his pocket for a pen. What he found there reminded him of a whole other issue, an issue he had been trying to forget. "Yeah, yeah I got a pen."

A sip of wine and two more tokes of marijuana later, Wally was drawing a picture of their neighborhood. It was from a rather high vantage point. It was elevated enough to include the building they were in, the one out the kitchen window, and the building south of that one. The building to the South faced out on Penn Avenue. Gia was sitting beside him watching him draw. When he had enough on paper to start talking, he began. "Next week Donnie and me are going to look at these two other buildings. His dad might come too. The real estate people are going to open them up for us. Do you want to come with us? I thought you might want to see them too." Gia commented, "Sure, if I'm not working. But you could ask me that without drawing all this. Why you have to draw all this?"

Wally was quiet again and looking to his left, out the window again. Gia sat to his right. He could feel her leg pressing firmly against his. It was quite some time before he said anything. When he did speak, it was another of those instances when the words came forth like obedient little soldiers, marching forward oblivious of the consequences. "I was trying to get my mind off you, Gia . . . trying to get my mind off getting' your clothes off." They just sat there looking at one another. Gia spoke: "I got hour and half before I have to be at work." She took Wally's hand. "Come on, we got time." She had no trouble leading Wally into the bedroom.

It was some time later. Neither Gia nor Wally were aware of the time. Gia was in the shower. She was singing the funny little Italian song she sang when she was happy. She had turned the hot water up. Steam was all around her. The steam made her think of an expression Secula had used, a literary reference: 'steaming wench'. Then her thoughts went to Wally. She was thinking about things Rupert said about them being sister and brother in Italy hundreds of years ago. She was remembering how good sex felt with him. Wally was lying in her bed staring up at the ceiling. He was thinking it had been the best sex he ever had. Thoughts of Secula weren't in his mind now. All he could think about was being naked with Gia, being inside her. He knew she was going to work at the bar. He was thinking that he might go over to the bar so he could be with her.

It was later on that day. Gia was behind the bar at Metropol. Wally was at Metropol too, on the other side of the bar. Gia was surprised to see him come in. He rarely came in at that time of day. He showed up just minutes after she had started her shift. Gia wasn't sure what this was about. Wally wasn't sure either. He just knew he wanted to be where Gia was. There weren't many people there yet. There were four people, guys, down at the far end of the bar. She had been talking with two of them. She politely avoided the other two. She had seen them before. They were not people she liked to have around. Looking to her left she noticed that Wally's beer glass was nearly empty. Without continuing the conversation with the two guys she had been talking to, she ambled down to the other end of the bar, nearest the stairs. Wally sat there smiling as she approached.

"Is the kitchen open yet, Gia?" Gia grabbed Wally's beer mug. As she was wheeling around toward the bar, she said: "I'm going to check in the kitchen. The cook got here couple minutes ago." Gia disappeared as Wally sat there with his thoughts. Thoughts of Secula were with him. He wondered what she was doing. He imagined her over at the house in her basement writing room. He knew she was working on a book on something. He wasn't sure just what. Gia reappeared. She had a cold beer and news from the kitchen. "We can do simple stuff now. If you want burger, fries, coleslaw, that takes 15 min. Other stuff on the menu will be a while longer." "Burger, fries, slaw – my kind of stuff – 87 octane food, that's my kind of cooking." "I'll tell the cook to go ahead with that, Wally."

Wally watched Gia disappear into the kitchen again. When she came back out she went down to the far end of the bar to check on things there.

Then three more people came wandering in. Wally sat there doing sketches on a napkin while Gia was busy. He was thinking about his project for the History and Landmarks Foundation. He knew that if he didn't jot ideas down when they came to him, they may not show up again. Some of the buildings he had to illustrate for that project had no visual references to go by. They had only mapping and written references to get him started. This required him to use his imagination quite a lot. As he sat there he worked on first rough sketches of two old downtown buildings that had been torn down in the 1890s. Then Gia was standing in front of him again. "I've been thinking about Secula; are you going to tell her, Wally?" That was a question that very quickly pulled Wally back to the summer of 2001.

Secula was sitting in her basement writing room. Before the phone call, she had been assembling parts and pieces of a story. It was about her ancestors in Italy. It was part fiction and part biography. Her fertile imagination had been cobbling together a story based on things she knew and things she had imagined. She was hoping that the planned trip to Italy would give her additional insights that might keep the story going. She was anxious to talk to relatives and others in the little village her family had come from. It was the village that Gia had come from last year. Then there had been a phone call. It was her dad, Dom Venturi. There was news. Her brother, Dominic Junior, would be visiting Pittsburgh. Could he stay at her place? Her mother, Maria Venturi, had disowned him when he came out gay, a few years ago in the mid-1990s. There was more news. Dom was thinking about going to Italy with Secula, Gia, and Wally. He wanted to bring Dominic Junior along on the trip so they could all visit the land of their ancestors and the remaining relatives there.

All of this was quite a surprise to Secula. She knew her mother would be furious about this. Maria had told Dom not to come back if he went to Italy. It would also postpone the trip a bit if Dom and Dom Junior came along. They would have to get visas for the trip; they both had passports already. She was turning all this over in her mind. She went upstairs to make tea. While the water was heating she looked out the back door into the yard. She wanted to see how the tulips planted that spring were doing. There were yellow ones and red ones. The red ones looked healthier. She was thinking she should water them when she noticed something she was not expecting. There was someone on the far end of her porch swing. It was a little fellow in an overcoat, an overcoat on a summer day. His feet didn't even reach the floor – Rupert.

Although Secula was glad to see Rupert, she went back to finish making tea before going out to say hello to him. As she stood at the stove she was recalling another day when Rupert visited. She had been making tea that day too. On that day she had rushed out on the porch right away to see Rupert. She forgot her tea until the kettle started to whistle. But she was very happy to see Rupert; she was also relieved. Now she would have someone to talk with about things on her mind.

Over at Metropol, Gia had a few free moments to talk with Wally as he was waiting for his burger and fries. "Wally, it feels like Rupert is around somewhere. It's not the same as when he is going to talk through me. That's something else. Sometimes, when Rupert talks to Secula, I can feel him around. What I feel is like that." Wally sat there looking thoughtful. "I wonder what Secula is doing."

Secula was, by this time, sitting on the left side of her back porch swing. Over on the right side was Rupert. *You shouldn't need your notebook for this. I just have a few thoughts to pass along. Sip tea and enjoy the nice day. I do not foresee everything that happens. Things with your cousin, Gia, and your friend Wally have entered a new phase. Yes, that is what I mean. Although it is an unexpected event, it should cause you no alarm. Their natures are stable and sincere. Don't expect them to go off on a personal, selfish romp and leave you alone. You may ask me questions if there is a need.* "No, I think I know what you're talking about." *Yes Secula, I think you do. Now, things in your family are likewise developing. Your brother will be coming to Pittsburgh for a bit. Perhaps he and your father will go to Italy with you. This may cause something of a problem for Gia as her father's health is rapidly deteriorating and she should get to Italy sooner rather than later. Your father and brother going on that trip with delay it somewhat for Gia.*

Secula sat there sipping tea pondering the matter. "I can see there are things that should be arranged." *For that reason, Secula, I am hoping we can gather the people involved when Gia would be able to channel me in their presence. Maybe you could arrange something for this weekend. Could you try to do that? And, are you still alright with your brother staying at your place? Given your mother's attitude toward his being gay, you know he is not welcome in the house he grew up in. If all goes as expected, he should be here by the weekend.* "I'm going to call dad later today to see what's happening with Dominic Junior. I want to talk to the both of them a bit before Gia channels you." *That's a very good idea. Seeing Gia talking as someone else could be very disconcerting for a person, unless some preparation work had been done.* "That's why I want to spend some time with them before Gia channels. Right now I want to talk to Gia. I want to make sure she'll be able to channel this weekend." *That's fine Secula, it would be best if you look away now, or just walk into the kitchen. I'd rather not disappear before your eyes.*

Secula got off of the swing as fast as she could with a cup of tea and saucer in hand. Back in the kitchen she did an about-face and returned to the screen door. She wanted to see if Rupert was still on her swing. He was gone. She knew Gia would be at work by now. At first she hesitated to call, but convinced herself that this was important enough for her to call Gia at work. At Metropol Gia was just bringing Wally's burger and fries when her cell phone rang. "Hi Secula, I was talking about you not long ago. I was telling Wally I felt Rupert around. Wally is here right now." Secula was a bit surprised that Wally was there. "Tell Wally I say hi. You were right about feeling Rupert around. We were sitting out on the swing talking. He just left. He has some things to say to all of us. Could you channel for him sometime this weekend?" Gia was quiet for a few seconds. Secula could tell she was thinking. "Sunday, Sunday Secula, that is a good day for it. I'm not working then." Wally interrupted his burger and fries to talk with Secula a few minutes. Gia grabbed his plate, taking it to the kitchen to the microwave.

Secula explained to Wally that she was going to make some phone calls to line up people for the weekend meeting with Rupert on Sunday. She also mentioned having had lunch with her dad and that he was very interested in going to Italy with the rest of them. Secula mentioned that this might delay the trip to Italy a bit, especially since her dad wanted to bring Dominic Junior along. After saying so long to Wally, Secula called the people who might be interested in a Sunday session with Rupert. Those who were going to come for the event, Secula also invited to dinner at her place. The plan was to have dinner, then have a session were Gia would channel Rupert some time after the meal.

Wally had finished his burger, fries and slaw. The bar was maybe half full now, and Gia was getting busier. Wally was jotting down some quick sketches and notes for this illustration project for the History and Landmarks Foundation. He always told himself that if he didn't jot down ideas when they came to him, they may not show up again. There was a building that had once stood on Market Square; he was trying to recon-struct that when his cell phone rang. "Wally, Secula. I've been lining up things for Sunday when Gia channels. Do you mind if I come over to the bar?" Wally's reaction was somewhat tinged with guilt. In the back of his mind was this dalliance with Gia that afternoon. "Not at all, Secula. You better hurry though; the bar is starting to fill up. I'll try to save a place for you."

Secula decided to go over to the bar wearing just what she had on. She felt less than pretty and fresh, but told herself she would not be the only woman there who looked a bit on the shabby side. She wanted to get a stool at the bar because she wanted to talk with both Wally and Gia. On the walk over to Metropol, she was having second thoughts about what she was going to propose to Gia and Wally. Arriving at the bar, she was glad to find Wally had kept the barstool to his left open for her. Gia spotted her coming in and was quickly on the other side of the bar from her. "You having Yuengling porter today, Secula?" Secula just smiled and nodded her head. She then started to fill Wally in on a few matters.

Gia was quick in bringing Secula's beer. Secula grabbed Gia's right-hand and slid her some money with her other hand. "Gia, I want to say a few things to you and Wally. When you get a few free minutes, come back over." Gia was nodding her head in the affirmative. "We can talk now, Secula. You and Wally are more important than the whole place here." First Secula told her two friends who else she had invited for the session on Sunday. Then she invited them both to dinner. Both said they would be glad to come for dinner and volunteered to help with getting things ready. What she said next left Gia and Wally just staring at one another. "Since my dad and brother want to come along to Italy, that will delay the trip a bit. I'm thinking about Gia's dad in Italy. He may not have a whole lot of time left. If you two want to go to Italy first, my dad, my brother, and myself will follow when passport and visa matters are cleared up." There was just a period of silence with Wally and Gia looking at one another wondering what Secula knew.

Eight

A Trip to Italy

It was Sunday. There was dinner at Secula's house. In addition to Secula, Gia, and Wally, there were others. Secula's dad, Dom, and her brother, Dominic Junior, were present. On the previous day Secula and her dad had met her brother at the airport. It had been arranged that he would stay at Secula's place since his mother had disowned him when he had come out gay several years ago. After Secula and her father and brother had arrived at her place yesterday from the airport, she felt a need to explain the Rupert experience to them. Since there would be dinner the next day followed by a Rupert session, she felt some advance notice was in order. Not surprisingly both Secula's dad and brother were completely mystified and had a raft of questions. She went to great lengths to fill them in and even showed them some manuscripts that Rupert had dictated. Now it was Sunday evening and both Dominics were very curious what would transpire as the evening progressed.

Also at dinner that Sunday were Secula's sister, Susan, and Donnie Diangelo; they had arrived together. George Willis was also there; he and Gia had been an item for some time. Since it was a summer evening, the meal was not a heavy one. There were several kinds of salad – one with pasta, one without. There were cooked beets and turnips, and there was barbecued chicken done on the fireplace in the backyard. Wally had supervised that project. The two main subjects of conversation that evening were the trip to Italy, and the arrival of Rupert. Donnie and Wally had been discussing the possibility of getting the two adjacent buildings that they were to see this coming week. Donnie mentioned that his dad would definitely be along for the viewing.

As the meal wound down, a cake Susan had made and some dessert wine appeared. By that time Dominic Junior was starting to become talkative. Previously, he had been very reticent. He started to talk about San Francisco, where he had been living. He was making comments on the music scene there, as he was a musician. He was also trying to elicit comments on the music scene around Pittsburgh. Donnie and George had a few enlightening comments for him. They talked about local bands that had caught their attention. Donnie asked Dominic Junior if he might want to see the new buildings that he and Wally were going to see that week. Young Dom seemed interested.

It was now close to seven o'clock and people were beginning to wonder when Rupert would make an appearance. For the benefit of both Dom Junior and Senior, people began to fill them in on what to expect from a Rupert session with Gia channeling. Everyone there except the two Doms had experienced one. Secula commented that the basement rec room – directly under the kitchen where they were sitting – would be the best place for the session. She contributed: "George has been working on that room; it is now very usable and a nice place to hold a session." There were words of assent. George began to carry some wine bottles to the basement. Secula brought glasses. The two Doms were all eyes and ears. They knew that something was about to transpire that they had not experienced before. The lighting in the basement room was muted for the occasion. Secula went back upstairs to retrieve her tape recorder and notepad. George decided it was time to fire up a joint, wondering how Dom Senior would react.

To George's surprise, Dom Senior moved closer to him. This enabled him to be the first person to get the joint when George passed it on. Dominic Junior was taking all this in. He was somewhat surprised, relieved.

Though it was summer, the basement was nice and cool. It wasn't long before Gia and everyone else was in the basement rec room. Eight people sat around waiting for something to happen. Things were mostly quiet. Gia was conscious that people were looking at her, waiting for something to happen. She put her head back in the rocker she sat in. She stared at the ceiling, not liking everyone looking in her direction. They had been sitting there five minutes waiting when Secula went upstairs to get something. Shortly she returned with a large, lit candle. It was aromatic, and the smell of pine began to mingle with the odor of marijuana smoke already in the room. By that time no one was smoking George's joints. They had gone up in smoke and people seemed comfortably spaced out. There were bits of disjointed conversation as boredom began to set in.

They had been sitting there some fifteen minutes when it was noticed Gia was sitting upright. Her lips were slightly moving; she seemed to be saying something, but it was mostly inaudible. Secula turned on her tape recorder just to be sure, but put it on pause. It wasn't long before words were heard, and Secula took her machine off pause. *Greetings to all, and especially to Dominic Senior and Junior, who have not taken part previously in one of our gatherings. Some of you are getting ready to make a journey across the seas. It will most likely involve a flight on one of the quick, powered, flying machines. You have no idea how lucky you are to be able to travel thus. In lives when I was physical, such a trip could have taken weeks, sometimes months. The conditions were not pleasant on such journeys and many times perilous on the high seas. But I think you should be able to get there in a matter of hours. Be sure to take advantage of the educational opportunities offered by such a trip. I do not speak here of book learning. An encounter with another culture can be a great eye opener. It can help you see the world from a very different point of view. This is especially true for those in the arts. Your vision can be expanded. You may begin to see the world in ways you never thought possible. It can open you to vistas of experience that can fuel your artistic production for years to come.*

Now, some here are considering a venture that will involve the acquisition of several adjacent buildings. I understand this is an effort to provide space where a community of artists will be able to grow and flourish. Providing facilities where artists may be able to live, work, and exhibit is an excellent project. What is even more important is laying a groundwork of thought that can infuse and inspire such a project. I point this out because the culture you live in has attitudes toward creativity that may not be helpful to your venture.

In your culture creativity is very often looked upon as a feminine trait, as is intuition. Power in your culture is seen as a male trait, or characteristic. In this biased cultural outlook, you have a world were males are deprived of creativity and intuition and females are deprived of power. Although it should be admitted that these attitudes are slowly changing, a cultural residue of several thousand years does not vanish overnight. In the real scheme of things, power is no more a possession of the male than creativity and intuition are of the female. These are only socially and culturally induced ideas and much in need of revision. I bring this up with reference to your art community because the entrenched attitudes or norms in your society do not help the functioning of such a project.

Gods in your millennia-long traditions have been male, and they have been gods of power. Female gods have been relegated to positions of historical curiosities, although there was a time when they were taken seriously. For the women in your community to feel they are fully empowered and enfranchised members, these attitudes need revision. For the men involved, a revised attitude toward creativity and intuition is needed. Many men feel embarrassed by being associated with creativity, feeling it to be a feminine trait. Women often are reluctant to accept political power in community situations, considering it a male prerogative. These attitudes help no one. As part of the baggage of the past, they need to be jettisoned to allow your project to move forward and flourish. This advice does not only pertain to the creative community you are considering; it should pertain to communities in general. Perhaps it is time I give you a short break. I have a few more things to say, so meet me here again in ten minutes or so.

Everyone made their way up to the kitchen. Gia was not long in coming out of trance. Secula was watching her and said: "let's go up to the kitchen." Up in the kitchen, George decided to fire up another joint. It was making the rounds when Gia and Secula came up the steps into the kitchen. Gia began talking to Dom Senior about Italy. She was explaining her father's precarious health: "that's why I want to go to Italy right away. If it weren't for my dad, I'd wait and go to Italy with you, young Dom, and Secula." She didn't mention the fact that she would be going to Italy with Wally. While Dom and Gia had been talking, young Dom had been standing by them listening. It was obvious that he wanted to say something to Gia. Gia, noticing this, looked over at him. Dom realized he had her attention. Gia slightly smiled and Dom Junior began talking. "That stuff you were saying about sex roles in our culture got my attention. I mean about male power and female creativity and intuition. How does that stuff apply if you are gay or lesbian?" Gia laughed audibly and sipped a bit of red wine she had just poured. "Dom, you might have a hard time believing this. Most of the time when I channel, I don't have a clue what I said when I come out of trance." Gia started looking for Secula. She spied her about 7 feet away talking with George. They were over by the sink. Gia went over there and asked Secula to come over to where she was talking with the two Doms.

George, Secula, and Gia moved over by the door to the front room where Dom Senior and Junior were standing. Others in the room noticed a kind of conclave forming there. There was a short fill-in session for George and Secula. Secula was quiet for a bit when she understood Dom Junior's question. Looking around at all she then spoke: "When we start the session again, I'll interrupt to ask a question. That's the best way to bring this to Rupert's attention." Secula then proceeded to get some munchies on the table. There were crackers, chips, dips of various kinds, and other good things. The odor of fresh cut pepperoni began to fill the kitchen and mingle with marijuana smoke.

It was more than fifteen minutes later. Everyone was again in the basement. Gia was staring at the white ceiling George had recently installed in Secula's rec room. She hoped that she would go into trance quickly, though it seemed a matter not much under her control. A few noticed Gia staring at the ceiling and did the same. There were stray fragments of conversation passing back and forth. An attitude of anticipation pervaded the room. All were hoping Rupert would soon return. Pittsburgh night noise occasionally filtered into the cool basement. Most obvious were the sirens and horns of fire department vehicles. Finally, Gia's lips could be seen moving. Secula again turned on the tape recorder. People seemed to be straining to hear something. It wasn't long till audible utterances came through.

It is good. It is good to see all of you here again. I do have a few more items to pass on – not a lot. It should not take up too much of your evening. All in the room noticed Secula stand up. It caught Rupert's attention through Gia's eyes. *Perhaps there is a question on the floor. I shall pause to see the outcome.* Secula took the opportunity. "Thanks for pausing, Rupert. Yes, I do have a question. It comes from my brother, young Dominic Venturi. He was reacting to what you said about male and female traits in our culture: power versus creativity and intuition. He asked how this relates to those of the gay and lesbian persuasions."

My thanks to young Dominic. Frankly, I am not always aware of everything. That is an issue I should have brought up myself, but neglected to do so. Yes, again thanks. The gay-lesbian community often points out by their behavior just how culturally based – and biased – the so-called male and female traits are in your society. Those born of the male gender but of gay inclination will often show the creative and intuitive traits usually only associated with females. This has to do with the simple fact that usual sex typing does not take in their case. A similar thing often happens to those born visibly female but of a lesbian inclination. They often will not sit quietly by and allow the male power prerogative to be possessed only by the males. They will often assert for themselves the need and necessity for political and social power. Again, sex typing in their case has not taken hold and they see no need to deprive themselves of what seems so naturally theirs. Much more could be said here, but I just wanted to pass on this little bit of advice relating to the creative community you are working on. There is no need to infect your community at its inception with attitudes that are to say the least, unhelpful.

In not so many days some here will look at the buildings you are thinking about for your creative community. I promote this project for a number of reasons. Some of these reasons have to do with issues larger than your own self that you are aware of. They relate to the larger human community that you are a part of. But this issue I speak of next is for you – yourself as an artist, if you want to hear it. Many artists live in circumstances that are not conducive to their art. Because of their focus on creative activity, they very often have to neglect taking care of what most think of as the necessities of life. I am speaking here of a stable and abiding place to live. The community venture you are now considering and have begun in the building some of you live in next door can be a helpful remedy. Having a stable place to live can be helpful to an artist in ways you may not be considering right now.

I bring up the subject of having a place to keep your artworks. This may seem paltry and insignificant to you right now. However, consider artwork you have already produced. How often has it happened that you were not able to bring a work to the happy outcome you had in mind at its inception? This happens often with artists. Now, instead of throwing the disappointing piece away or painting over it, keep it. The person you are today is not the person you will be in the future. In the course of life people learn things. What you are not able to do today may be possible for you in time to come. The things you will learn in the future can enable you to do things you may not be able to do today. Keep the works that disappoint you now. Do not discard them. The day may come when you might look at them and know exactly what they need to make them right. If

112

you have a stable home and place to keep your works, you will have them when the time comes that you have progressed to the point of being able to bring them to completion and perfection. Don't give up. Never give up.

In what I said above, it may seem I was only speaking to people working in the sensuous medium of paint. I was not. I was speaking to people working in any medium of creative activity. I used the example of a painter to illustrate my point. If you are a writer, keep what you have written. If you are a sculptor, do the same. I speak here as much to the filmmaker and basket weaver as I do to anyone striving to complete a creative work. In what I say next, I again use the painter as an example but recall, this applies to anyone working in creative media. The exemplar I will use is the lady who speaks for me now. You know her as Gia, a beautiful lady who does good things. Support her efforts. She deserves your support and encouragement. In many lives in many centuries I've been a teacher. I have learned the wisdom of using examples to teach. Another pedagogical method I have learned the usefulness of is: "Repetitio est mater studiorum." Repetition is indeed the mother of studies. I go on at length to inculcate the importance of matters I present. I have not so much the need to go on about these issues as you have to learn them.

The good lady who speaks for me, Gianella Francesco, whom you know as Gia has been doing painting in the building where she lives next door. It came as a surprise to her how her art changed since moving into the place where she lives now. Prior to living there, she was doing what would be called representational artwork. It was representational in the sense that it re— presented things in your visible world. It re— presented them in the two dimensional media of drawing and painting. Much of what she re— presented was architectural in nature. She likes the structures of your built environment and has worked to re— present them in the media she is familiar with. After moving into the building where she now lives – an old factory – her art changed greatly. Although she continues to do representational art, something new has happened. She has begun to do what can rightly be called non-objective art. I bring this up to point out to you – no matter what kind of creative type you might be – how important the environment you function in is to you. Do not discount this

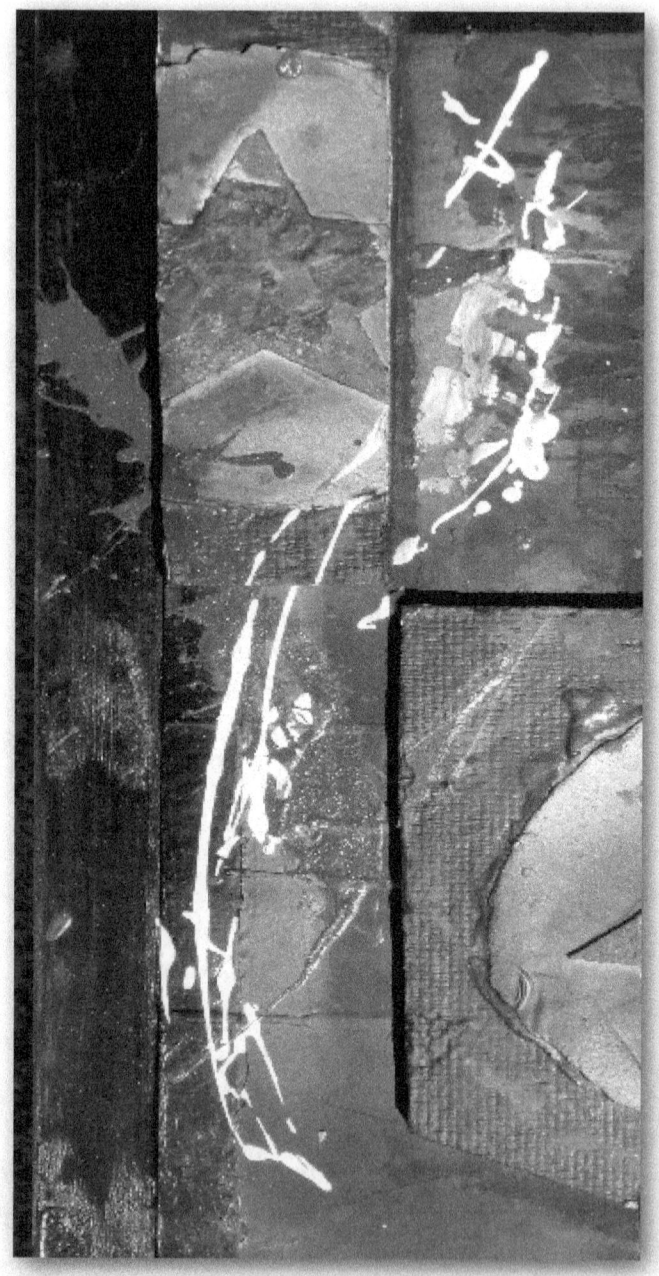

One of Gia's 'non-objective' paintings done in the old factory.

simple fact. No matter what kind of art you are involved in, the circumstances in which you work matter greatly. What is around you influences what you do. I might also say that who is around you is also a potent factor in your creative environment. I will not say more on that subject right now.I mentioned a word that may not be familiar to some of you. In talking of Gia's painting, I used the term non-objective. This type of painting is work that some may want to call abstract, but it is not. Abstract art derives from things – objects – in the visible world of your experience. The objects are then usually modified in some way. Often the objects are simplified in an attempt to pare them down to their very essence. On the other hand, sometimes distortion is used to express how the artist feels about the subject. Distortion of form and color is common in abstract art.

Now, turning to the type of art I spoke of as non-objective, the real difference here is that this art does not derive from anything – object – in your visible world. There is no attempt to modify or distort things encountered in the world of your experience. Non-objective art is a putting together of the elements of design: form, color, texture, line, etc., in a way as to create visual presences in your world that in no way refer to, relate to, or try to re-present the things of your visual experience. Works of non-objective art are new creations in your world that make no attempt to relate to or re-present other objects. Although many people are hardly aware of non-objective art and call it abstract, it is an art form of its own. It has been around for close to a century now. The battle to legitimize non-objective art has been fought and won in Europe in the early 1900s. It is time to accept and recognize it on its own merits.

I have almost said enough to you tonight, but there is one more thought I want to leave with you before I say good night. This too has to do with the community of creative types that you have in mind. It is an unfortunate stereotype of your society that the artist is often seen as a bizarre fringe dweller of your culture, who is not able to cope with the demands of life. One of the sources of this attitude toward the artist is that artists often find themselves in situations of isolation. Prolonged periods of isolation can produce traits of bizarre particularity in any individual, artist or not. Artists can be prone to become isolated because of just what it is that makes an artist and artist. We may speak of artists as ones who have, on the one hand, a unique insight into the world they live in. On the other hand, they have the ability to express that insight in some artistic medium. That unique insight they are blessed with can at times be a curse and a contributing factor to their isolation. In as much as they do not share a common outlook with many of their contemporaries, they are often at a disadvantage in relating to them. The creation of a creative community can bring together types who may have more in common. Isolation can be less of a problem if there is more common ground.

If being part of a creative community can be helpful to the artist, it can also be helpful to that artist's art. I say this as much to writers, filmmakers, digital media artists, as to those in the more traditional arts. Working as a solitary, isolated artist, it is all too easy to nourish and cherish illusions about one's art-work. Without outside input the artist can come to see his or her work in categories of excellence that the work might not merit. Exposing one's work to the scrutiny of other creative types can be helpful to see one's work in more sensible terms. One can see one's work as others see it. For this reason, I suggest making use of some portions of the new buildings for exhibition/performing space. It becomes very difficult to maintain illusions about your work when it is placed in a more public context. Once the artist places his/her work in a less private space, it becomes possible for that person to begin to see their work as others do. You might also apply this thought to another public format that has recently opened up, the Internet. Here you can come in contact with individuals from all over the world, opening you to a new level of cultural facilitation. At this point, I have said enough – more than enough. I bid you a fond good evening.

As Gia was slowly coming out of trance, the others were getting up and moving about. Wally wanted to talk to Donnie Diangelo about the buildings they were to look at later in the week. He moved over to talk to Donnie. The two of them signaled to Dominic Junior to join them. He had expressed interest in coming along on that venture too. When Dominic Junior joined them, he suggested asking Gia if she wanted to join them; she had said she might come along. Wally began passing along information when Gia was part of the group. "Thursday afternoon will be the time that the real estate people will be there to open the buildings and show them. We'll start, or meet, at one o'clock in front of the building beside the one I live in. You might want to bring flashlights – maybe pencil and paper." Donnie commented that he would pass the information along to his dad, who was also going to be along. He also suggested making note of questions they may have: the kind of heating system; whether utilities were still connected; amperage of breaker boxes; city code violations, etc. Being an architecture student, these things came quickly to mind. At that point, Secula, her dad, Susan, and George were leaving. Noticing this, they decided to break up. They agreed to meet in front of the new building on Thursday.

Although Gia had been scheduled to work at the bar on Thursday, she was able to trade days with Andrea Sandusky; this made her able to come along. She liked the idea of a creative community right where she lived. She was talking it over with Secula. Secula wanted to come along too, but Thursday was a bad day for her. Gia also thought that George should come; his background in the construction business could give insights into structural matters and possibilities for improvements. George was involved in a project downtown; it was also a bad day for him. Thursday dawned as a sunny day. Although there were hints of rain in the morning, nothing materialized. About ten till one Gia was coming down the stairs from her top floor apartment. Wally, hearing her on the landing, came out quickly. "Gia, can you hang on just a sec? I'll go over with you." Wally retreated into his place, then quickly came out to join Gia with a flashlight and sketch-pad. The two of them headed down the steps. Gia and Wally were the first to arrive in front of the new building. Since there was time, they walked around the perimeter of the place to scope out details. While they were doing this, Secula's brother, young Dominic arrived. "This is a pretty impressive place. Is that building to the back the other one we're supposed to see?" Wally and Gia assured him that it was. The three of them continued to walk around the building taking notes of the things that it might be wise to pay attention to. Wally was pointing out a broken window on the third floor when a stylish looking white Cadillac pulled up in front of the building.

Donnie Diangelo and his dad got out of the car and joined the three already there. Donnie proceeded to introduce his dad. As he had served as attorney for the parties owning the building Wally and Gia lived in, they had met him at closing. That had been a rather formal affair. This one was less so; he insisted that everyone call him Mike. Michael Diangelo had spent his working life in Pittsburgh as an attorney. He was now retired and quite well-off. He was looking for an investment where his money might be put to work at some good purpose. He was not now so much concerned with monetary return on his investment. Having spent his life making money, he felt the need to put it to good use. A community of creative types seemed to fit into the category of a 'worthy project'. Now there were five people walking around and looking at the building. Around back, Wally pointed out the other building of interest. Very little could be seen of it than its back wall. Of note there was a door on the ground level giving entrance. Wally was hoping the real estate people would have a key for that door. Otherwise, all of them would have to traipse around to Penn Av. were the building fronted. Just as Wally was thinking about the real estate people, another car pulled up out front. It was 1:05 PM.

Margie Sloan introduced herself as representing City Commercial Properties. She also introduced a twenty something understudy, Melanie Zappone. Donnie's dad, Mike Diangelo, seemed immediately infatuated with the younger girl. As it turned out, he had once done business with the older lady, Margie Sloan. Gia and Wally looked at one another. Their knowing glance said that things were getting off to a good start. The jingling of keys was heard.

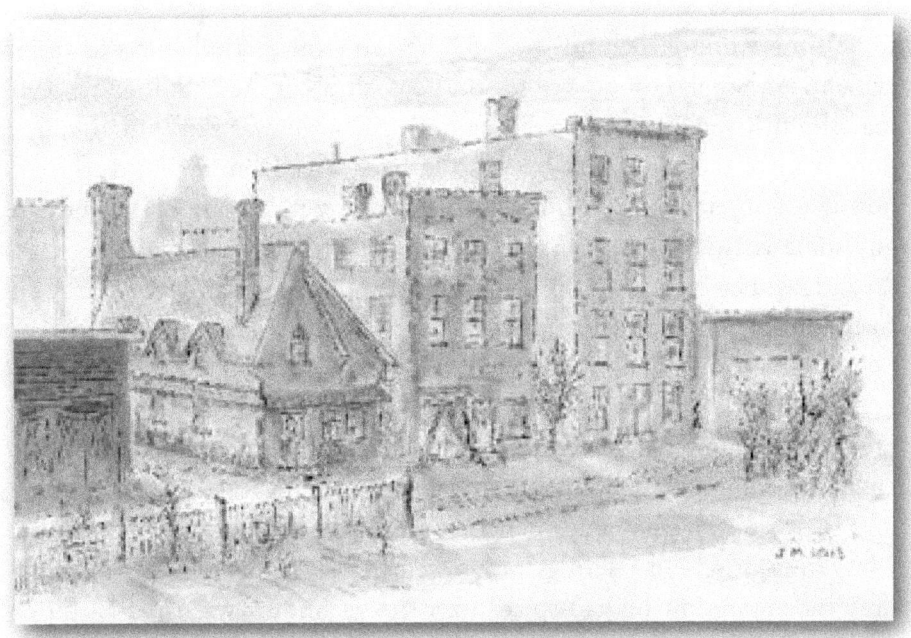

The buildings they looked at that day.

There were two locks on what seemed to be a rather substantial front door. Going in the door, Margie Sloan commented: "I've been here once before." She went on blithering as she scurried to a small room that contained service equipment and breaker panels. Her understudy followed her in as did Mike Diangelo. Mike seemed more interested in the understudy, Melanie, then the service equipment. He kept trying to strike up a conversation. Wally and Gia smiled as they took it all in.

Lights were coming on revealing the first floor of a building that seemed pretty much intact. Wally commented to Gia: "this one looks in better shape than the one we bought." Gia nodded in agreement: "that means it costs more. It's bigger too." Wally wanted to get Mike's opinion on the chances of using this place for living and working space for artists, but could tell Mike was busy with Melanie. Gia was noticing this too. As she looked at Melanie, the word bait kept coming into her mind. Having spent some time working behind the bar, the economics of all this was quite evident. Although it bode well for the acquisition of the building, her feelings about it were quite mixed. Gia notice Donnie was sketching a quick floor plan of the first floor. She also noticed that Donnie was distracted noting the interaction of his dad and the young real estate understudy. A guy somewhere between 60 and 70 was making out with a girl between 20 and 30. Having grown up around his dad, Donnie was not the least bit surprised. He just wanted to keep an eye on things.

The second floor was shown next. Dominic Junior had come along. He seemed interested and was taking pictures. Donnie pulled him aside and asked him to get a picture of his dad and Melanie together. "Make sure it's not obvious. It's not an evidence thing. My mother divorced him when I was in high school." Things progressed to the third floor. Wally found the broken window he had spied from the ground. It was the first bit of obvious damage in an otherwise mostly intact structure. After a quick look at the fourth floor, all went to the roof. Margie Sloan commented: "This completes the tour. There is another building to see."

Wally was quick to jump in. "Doesn't the place have a basement? I haven't seen a furnace yet." Margie Sloan had another appointment that afternoon and hoped they would forget the basement: "Umm, maybe it does. We'll have to look." The seven person parade marched to the basement. It was not hard to find. Wally had his flashlight, but there was no need for it. The lights down there were in good condition. Wally and Donnie found the boiler for a hot water heating system. Things looked intact and up to code. There was no knob and tube wiring. It was time to see the other building.

Although the building had a back door, all left by the front door they had come in. They walked around a garage that sat beside the building on the downtown side. Margie Sloan stopped the group to point something out: "The garage and lot here is part of the parcel. It comes with the building." Wally noted the faint outline of what had once been the basement of a building behind that garage on the property. They moved on. The parade moved to the back door of the other building. That door was some 30 feet opposite the back door of the building they had just been in. There was a key for the lock. The open door led to a dark corridor some 20 feet long. Gia was toward the back of the group going in. She noticed Mike fondle and grope Melanie along the dark hallway. She also noticed Melanie didn't seem to mind. Along the hallway were rooms. Switches turn the lights on. Unlike the other building, the power was on here. Margie made a comment that she had not seen this place before.

Going from back to front led to a large open space that had once been a store. There were high ceilings. Donnie commented that this could be converted to exhibiting and performing space. In all, the place seemed to be in poorer condition than the one they had just seen. Margie Sloan was talking 'location, location' and 'potential'. The place did front on Penn Av., for what that was worth. Wally and Donnie opened the front door to see the place from the street. Soon everyone was out there. Store windows on the first floor were under a four bay façade of three more floors. The place was not prime real estate, but was still a substantial building. There was considerable street traffic out there. Margie herded them back into the building to find and explore the upper floors.

Spaces up there gave the appearance that they had once been lived in. Again all ended up on the roof. Wally and Donnie noted the tar and gravel roofing. They also had noticed interior leaks on the fourth floor ceilings. Mike seemed not concerned with much other than Melanie. This time Donnie suggested a trip to the basement, and all descended the creaky stairs to the fourth floor. Little of note resulted from the trip to the basement. The building was locked and all returned to the front of the back building where their cars had been parked. Mike began talking to Margie, asking if there was a firm price yet. Mike asked Margie and Melanie out to dinner. Margie declined, mentioning her next appointment. It was not clear whether Melanie would go or not. Wally talked about getting Secula's uncle Louie to go through the buildings. Gia and Dominic Junior sauntered back home as discussion on the street continued. As they walked along, Gia said to Young Dom, "It looks like something gonna happen there."

Nine

ITALY

Secula Venturi was putting a few things in her purse prior to a trip to Pittsburgh Airport. The cell phone might come in handy. Extra cash might be needed. She grabbed some Kleenex and the keys to her BMW. Walking across the porch, she stopped for a second to think about what was going on, what she was doing. There was no rush. Gia and Wally were to meet her at her garage in a few minutes. She could see them from the porch if they arrived. She sat down on the swing. Events of the last few days were going through her mind. Two days ago Gia had come over for a visit. They were sitting in Secula's kitchen. Although neither of them were expecting it, Gia got that far off look that happened before she started to channel. Gia's lips started to move. Secula went to the kitchen cupboard to the left of the sink and got out a legal size tablet of yellow lined paper and a black ballpoint pen. She sat down and waited to see if Gia would say anything audible.

It is . . . it is getting to be that time when a trip to Italy should be made by Gia. The others can go any time, but for Gia it is important to go sooner rather than later. Gia's father clings to life. He hopes to see his daughter before it might be over. Gia and her father have been associates in at least two other lives in previous years. They are members of the same entity and their lives resonate with one another. Rupert's comments were brief this time. To Secula he commented that it was not as urgent that she go to Italy right away. Rupert mentioned that if Secula wanted to wait until her father and brother had the necessary passport and visa materials collected, she could travel to Italy with them. Rupert did not mention Wally.

Secula sat on the back porch pondering this. Weighing heavily on her mind were the implications of what she was about to do. She would be driving her boyfriend, Wally, and her cousin, Gia, to the airport for a trip to Italy together. She was recalling how happy she had been to get together with Wally. He was not the typical kind of guy she had been meeting lately. He was a cut above the rest, someone she liked having around. Earlier, she, Gia and Wally had been planning to go to Italy together. That was before Dominic Junior showed up and Dominic Senior decided to visit Italy. She felt she should go to Italy with her father and brother. She had told Gia and Wally to go ahead to Italy and the Venturis would meet them there when all was ready. She was pondering the wisdom of all this, sending her boyfriend to Italy with her very attractive cousin. And there had been the things Rupert said about Wally and Gia being associated in a past life – in Italy. She had noticed some chemistry between them during that trip to Cambria County earlier in the year. She was sitting there looking out into her backyard when she spied Gia wheeling a luggage carrier over to the garage.

"Wait Gia, I'll help you with that." Secula came down off of the porch just as Wally came down the driveway carrying his things. "Hi Secula, I'll have to make two trips." Secula went back into the house. Coming back out, she was carrying a wheeled luggage carrier. "Wally, take this. If you have to make two trips to carry stuff, you'll need it." Wally was all smiles. He had not been too sure how Secula would be about him going to Italy with Gia. Secula's generous gesture made him feel better. Gia had gotten the garage door open. Secula unlocked the trunk of her BMW. When the luggage was aboard, Secula backed her car out into the driveway. Wally called out: "Did you lock the house up Secula?" Secula nodded yes and Wally crawled into the back seat. Gia, who had mostly been watching things, got into the front seat with Secula.

There were some awkward silences as Secula drove downtown then headed out toward the airport. Going across the Fort Pitt Bridge, Wally asked Gia if she had called Italy to tell her family they were coming. Gia had been looking down at the river traffic. "How the boat pushes so many barges amazes me. I called them last night. They know we're coming. It's okay for us to stay there. We can rent a car at Venice airport. To drive in straight line is about 50 miles to Borgo. Maybe about 90 km driving. By the time we get to Borgo, it will be night." Secula was curious if they were going to keep the rented car or return it at Borgo. "No, can't return it at Borgo. Trento is not too far away. We can return it there, but we might want to keep it."

It was hours later. Things at the airport had gone well. The flight was on time. Gia and Wally were now over the Atlantic Ocean. Gia had encouraged Wally to go to sleep telling him that they would have to drive to Borgo once they landed at Venice. Wally had managed to fall asleep. His leg rested against Gia's, and Gia was aware of this. Despite the fact that she had sex with Wally, she wanted to keep on good terms with her cousin, Secula. It did cause a certain kind of tension when she was around Wally. She was wishing she could go to sleep too. She paid attention to the other passengers around her. Across the aisle were two in their early teens. Gia thought they were too young to be traveling together, but she couldn't see anyone with them. In the seat in front of them were military types. Gia was curious where they were headed. A well-dressed, portly businessman lumbered down the aisle. Gia consider him especially uninteresting. In seats further back, Gia could hear a couple speaking Italian. She could make out that they had been in America on vacation; it had been their first time in America. She almost wanted to talk with them.

Her thoughts drifted to just where she was. She figured she was higher than a mile above the Earth. Burning jet fuel and the aerodynamic effect of the Earth's atmosphere rushing past the wings kept her up there. She thought about her ancestors from before the time of airplanes. She wondered how they would process all of this if they were suddenly scooped up and put on an airplane. She was now getting drowsy. Half of a dream was bouncing into her consciousness. Somehow it mixed with the sound of the jet motors and the plane swiftly moving through the sky. There were clouds, multicolored clouds the colors of the rainbow. She was floating among them, not in a jet plane now. She was flying on her own power amid these beautiful clouds. Her flying took her deeper into sleep land. She was noticing other people flying in her sleep land, others dancing on air amid the rainbow of clouds. There seemed to be a place where she was coming to, a place amid these colorful clouds. Arriving at the place, she was more stationary now. She could move about, but it was more like walking. She was noticing others there just as she had noticed other passengers on the plane. Some of these were ones she knew. There seemed to be a gathering over to her left. In particular, she noticed her father among them. Others of her family were there – departed ones. Then she spied Rupert among them. He appeared as Secula had described him to her. The long overcoat, the short stature, the bushy eyebrows were components of the presence that she took to be Rupert. She was drawn to join the gathering.

Amidst the gathering now, Gia felt herself surrounded by her family. It was a good feeling, like she remembered from when she was a child. This time it was all grownups around her. She watched Rupert introduce her father to people from the past of his family, people who had died before he was born. Rupert went to what looked like a roundtable - a table amid the clouds. He sat down. He then invited Gia to sit beside him. The others came and sat too, on chairs amid the clouds. This time it was Gia's turn to be introduced to relatives she had never met. Rupert introduced them one by one and mentioned when they had been on Earth. For some he mentioned where they had lived in the village Gia had grown up in and how she was related to them. Some asked her questions; some told her things they thought she should know.

After introducing Gia to her relatives, Rupert spoke to the whole group as they sat at the roundtable. Gia listened carefully; she could tell the things Rupert said were important. As Rupert spoke, a late- comer appeared. There was still room at the table, so she sat down. Gia was very surprised that this was the woman from her childhood that all had called *strega* – witch. Gia was even more surprised to learn that she had been a distant relative. Her family had never told her this. The lady had been ostracized because the Church had looked upon her as having powers coming from the Devil. She had lived a life apart in the village, even apart from her family. Gia felt a need to get up and go over to her and greet her personally. She did this, and talked with her for some time.

Rupert and the others watched as Gia talked with this lady. Gia had things she wanted to say. She really felt bad about the way this lady had been treated in her village. Just because this lady had powers others didn't have, she had been excluded from contact with her fellow humans – even her family. Gia was especially responsive to her situation because she had not so long ago come to realize her ability to speak for someone 'on the other side'. As Gia was speaking with this woman, she was conscious of someone tugging at her arm and shaking her. Other sounds and sights began to fill her consciousness and replace the wonderful environment among the colorful clouds. The sounds of jet motors and twittering passengers came back again. The others on the plane became visible. Wally was shaking her arm trying to awaken her. "Gia, Gia, we'll be landing at Marco Polo Airport soon; it's time to fasten your seatbelt." Gia looked at Wally: "I had such a nice dream. People from my family, living and dead, were there, Rupert too. I could have stayed there forever. I wish you could have been there." Wally wasn't sure what to say. He just looked at Gia for a bit, then said: "I wish I could have been there too Gia."

Gia fumbled for her seatbelt a bit, then found it. Just then a stewardess came along. Seeing that Gia was belting up, she moved on. There were some announcements from the cockpit. Quiet hung heavily in the cabin as all anticipated the landing. As Gia had the window seat, she looked for evidence of the land where she had been born. In not so many minutes the plane came out of the clouds. During the dream Gia had lost track of time. She was now becoming aware that it was evening as she looked out the window at the Italian countryside. There was some disturbance in a seat near the front of the cabin. Several flight attendants clustered there trying to make sense of the matter. Shortly all was quiet again and everyone resumed landing positions.

On the ground, there were procedural matters to attend to: visa, passport, customs, etc. once baggage had been retrieved, Gia and Wally were in the terminal at Marco Polo Airport looking for a place to pick up a rental car. There was a lot of confusion there and Gia just wanted to sit a while. As they sat there and caught their breath, a sign was spotted. It was what they had been looking for, a place to pick up a car. The quiet little mint green Fiat sounded more like a sewing machine than a car, but they were in motion. Gia drove. She still had her Italian driver's license. "When we get out on the road, you can drive. It's best I drive here." They were still making their way through a large parking area. When they got out onto what looked more like a street, Gia pointed a few things out to Wally. "There is Santa Lucia Train Station. That's where we would go if we didn't have a car. Across here is western end of Venice's Grand Canal. The church across the canal is San Simeone Piccolo. I know you want to see Venice, but we can do that later. Right now I worry about my dad. When the time comes, we'll come back to Venice.

As Gia drove, Wally noticed that as Venice disappeared in the distance, they were approaching an area that was beginning to look like the Italian countryside. As they drove on, it got dark and there was less for Wally to look at. Gia began to tell him a few words in Italian that would be helpful

Gia

in dealing with her family. "*Grazzie*, that one is the magic word; you need it a lot. That's how you say thanks. *Grazzie mille*, even better is that one – thanks a bunch."

Gia continued to tell Wally words and expressions that would be helpful. He eventually said: "I know some of this you've been telling me from a book for travelers I got in Pittsburgh. Hearing it from you is a lot better. I can get the pronunciation down. If you want me to drive just let me know." Gia turned this over in her head a bit. "Not yet, there's still some places I'll want to turn off. It might confuse you. When we get to an area with a long stretch with no turns, you can drive. Wally mumbled a quick *grazzie*, then started to fumble with words – in English. Gia could tell he was having a hard time with something. "Just say it, Wally. You are not going to say anything that will surprise me." Wally nodded his head. "Yeah Gia, I'm just wondering how much your family knows about us. I mean with Secula, and all." Gia could understand now what it was all about. Wally didn't have to say anymore. "It's okay Wally. I explain things on the phone. My old room is still empty, and there's an extra room on the attic for you. They know you and Secula have been together for a while."

Wally seemed relieved and asked her more questions about her family. He was curious about her six siblings. They talked until Gia pulled over to let Wally drive. "You drive now. If I'm sleeping when you see signs for Borgo, wake me up." Wally was driving through the dark. He put on the radio. Some of the stations he tuned in sounded like things he could pick up around Pittsburgh. He put on some hard rock to keep him attentive to the road. He couldn't help notice that some of the drivers went at a rate of speed that made him seem to be standing still. He didn't push the little Fiat hard. He went at a speed that made him feel comfortable. He was thinking that some of the drivers passing him might feel more comfortable at the speed of light. They went on and on through that warm summer night in Italy. Gia had not gone to sleep. Her dad was on her mind. She sensed that it was sometime between two and three in the morning in Italy; all that was

129

relative now. There was some confusion with the time. Having flown east she knew it would be later in Italy than where she had been living. They had been on the road for a while now. She had been on this road before. Although she couldn't see much in the way of landmarks, she felt that signs for Borgo should show up soon.

"Wally, I'm not sure, but I think Borgo not far away now." Wally turned the radio down – almost off. "Thanks, Gia. That'll keep me awake. Did you check the odometer when we left Venice?" Gia was quiet and said nothing. She was thinking she should have done that. They drove silently through the night for maybe 5 or 10 more minutes. "There Wally, the sign. Get ready for next turnoff." Wally slowed down a bit. "After you turn off, look for a place to pull off. I want to drive." Wally felt a sense of relief. Driving in a strange country a night set him on edge. "Right up there Wally, lights, a place to stop. Not long now, don't know if anyone up at home. I still have keys." Wally saw the place they pulled into as an Italian version of a convenience store and gas station. Gia saw it as almost home. Out of the car they stretched a bit and looked at the stars. "Look Gia, the moon – almost full." They stood there staring at it. Wally wanted to hold Gia's hand. There was still all the tension about Secula; he was supposed to be *her* boyfriend. Gia reached out and held Wally's hand. They both felt so much better as they looked at the moon that night. Gia started to sing the funny little song in Italian that she sang when she was happy.

It was one of those times when people get lost staring into the heavens. They stood there for some period of time they were unaware of. A comet streaking across the sky brought them back to Italy in the summer of the year 2001. "I wonder if that means anything", was Wally's response. Gia was silent for a few seconds, then said: "I hope not, am thinkin' about my dad. Let's get movin'." Back in the little Fiat they were off again into the dark night. Gia was driving. Gia felt a need to distract yourself from worries about her dad. She started talking about the place where she grew up. "Borgo, Borgo Valsugana, is old place. It was here in Roman times. A

Roman road went through it on the way to Augsburg in Germany. A river, the Brenta, runs through it. There are more than 6000 people in the town now. You like archaeology, and there's still some old things here – stuff to paint too. In the 1860s there was a bad fire. It took away a lot of the old wooden houses." Wally was commenting that parts of the town looked very new. Gia resumed: "There is the old and the new. The Italian Alps bring in a good tourist trade. Hotels, motels, restaurants grew up to service visitors, so parts of the town look more modern to you. Tomorrow, when it's light, you can see the older parts of town. You brought your paints. You might want to paint outside. Not too far from our house is material for your brush. I turn onto Via Liverone now. We're almost home."

Wally was surprised that, right in the middle of Via Liverone, Gia turned her lights off. She then made a right turn and wheeled into a lane that ended at a house mostly shrouded in darkness. "I turn off the lights so I don't wake anybody up. Let's go in. We can get luggage later." Then Gia started to mumble something about the Province of Trento. Wally was hardly listening. He was trying to get a look at the house Gia had grown up in. He followed Gia around to the back of the place. The back door had two panes of glass in the upper part. Through those two panes a friendly, but subdued, light greeted them. They stood there at the door peering into the kitchen. Maria Visconti Francesco apparently had been waiting up for her daughter and fell asleep. She was slumped over at the table, her head resting on her forearms. Gia very quietly tried to turn the knob on the back door.

They were in the kitchen now. Gia's mother was still asleep at the table. Wally was registering impressions of the kitchen. He thought it rather large. In some ways it reminded him of Secula's kitchen in Pittsburgh. There was a mixture of the past and the present with the past predominating. His eyes went to the shelves to the left of a good-sized refrigerator. There were a lot of jars on the shelves. Most were full of vegetables. Wally got the impression that Mrs. Francesco did home canning; she probably canned things she grew herself, Wally thought. Wally's visual exploration of the kitchen was interrupted by an explosion of Italian. Gia had awakened her mother. She was standing now with their arms around Gia. Wally couldn't make out a thing she said, but he could tell she was happy.

Gia was happy too. Her mother went over to the refrigerator and pulled out a big jug of wine. Setting it on the table, she suddenly noticed Wally. There was another barrage of Italian; Wally found himself in the arms of Gia's mother. They were both laughing – probably too loud for that time of the morning. A knocking was heard from above. Someone was pounding on the floor above the kitchen. Mrs. Francesco said something to Gia. Gia explained to Wally: "Dad is upstairs; we got him awake. I'm going upstairs. Stay here."

Wally was ushered to a chair at the kitchen table by Gia's mother as Gia went upstairs. Wally sat down and a large glass of wine appeared in front of him. Maria Francesco was gesturing to herself saying: "Maria, Maria." Wally, picking up on this, pointed to himself saying: "Wally, Wally." In very little time a big plate of cheese and vegetables appeared in front of Wally. Maria sat down across the table from him and poured herself some wine, though not as much as she had poured for Wally. She was curious about this guy her daughter was traveling with. Gia had told her that Wally was Secula's boyfriend. Maria Francesco knew that these things were not always clear-cut. Wally could tell that Maria Francesco was sizing him up. Despite the language barrier, Wally and Maria could communicate in a very basic way. During that early morning when they had just met, a kind of understanding developed between them. They came to understand that they liked one another and had a common interest. Gia was what they had in common.

Upstairs something very different was happening. Vittorio Francesco and his daughter were talking. They both knew that this was no ordinary moment. Rupert had said that they had connections from lives past, being members of the same entity. As they looked at one another, things were said that father and daughter normally don't usually say. Both knew that Vittorio Francesco would not be much longer in this world. For these two there was no need for apologies or large explanations. They had each been their best person for one another and both knew it was time for good-byes. Both cried. Both laughed. Holding one another's hands, they looked deeply into one another's eyes. They both knew it was the time to let go of one another. Vittorio had waited until his daughter came home. She was home now. He could go.

Downstairs in the kitchen Wally and Maria were trying to communicate. From across the table they threw words at one another. Wally threw English. Maria threw Italian. To explain what their words meant, they made gestures or pointed at various objects. Some common ground was being established. In the midst of this exchange, Gia came down the steps into the kitchen. Maria Francesco looked at her daughter. The tears coming down Gia's cheeks and the expression on her face told Maria all she needed to know. Maria stood up suddenly, stiff as a board. She looked at the ceiling, then started screaming. "No, no, no. . . " Stumbling to the counter beside the sink, she picked up a plate and smashed it on the floor. She was still screaming "No, no, no . . ." She picked up another plate which she threw to the floor. Gia wanted to stop her but thought better of it. As Maria was smashing more plates and screaming, the two children who still lived at home came down the steps. They stumbled wide-eyed and dazed into the kitchen. On the part of those who had just come into the kitchen, there was the dawning awareness that their father was no longer in this world.

Maria quieted down. The two who had just come downstairs greeted their sister, Gia. Then quiet filled the kitchen like a big, dark cloud. Maria Visconti Francesco walked upstairs first. Her children followed, then Wally. Strangely, Wally did not feel like an outsider. He could not understand why he felt much like a member of the family. They all filed into the room were what had been Vittorio Francesco lay upon a bed. The youngest child, Gabriella, looked at what had been her father. Her flat palms were spread out on the sheet beside her father's head as she cried. Her brother, Vittorio Junior, a boy of about 20, looked out the bedroom window into the dark night. Gia looked at him thinking it was hard for him to accept the death of his father. Gia's mother was more placid now. She sat on a chair beside the bed, just staring into space. Wally stood in the background, registering impressions of the scene. Gia started to talk to her mother in Italian. She wanted to bring her back into the present moment. She did this by beginning to talk about the people who should be contacted. This caught young Vittorio's attention; he came over and joined the discussion. 18-year-old Gabriella dried her tears and walked out of the bedroom. Gia got paper and pen. She and her mother and brother worked on a list of people to contact. An argument ensued between young Vittorio and his mother about using the old-fashioned black edged envelopes to announce the passing of the head of the Francesco family. Vittorio Junior thought it was too old-fashioned.

As Gia was trying to moderate this quarrel, Gabriella walked back into the bedroom carrying rosary beads. In a gesture that seemed to make no sense, she placed the rosary beads in her father's hands. In her other hand she had two large coins. She placed these on her father's eyes, already shut. Gia asked her mother were Gabriella had learned this. Her mother just shook her head. Gia started to become aware of Wally again. She knew he was tired, and there was no reason for him to stay awake for this. She took him out in the hall and showed him where the bathroom was. Then she took him to the attic to show him his room. They both came back down to retrieve their luggage from the car. Gia stopped in the kitchen to pick up the shards of the ruined plates all over the floor. Wally ended up bringing in all of the luggage himself as Gia tried to bring back some order to the kitchen. Gabriella, still in pajamas, came down to the kitchen and helped her sister. As they talked, Gabriella started crying again. She had been telling Gia how much their father wanted to see her. They both cried.

Wally was off to bed after what had been a very long day. In the kitchen Gia and her sister sat down at the table after a modicum of order had been restored. Gia was telling Gabriella about the flight over and the dream she had on the plane when young Vittorio and his mother came down the stairs into the kitchen. They sat at table too. Gia repeated the dream for them. She didn't include Rupert in the story though. She finished the story saying that Papa was now again with the people she had met in the dream, the people of his family and the village from days gone by. Vittorio thanked her, telling her it was a nice story. Then he remarked that she must be tired and need some sleep. Gia could hardly disagree with that. Vittorio commented on all the things that should be done when the sun came up. Maria said she was going to sleep downstairs on the couch. There were still some hours for people to sleep before what would be a busy day.

Ten

A Funeral

Some days had passed. There were more people in the house now. Gia's brothers and sisters who no longer lived at home were now in the house too. There were three little kids, the next generation. Gia called Secula telling her that her father had passed away. She wanted to know if passports and visas were in order yet. She told Secula that a neighbor lady had room in her house and would put them up on very reasonable terms. She said a funeral would be a good time to visit. Many members of the family would be in for the funeral. Wally heard her talking to Secula on the phone. When Gia said goodbye to Secula, Wally wanted to talk to her. "How are things with the American Venturis?" Gia shook her head. "No, they don't have papers yet." Wally had another question: "What you said about the neighbor lady, would she have room for me too? I feel like I'm just contributing to the confusion here."

There was a long silence. Then Gia said, "We'll go for a little walk – just three doors down the street." It was a warm summer morning. Wally was looking up at the hillside beyond the houses as they walked. "That might be a good place to do a painting from up there." Gia seemed to agree. "No one would bother you up there. When I was a kid, I went up there a lot.

Gia

There are good views up there. The old deserted house on the hillside, and the rocks beside it with the village below makes good composition. Maybe I'll go up with you." They had arrived at the neighbor lady's house. She was in the backyard hanging clothes and saw them coming. She seemed happy to see them. Maybe the prospect of additional income brightened her day, or maybe she was just glad to see someone. Wally noticed the house. It was big. They met and there ensued a lot of babble in Italian. In the midst of it, Wally was introduced. They went inside. Secula explained things to him: "Giovanna's husband passed away five years ago. The kids have moved away. There is much more room than she needs here. Her daughter was a friend of mine at school. I've not been in here since then."

Wally liked the place. The room he was shown was much cooler than the hot attic room where he was staying down the street. There were still at least three more rooms available for the Venturi family. There was some conversation about whether dollars or Euros would be better. A deal was made. Wally would have to go back down the street to fetch his things, but Giovanna told him to hurry back. It was getting close to lunchtime; she seemed happy to cook something for him. She invited Gia too. Gia and Wally made several trips ferrying Wally's things down to his new digs. Gia brought along her sketchpad and some colors. She planned to go along with Wally on his excursion up the hillside to draw.

Gia was somewhat relieved to get out of the house for a bit. All of her family and the kids were only part of what was happening there. Neighbors were stopping in bringing dishes of food. Relatives she hadn't seen in years showed up. Although she was glad to see them, she needed a breather. Lunch with Giovanna was a pleasant affair. She had gone out to the back-yard and brought in flowers for the table. There was pasta with a cheese sauce. There was veal, asparagus, and a salad. There was wine, an Italian red. Giovanna seemed happy to have people in the house again. She talked about the Venturis, and said something Gia didn't know. As it turned out, she was a distant relative of the Venturi family. It was a small town, and it seemed some families had been there forever. Gia paused to explain things to Wally; he was starting to pick up bits of Italian, but still needed the sense of things explained. Gia and Giovanna talked about the daughter Gia had gone to school and grown up with. Wally listened intently trying to pick up what he could.

During lunch it clouded over. A gentle summer rain came down. Lunch was not a hurried affair. The sketching expedition was delayed. There was more wine, more talk; no one seemed in a hurry to go anywhere or do anything. As the table was cleared, Wally insisted on doing dishes. He was at the kitchen sink looking out into the backyard and doing dishes when he noticed the rain had stopped. By the time the dishes were done, the Sun was shining again. The sketching trip was beginning to look like a possibility again. It was not yet 2:00. By 2:30 Gia and Wally were trudging up the hillside behind the houses where Gia had grown up. They got to the area where the old abandoned house sat, and continued to climb a bit further. There was a natural landform close to the top of the hill that suggested stopping there. Gia commented that it had been a place where kids played when she was young. They both agreed that this would be the place to sit and scope out scenes they would like to draw. Wally positioned himself so the old abandoned house to his right and down the hill a bit could be part of the composition. Gia, sitting some three or 4 feet to his left, sat so the tops of the trees on the hillside and houses in her hometown were visible. They sat quietly for a bit just looking. Wally punctured the silence after about 5 min.: "some of the Oriental artists would look at a mountain for days before they started to put a mark on paper." Gia was nodding her head, "I used to sit up here when I was a kid – just looking down. Now I can draw." They drew for a while. Although some of what they drew was the same territory, Gia's view was further to the left and Wally's further to the right. Gia's view included more of the town. She was noticing a kind of haze over the more distant parts of the town, and a kind of purplish tint in the distance.

After about 15 minutes Wally had his composition fairly well structured. The hard work was done. He started to work in detail in the various areas, paying attention to value – light and dark differences. Being on this hillside alone with Gia was starting to dredge up the memory of the day they had made love in Gia's bed. Wally was trying to redirect his attention to his drawing; he pulled out some pastels to add a bit of color. Gia was having similar thoughts. Totally unrelated to that, she asked Wally a question: "I see in the distance a kind of haze; it looks a bit purple. If I use this drawing to do a painting from, how can I get that purple haze in the painting?"

Wally didn't answer right away. Gia could tell he was thinking. He was using some yellow and green pastel colors on the foreground trees in his composition. Then he put down the pastels and looked at Gia: "You've heard about perspective before, the kind that uses a vanishing point and structures your composition like a camera lens. What you are bringing up is quite another type of perspective. Sometimes it is called aerial, or atmospheric perspective. It's used to show distance by diminishing the saturation of colors and introducing the purplish haze you are noticing. Camille Corot, the French Impressionist, understood it well." Gia responded to that; she liked Corot. "Thanks Wally. You and Corot are good teachers." Wally continued: "I've been working on a way to paint that kind of aerial perspective. I call it Corot in a can. I get a spray can of light gray automobile primer at an auto parts store. I spray that on the painting in the areas in the distance to get the hazy effect I want. When it's dry, I mix up a glaze of mostly solvent, putting in just a bit of dioxazine purple and maybe a dash of linseed oil. Mix that up good and paint it over the areas you've sprayed with primer. When it's dry, if the purple isn't strong enough, put on another layer of the glaze. Keep doing that until it's the way you want it."

Gia was making notes in her sketchbook as she listened, writing down things Wally said. She was also noticing the light. It was getting dimmer as

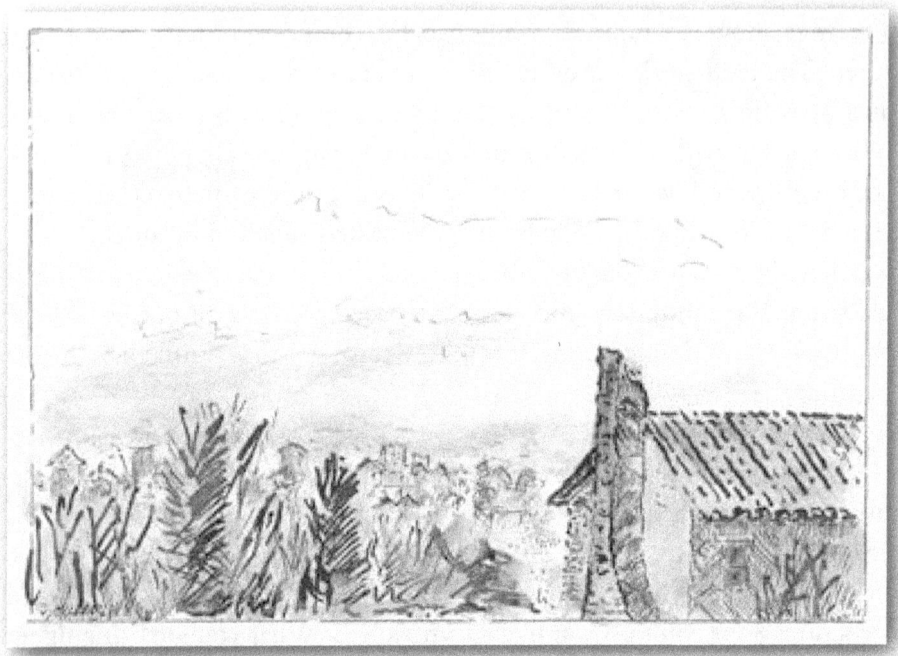

Drawing from the hill above BorgoValsugana, before the rain.

it reflected off of the white paper she wrote on. Then there were little drops of water that appeared on her tablet. She looked over at Wally. He was busy closing his sketchbook to keep it dry. She did the same and looked back at Wally. He was looking at her now. Then they both looked at the sky. Gia was recalling how the winds could quickly bring in moisture laden air from the mountains. "The old house down there still has roof. Let's go there." On the way down to the old house, the drops became more frequent. Wally was noticing the reddish tiles of what was left of the house's roof darken. Cloud cover was increasing as was the rain. In the last 40 feet to the house the drops became a downpour. Gia and Wally were running and drenched as they came in the back door of what had once been a nice piece of real estate. Standing in what had once been a kitchen, they peered out through a broken window into the rain, with the falling rain's sound as background, Gia was telling a story about how this place came to be deserted. It involved the death of an old woman. There were many quarrels amongst her children over who should have the house. Bitterness ensued. The children no longer spoke to one another. The house was allowed to slide into disrepair. Gia did not know the whole story, but the house had been derelict since she was a child.

As Wally was watching the rain come down, he was recalling something George had given him back in Pittsburgh for the trip. In the Army backpack that he used for art materials, there was a tin box of Conte crayons. In addition to the crayons, it contained three fat joints from George. Gia was watching: "You have matches, Wally?" Wally smiled and nodded in the affirmative. It wasn't long till marijuana smoke wafted through the kitchen. They were both wet and uncomfortably so. The moisture laden air from the mountains had brought in colder air with it. They were not just wet, but cold too. An old cast iron stove still stood in the kitchen. They began to scavenge wood. Old newspapers, broken furniture, and anything that would burn found their way to the stove. Some coal was still in the basement.

It was one half hour later. Gia had found some rope and stretched it above the stove. Gia took off her wet blouse and put it on the line to dry. Wally took off his wet T-shirt and put it there too. Some cardboard was placed over the broken window. The rain still poured as they hovered around the stove for warmth. Wally decided it was time for another joint. While they smoked the second one, Wally brought up more coal from the basement. He also decided to take off his pants and socks to dry them out over the stove. Gia thought this a good idea and did the same. Since it was very chilly with very little on in the way of clothes, they held one another to keep warm. Without the marijuana, there may have been inhibitions that would have stood in the way here. After the second joint, Gia stoked the fire a bit and Wally brought up more coal. They listened to the rain a bit, then Wally decided it was time for the third joint. By the time the third joint was nearly gone, there were panties and a bra hanging on the line above the stove. Wally saw no reason why his boxer shorts shouldn't be on the line too. The holding and touching was now more than just keeping warm. Though there was nothing to lie on in the kitchen, Gia and Wally enjoyed some real afternoon delight that day.

Walking down the hill Gia said: "the funeral is tomorrow. Usually the priest comes to the house the night before to say the rosary." Wally had to ask what a rosary was. Gia explained all that, then said, "I hope the priest does not come." Wally was curious about that too and asked Gia why. She took her good old time to respond. When she did, she told Wally the story of how she had worked for the parish priest, how he had gotten her pregnant, then fired her. Wally was seething with anger when Gia finished the story. "So that's the priest you told me about. I'd like to punch that bastard in the balls." Gia was quick to respond. "You mustn't tell anyone about this. No one in my family knows. If the priest does come to the house, I'm gonna go somewhere else – maybe see you." Wally seemed quite happy with that idea.

Gia was thinking about Secula and her father and brother. "I wish Secula and the two Doms could be here for the funeral tomorrow. It would be the perfect time for them to come. So many people they are related to will be here." This got Wally thinking about Secula. "I have so many conflicted thoughts about your cousin Secula. We're just coming down the hill from that old place where we had so much fun. Secula, who is supposed to be my girlfriend, is still in Pittsburgh. I wonder what she's doing. Then there's George. He's been my friend since I moved to Pittsburgh, and he's supposed to be your boyfriend. It's funny; I don't feel anything wrong about the situation with George. It's only Secula that bothers me. I wonder what she is doing now."

In Pittsburgh it had been a rainy day. Secula was in her basement writing room at the typewriter. Normally she used her computer, but today she felt the need to use her old style typewriter. Her brother, Dominic, had been staying at her place, but he was out. She was thinking

Gia

about George and what Rupert had told her about George. According to Rupert she and George had shared lives together in other dimensions of time, been lovers and had children. Secula had never told George about this. She had the feeling that she wanted to tell him. From where she was in her house's basement, she could hear him running the rip saw in the building next door. He had built a shop in the back of the building on the ground floor. It was the floor he lived on. She knew he had been working on a project downtown; he had to do a lot of precut pieces of wood for that job.

Secula got her flashlight from the top left desk drawer and went over to the concealed door that George had built into the paneling on the wall of her writing room. Opening it she proceeded down the tunnel that led in to the subbasement of the building George lived in. The flashlight was a necessity because there was still no electricity in the tunnel or the sub-basement. Coming up the stairs into the basement proper, she located the switch that transformed the dungeon like-basement into a more accommodating place. Finding the stairs to the first floor, she proceeded. The rip saw was still singing its strident, high-pitched song as she came into George's workshop. She just stood there until he was finished with the cut. Intent upon the saw blade and board, George did not notice Secula. She watched the waste piece of board tumble to the floor as George hit the switch to turn off the saw.

Secula was standing there flashlight in hand as George reeled to his left. "Jesus, Secula, you scared the shit out of me. How long have you been there?" Secula was laughing. "Not long – I just watched you finish that last cut. I snuck over through the tunnel and subbasement. I was sitting over in my writing room and thought about something I wanted to tell you." George, never missing an opportunity, went over to his jacket hanging on the wall. He grabbed a baggie, papers, and matches. He started rolling a joint right on the saw table. "How did you ever get so good at that?" George laughed sheepishly. "You know the old saying, 'practice makes the

143

master.'" Secula just laughed as she watched George finish a perfect, tightly packed joint.

After two tokes on the joint, George passed it to Secula. He was getting curious about what Secula had to say to him. "What's on your mind, Secula? You know I'm not hard to talk to. Actually, I'm glad for the break. That sawing gets pretty old pretty quick." Secula, still smiling, shifted back and forth from left to right foot. She was thinking how she wanted to say this . . . or just what she wanted to say. "Would you like to come over for dinner? Dom, my brother, may or may not be there. We can still talk even if he does show up." George, after a long toke with a thoughtful look on his face, came through with: "this sounds a bit mysterious, Secula. I'm getting curious. Is there some reason we can't talk about it right now?" Secula tried to avoid George's direct line of questioning. This was an issue she had a hard time talking about. "Maybe it might be easier to talk about over dinner, but we could talk about it right now. It's something Rupert told me one time. It's not that it's a big deal. It's just hard for me to bring up. I thought it might be easier with a good dinner and wine." George was now really curious. "I can wait till dinner, Secula. Let's have another joint." During the course of the second joint, Secula was thinking she was being ridiculous putting the matter off.

Secula and George were now sitting on folding chairs. Secula thought the shop to be a more comfortable place than when she had first come in. They were talking about their friends in Italy. Secula was thinking she should just tell George what was on her mind. Time had lost its icy grip. Secula was no longer sure whether it was morning or afternoon. She had become sure she was ready to tell George what Rupert had told her. "George, Rupert told me that we knew one another in other lives. I know you are interested in history. This was before history, prehistoric. We probably didn't even have last names. There was not just one life; there was more than one. We had children together in that dim, dark past Rupert talked about." George was wide-eyed with amazement. "Why didn't you tell me before?" She looked out the window toward her house before saying anything. "I thought you might think I was making it up." That prompted George to roll another joint. Time passed. Shadows from the sun outside moved across the floor. No one had said anything for a while. "George, will you still come over for dinner? I was over in the Strip. I got some good things. I think you would enjoy dinner." George was slower to respond than usual. "Secula, I'd love to come over. I need a shower. Give me some idea about what time."

Their friends in Italy had gotten to the bottom of the hill. Wally and Gia paused at the Via Liverone. "Wally, do you want to come over to the house this evening for dinner?" Wally had a thoughtful look on his face. "You talked about that priest coming over. That's not the kind of company I like." Gia was shaking her head. "It's not my idea of a good time either. If that person shows up, I won't be there. When I get over to the house I'll find out what's happening and call you." Wally was now smiling. "That sounds like a plan. Try to get through in time so I can tell Giovanna what's happening. She goes out of her way; I don't want to take advantage of her good nature."

Gia and Wally parted company then. He went to where he was staying and she went to what was now her mother's house. Coming in the door, Gia found a lot of people at the house. There were new faces, and her sister she hadn't seen for some years. "*Cristina que se diche?*" Gia and her sister hadn't had an opportunity to catch up on one another's lives for some time. Cristina was one of those people Gianella was genuinely glad to see. She had been living in Florence with her girlfriend, Renata. Much water had gone under the bridge and many miles had been traversed. Gia filled Cristina in on her life in America. Cristina filled Gia in on her life in Florence: all about her partner, Renata; the gallery world in Florence; gossip about others in the family; their friends growing up and what they were doing. Cristina told Gia about the art gallery she worked in. She also invited Gia to come to Florence if she had time on her visit. Gia began inquiring if Cristina had heard what was going on at the house that night. Cristina had heard. The priest had called with some excuse why he couldn't come over for the rosary. This may Gia very happy. She excused herself for a minute to call Wally.

First Gia found her brother, Vittorio, in the kitchen. She wanted to know if there would be room for Wally at dinner. There was plenty of room. Next she asked Vittorio how her mother was doing. He told Gia that she seemed relieved, now that it had sunk in that Vittorio Senior had actually died. Gia found her mother in the backyard with relatives from her side of the family. After greetings had been exchanged with at least five people Gia hadn't seen for a while, she explained to her mother that she was going to ask Wally for dinner. She really wanted to see how her mother was doing. Satisfied that her mother was pretty much as Vittorio Junior had told her, she proceeded to call Wally. "Hey, no priest here tonight. Come over for dinner." Wally was happy to hear from Gia. He asked how he should dress and if he should bring anything. Gia just laughed and Wally caught on, realizing that if he just showed up with clothes on, he would be welcome. Gia mentioned that there would be about 30 people for dinner, and he would not have a problem blending in with the crowd. Tables had been set up in the house, on the porch, and in the backyard. Wally volunteered to be a waiter. Gia at first refused, then told him to come over and they could talk about that.

Once in the house, Wally was caught up in a whirlwind of people to meet and confusion about the Italian that was being thrown at him. Gia noticed his perplexity and came over to him to translate. This in itself caused some confusion. Many of Gia's relatives took Wally to be her boyfriend or husband. Explanations had to be made. It turned out that Wally was good at waiting on tables. He and four or five of Gia's relatives brought food out from the kitchen. When everyone was served, Wally sat with Gia and her sister, Cristina. She was very interested in the fact that Wally was an artist. Wally told Cristina things about the art world in America, and what he was working on. In a rather tactful way, Cristina explained that she was lesbian and lived with Renata in Florence. She invited Wally and Gia to come to Florence, where they would be welcome to stay with them. She suggested that the art scene in Florence might be a worthwhile experience for the both of them. Both Gia and Wally took this to be a very attractive proposition. They told Cristina that, if at all possible, they would visit them in Florence.

As the evening went on, even more people showed up. These were mostly people from the village. Some brought food, others wine. Wally had an opportunity to observe goings-on at a genuine Italian funeral. In the backyard Vittorio Junior was involved in a heated discussion with one of his cousins. It involved a girl. Much wine had flowed. It was dark. Insults were traded. Someone threw a punch. In the melee that ensued, most of the activity revolved around separating Vittorio and his cousin. It all ended with both of the combatants pinned to the ground with a good number of their relatives screaming in their faces and threatening them with further violence if they didn't show proper respect and stop fighting. For some reason Wally found it funny and was laughing as he sat on the porch watching. Gia was not at all amused and cast an evil eye at him for levity in the midst of such scurrilous and thoughtless behavior.

Following the fisticuffs there was a lot of discussion about why the priest did not show up for the rosary. Gia was tempted to divulge how she had been treated by that priest; that was no doubt the real reason he didn't show up. She talked with Wally about this. He quickly told her that if she did make that information public, she would likely regret having done that tomorrow. Tomorrow would be the day when they would all politely file into church for Vittorio Senior's requiem mass. After that they would take the body into the churchyard and lay him among his ancestors. Upon more sober reflection, Gia agreed with Wally that the prudent course would be to leave things as they were. The night ended in a cacophony of noise and forgetfulness. Gia was glad that her mother, surrounded by her family, seemed reconciled to her husband's passing and was taking it all better that Gia had expected. Gia and Wally said good night around 11:30. Wally walked down the street to his place. Gia went to her old bedroom where she spent a quiet night.

In the morning, breakfast at the Francesco house was rather early considering the previous night. Around 8:30 Gia walked down the street to where Wally was staying. Giovanna greeted her at the door. They walked to the kitchen where Wally was finishing breakfast. Giovanna poured coffee for Gia and they all sat down. Over coffee Giovanna asked Gia why she had stopped working at the church. Gia looked at Wally. He gently smiled. Gia stared out the back door for a while; she then started speaking. In Italian she explained to Giovanna how the priest had gotten her pregnant, then fired her, denying that the child was his. Having said this, Gia knew that this would be public information throughout the whole village within days. She was glad she hadn't published this information last night; it would have soured the morning's funeral solemnities. Giovanna was in something resembling a state of shock. With what composure she could muster, she grabbed the table and stood up. She made her way to the back porch. Gia and Wally were left sitting there staring at one another.

By 10:00 all had assembled in the village church for Vittorio's funeral. These affairs usually took place on time. By 10:05 Gia and Wally were looking at one another. Gia was not with the group that comprised her family. She and Wally had arrived at the last moment so they could position themselves toward the back of the church. There was some twittering going on throughout the building: "why is the priest late?" It was nearly 10:10 when the priest finally came out in black vestments. The organ in the gallery wheezed. The choir sang. Incense smoke drifted through the church. The priest seemed preoccupied through the whole slow moving ceremony. In lieu of an actual sermon, he mumbled a few paragraphs from the Protestant theologian, Dietrich Bonheoffer. The mass being over, the funeral moved to the churchyard. The priest studiously avoided looking at Gia and Wally. Though they stood directly opposite the casket from him, he would not look at them. People were beginning to notice his sideways glance. Giovanna moved through the mourners pointing an accusing finger in his direction. Twittering followed in her wake. When the priest was finally finished he hurried away. Gia and Wally hurried away too. They could tell that the public information campaign had begun.

Days passed. Gia and Wally made more excursions to old parts of the village to do sketching. Some days Gia stayed home with her mother. She knew that her dad's passing would have an effect on her mother. She wanted to be there in case her mother needed her. Gia's sister and brother still living in the house were a helpful influence. And Gia's father being sick for quite a while had prepared her mother for his passing. One day when Gia was out shopping her mother's sister stopped in. She was Gia's aunt and also her godmother. She had stood for her at baptism. At that point, Gia's mother had still not heard the gossip spreading through the village about Gia and the priest. Since she hadn't been going out, she had no opportunity to hear that noise. Gia had planned to tell her, but felt she should give her time to process her husband's death first. The arrival of aunt Fiorenza that afternoon introduced a complication to Gia's plans to keep her mother unaware for a while.

Gia had been to market to pick up some items for dinner. Coming in the kitchen door, her mother and aunt greeted her with silence. Gia thought this strange. Then her mother got up and, going to the refrigerator, got a bottle of wine for the table. Gia thought this too was a bit unusual in the mid afternoon. That was when it started to come into her awareness that aunt Fiorenza had probably told her mother the story about her and the priest. While Gia was putting away her acquisitions from the shopping trip, her mother put glasses on the table and poured wine. Gia saw three glasses there. She was guessing that she would have to tell a story – a true one.

"What you heard is true aunt Firenze. I don't know exactly what you heard, but that man did get me pregnant. He told me he was leaving the priesthood and wanted to marry me. I didn't know he was lying to me. When I got pregnant and told him, it was like he was another person. He called me a whore and said I should not be working for the church. In little more than a week he fired me." Gia told her mother and aunt about the miscarriage. Then she explained how she planned to wait to tell her mother, since she was just getting over losing her husband. "When I went to America I left all the shame here in Italy. Now I am back here. I must claim it as mine. More than all this, there is something else important that should be said. I found out that the priest has another young girl working for him now. Someone should tell her about this priest. He is not a good man. The old priest I worked for when I started at the church was a good person. This young priest is not a good man. He is a liar and worse. Someone should tell that young girl about him."

Aunt Fiorenza and Gia's mother quietly took all this in. Then aunt Fiorenza spoke: "I know this girl's mother. We went to school together. We live in a small world here. If this girl is willing, will you talk to her? You are the best person to tell her. If all this is true, she should know." Gia quietly agreed. That evening there was another guest at the house, the girl who worked for the priest. At first she didn't want to hear the things Gia was telling her. On her third glass of wine there was a shift of attitude evident. She started to talk. The priest had been telling her he was going to leave the priesthood. He wanted to marry her, and he had been trying to get her in bed. At that point the girl started to cry. Gia could understand what she was going through. She gave her some good advice. "Better get on birth control if you are not already. If you get pregnant, the love affair will be over really quick." Gia could tell that the girl still didn't want to believe all this, but she was beginning to open her eyes. They talked for more than an hour that night. After she left there was a phone call from America. Secula's father and brother had gotten their passport and visa materials together. They would be landing at Venice's Marco Polo airport in a few days.

Eleven

Road Trip

G ia and Wally still had the little Fiat rental car that sounded like a sewing machine. They decided to drive down to Venice. Wally had been
waiting to see Venice for some time. It was morning and the little Fiat
was packed and ready to go. Gia's mother, sister, and brother were in the
driveway to say so long. Giovanna was there too. She had brought a lunch
for Wally and Gia. She was expecting to meet the American Venturis when
they returned. When they pulled out onto the Via Liverone it was about
9:30 in the morning. When they got out on the highway, Wally offered
to drive. He knew Gia would have to drive when they got close to Venice.
Conversation during the first part of the trip was mostly about Secula and
her father and brother. As they got closer to the city, they talked a lot about
Venice. Wally knew that Gia had been there a number of times; he was
interested in the things there that fascinated her most.

"The big church, San Marco, of course takes my attention first. The
canals and the parts of Venice they show to me are a big attraction too.
Maybe – above all – are the ancient little alleys that lead to places so strange
you think you are in a movie. There are still islands you can go to only in
a boat. Some of these are more than fascinating. You have to be careful

here. Some of the islands, and some alleys, or also dangerous." Wally was talking about the struggle of Venice with the water. "I've often read about how Venice has to battle with the water. It seems they've never really solved the problem, despite valiant attempts to keep it at bay." Gia took Wally up on that one. "At bay, Wally, was that a pun?" Wally looked surprised. "I guess it is, but I didn't even realize I was doing that. Something what fascinates me about Venice is the early history, more than 1000 years ago. I understand it was a place for people in trouble with the law to hide out. The bunch of islands and swampy marshlands made it almost impossible to find someone who didn't want to be found. I'm talking about a time when it was hardly a city yet."

Wally was driving. Gia seemed thoughtful for a while, then spoke. "I think that was before Venice was a city. *Veneti. . . Venetia,* maybe just an area of early Italy. It was before the islands were connected. To make a city, many of the little islands had to be connected. The lagoon was dredged to let the big ships come in. Some of the dirt they bring up from the lagoon was used to connect the islands. Much work for hundreds of years was done to make it a city. It's one of the things I like about Venice. It seems the spirits of the people who built the place are still there and talk to you." This got Wally thinking. "Do you think Rupert will talk to you while we are here?" Gia laughed. "I never know about that little guy. It would be nice if he would talk to us about Venice. I'm starting to think about where to stay in Venice. We haven't talked about that yet. Something else, Wally, I should start driving now."

Wally was more than happy to let Gia drive. He could feel his stomach and hands getting tense. That always happened when he approached a city, even Pittsburgh. He found a place to pull over. Some lunatic in a Ferrari started honking wildly as he slowed down. Wally seemed to enjoy pissing him off and took his time getting off the road. He brought the little Fiat to a stop beside some scrubby pine trees. Fifty feet down over the bank were some remains of old buildings that caught his attention once out of the car.

Gia, noticing his attention, came over to the edge of the bank to get a look too. They stood there a couple minutes just looking. It wasn't the quietest place to talk, but Gia wanted to say something about where to stay. At that point, they were under the impression that the Venturis would be arriving the next day. "I'm thinking about leaving our car at the airport parking lot. We can leave most of our stuff in the car. We can carry just a few things we'll need overnight. The Grand Canal runs not too far from the airport. We can get a boat into the city on the canal or take a taxi." Wally was nodding. "That sounds like a plan, Gia. I'm thinking about staying at one of those ancient little hotels by a canal somewhere. It's the kind of place that only exists in my imagination, but maybe such a place really exists." Gia was laughing. "You will be surprised Wally. Venice is a place for people with good imagination. Maybe we find the exact place you're looking for."

In just a few more minutes, they were on the road again with Gia driving. Traffic was getting heavier approaching Venice and the pace was a bit slower. Wally was thinking about whether they should get separate rooms or room together. He had hesitated to bring that up when they were standing by the road some minutes ago. He was still dealing with conflicts about feelings for his friend Secula and his erotic desires for the girl he was traveling with. He was thinking that it might be better to settle the issue while they still had time to talk about it. "What do you think we should do, Gia? I mean about a hotel. Do you want to get separate rooms, or room together" "I've been thinking about that too, Wally. It's gonna be cheaper to get one room; if you want, we can get two." Wally realized that the decision was his. It had been some days since they had sex in the abandoned house during the rainstorm. He was wanting her again – badly. "One room is okay with me, if it's okay with you." Gia just smiled and looked over at Wally. He was smiling too.

Marco Polo Airport at Venice was within sight. Gia was thinking they would pick up the two Doms and Secula there the next day. It got her thinking about Secula. "I wonder what Secula is doing today." Wally just nodded, registering a tinge of guilt. In Pittsburgh Secula and George were still in bed, together; they had slept in. They had spent the night together for the first time. "I'm getting up, George. Are you interested in eggs and bacon for breakfast?" "Yeah, I'll make some toast." There were clothes strewn all over the floor of Secula's bedroom. George was thinking about the job he was working on. "I better call downtown to explain a few things." Secula was picking clothes up off of the floor. She was fully clothed when she came downstairs into the kitchen. She was hungry, and it annoyed her when her cell phone rang.

Secula's father, Dom, was on the phone. He was upset. "Secula, things here are not good. Your mother has been having a hissy fit about me going to Italy. She's been screaming that I shouldn't come back if I go to Italy with you and Dominic. This morning she started drinking before I got up. I got awake to the smell of smoke. She had the kitchen on fire – again. The fire company just left. The kitchen is unusable. I'm going to have to spend some time putting things back together here." Secula was adding disappointment to annoyance. She had been planning on this trip to Italy with her father and brother. "Dad, can you still go to Italy? How bad are things there." She could hear her dad breathing. He seemed out of breath. "I'm still going Secula. I may have to delay things a bit. Can you cancel the flight for tomorrow and reschedule it on a later day?" Secula was very quiet. She could hear George coming down the stairs. "All I can say, dad, is I'll try. I'll let you know when I know. I'm going to have to call Gia in Italy to let her know. She and Wally were planning on picking us up at Venice tomorrow." Dom seemed apologetic and said so long.

It was late morning when Gia and Wally found a place to park at the airport. They rummaged through their things so they would have sufficient for an overnight stay. They were in a gondola in the middle of the Grand Canal when Gia's cell phone rang. It was Secula. She had cancelled the flight for the next day and gotten reservations on a flight that would come in on Saturday. Secula explained about the fire, with apologies,

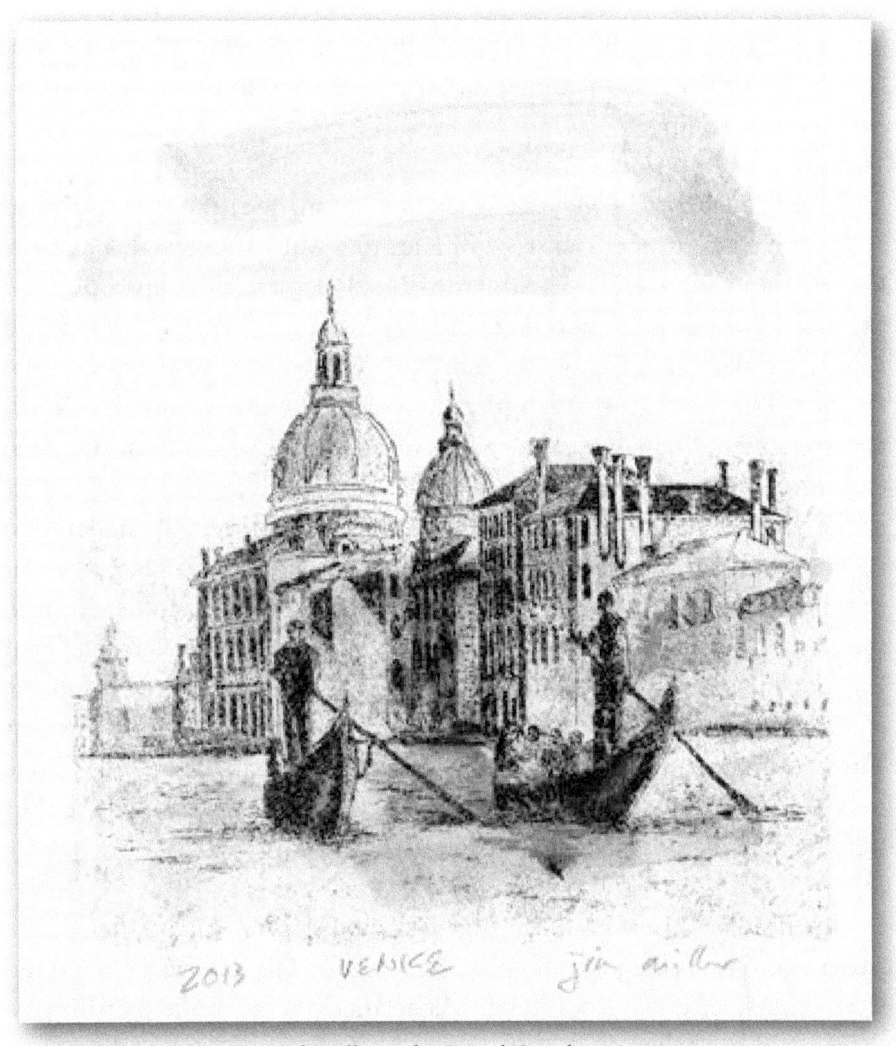

Gia and Wally on the Grand Canal in Venice.

saying so long. After saying goodbye to Secula, Gia looked at Wally. He was understandably curious; he could tell something had happened. "We get a longer stay in Venice that we expected. Secula's mother got the house on fire again. Secula and the two Doms will be coming in on Saturday. To tell the truth, I think it's okay. Venice is a big place. Today is Wednesday. We have more time to see the city." Wally was smiling. Gia could tell he wasn't at all upset. Wally was thinking that not only would he have more time to see Venice, but the thought of spending that time with Gia was also extremely appealing.

The boat they were in was of the old-fashioned variety. That is, it had a guy in back to propel it instead of a motor. Wally thought that the guy looked about his age. The boatman seemed glad for the opportunity to practice his English. When he couldn't get the English right, he would slip into Italian and Gia would translate. Wally had his camera out and the gondolier would give lengthy discourses on the scenes that Wally photographed. Wally had an idea. He started to explain to their boatman the kind of hotel he was hoping to find. Gia chimed in with Italian some of the fine points of their quest. The gondolier told them in Italian that he knew the perfect place for them. What he didn't say right away was that it was his aunt who ran the place. The boat made a sudden turn to the right. It went off of the Grand Canal and onto a smaller one. That was not the only turn. There were more. When they came to a mooring place, Gia and Wally were confused as to where they were in the city. The boatman, named Michelangelo, gave them a map. It had his phone number on. He told them to call him anytime, showed them where they were on the map, then said: "now we meet my aunt."

Michelangelo made a call on his cell phone first. Then he helped his passengers onto solid ground. For some minutes, Gia and Wally just stood there outside of the ancient hotel. Michelangelo went inside, but his passengers did not follow. Gia, and especially Wally, were just standing there in amazement at this strange little corner of Venice they had just docked at. Pungent odors wafted up from the canal. Once on solid *terra firma*, other odors manifested themselves. It was obvious that someone had taken a piss outside the hotel, perhaps during the previous night. Vaguely, the scent of incense wafted from inside the hotel. Gia and Wally had been looking for a place to stay that was not in the mainstream of Venetian tourist life. They had certainly found what they were looking for. Wally was noting the façades of the buildings along the canal. He had been taking note of these since first getting in Michelangelo's gondola. "Gia, have you noticed how many buildings in Venice have false fronts – façades? They seem to work at hiding what a building really looks like." This brought Gia out of her reverie. "Yeah, they are very much like the false faces people wear in the carnivals at Venice. People, like buildings, can pretend to be something other than what they really are. As styles changed and the old buildings became outdated, they put on false fronts to make them more like current styles. It's a good . . . ." Michelangelo was in the doorway calling to them to come in.

The lobby of the hotel was a *mixtum compositum* of debris from ages past. Some of it could qualify as artwork. Some was unusual junk. Some was useful furniture. Other things were objects that defied description. There was a layered effect on each of the walls made up of the *accumulata* of untold ages. Michelangelo, noting his passengers' amazement at the place, commented: "over the years, many guests at the hotel were not able to pay. When they checked out, they left things that they considered valuable. Sometimes they came back, paid the money, and redeemed their treasure – like a pawn shop. Most of the stuff stays here. Since I was a little boy, this has been one of my favorite places. Even now, grown-up, I like to spend as much time here as I can. Although some of it is just junk, for me it is a treasure. And there is more, but not in this room."

From behind the counter, parallel to the wall of the building that held the front door, there was a small person clearing her throat. Michelangelo's passengers took this to be his aunt. She seemed annoyed that her nephew had upstaged her. She started speaking in English, or trying: "what room, what room you . . . ." Gia quickly came back at her in Italian. ."*Bongiorno* . . . ." Gia went on to assure the lady that English was unnecessary. The lady seemed immensely relieved. Gia took care of the transactions. The lady disappeared into a back room. Gia conferred with Michelangelo: "your aunt doesn't charge us enough, I think."

Michelangelo only laughed. "She doesn't have to worry about money. Since my uncle died, much as come to her. She is glad you are here. But I forgot to introduce you." Almost on cue, the lady reappeared with wineglasses and a bottle. She placed these on a table near Gia and Wally.

Very quickly Gia and Wally learned her name was Lucia as Michelangelo took care of introductions. In Italian she told them to sit. Michelangelo, Gia, and Wally sat and Lucia disappeared again into the back room. The three at table sipped wine and talked. Michelangelo was talking about a party on an island he was going to on Friday. He knew people there and he was bringing his girlfriend. Suddenly Lucia appeared again with a big plate of goodies. Placing it on the table, she sat down. Michelangelo poured wine for her. She wanted to know where Gia and Wally came from and what they did there. She was surprised to find out Wally was an artist. Gia had to do translating for both Lucia and Wally.

Michelangelo's cell phone rang and he said he had to leave. Before he left, he told Gia and Wally they would be welcome to come to the party on the island. He told them to call him if they were going. Gia and Wally were very grateful and told him they would let him know when they figured out what they were doing. Wally wanted to take his things up to the room; he took Gia's things up too. "I'll be right back; I just want to get rid of this stuff." Gia began telling Lucia where she had grown up. This caught her attention. Lucia told Gia about relatives she had not far from Borgo. Gia was interested in places within walking distance that she and Wally could go to that afternoon. Lucia got up and went back behind the counter again. When she came back she had pen and paper. Before she sat down, she asked Gia if there was anything she needed to eat that wasn't on the table. Gia told her she was fine. Despite that, Lucia put the paper and pen on the table and disappeared again into the back room. When she returned she had with her another plate with cheese and sliced ham. Then Lucia sat down and started to draw a map for Gia and Wally. She pointed out things as she drew them, making notes as she drew. She explained to Gia that she was only drawing places they could go to without a boat.

During the course of Lucia's map making, Wally reappeared. He was very fascinated with what she was doing. Gia filled him in on details. He started to compare Lucia's map with the one Michelangelo had given them. They sat there quietly until Lucia finished her map. Then Wally talked: "Gia, could you ask Lucia for me what it's like when it floods in Venice?" Lucia started to laugh. Then she launched into an animated discussion in Italian that Gia translated for Wally. Wally was informed that Venice was a good place to sell boots and umbrellas. Lucia began recalling 1966. She and her husband were running the hotel then. It was the year of the big storm. She went over to the wall to point out how high the water had come up. It rose more than 6 feet above its usual level. She laughed and she cried. She started talking about how there were more floods now than there used to be, but not as bad as that one in the 60s.

After Lucia's discourse on flooding, Wally got Gia to ask her where would be a good place to start their explorations of the area Lucia had indicated on her map. Lucia started to talk about a bridge. That much Wally could understand, but he had to wait for Gia's translation for the whole story. Lucia poured more wine for all of them. They sat there for a while listening to Lucia's comments on places they could walk to. In addition to notes about churches, museums, shops, and galleries, there was a long description about an alley for lovers. Wally was starting to get very interested as Gia translated that one for him. Lucia poured one more glass of wine. Wally was curious if she had lived all of her life in Venice. Gia translated. Wally learned that she had been born and grown up in Venice. Her family had lived here as long as anyone could remember. They had been in the glassmaking business.

Lucia mentioned that she had some old paintings that she wanted someone to look at. Knowing that Wally was an artist, she got Gia to ask him if he would give his opinion on them. After listening carefully to Gia's translation, Wally said he'd be glad to but not right away. Tomorrow morning might be a better time. He asked Gia to tell Lucia that he was hoping to see some more of Venice while there was still good light. It wasn't long before Gia and Wally were out on foot with Lucia's map in hand. They were headed for a bridge on Lucia's map. In the process of making their way there, they went past a little cubbyhole of an alley. Having gone past it, Gia stopped. "I think that alley we just went past is the one on Lucia's map." Saying nothing more, she did an about-face. Wally followed. In about 30 feet Gia did a quick 90° turn to the left. She was entering the alley for lovers. Again, Wally followed.

An old lady dressed in black was coming in the opposite direction. She started to talk to Gia in Italian. She was telling her about a hallway that led off of the alley. She mentioned it was a good place to be alone with your boyfriend, and: "no one will see you." Gia, smiling, thanked her and passed on. Wally said, "what was that all about?" Gia told Wally that it had been a confused old lady not knowing where to go. Wally thought that didn't sound right, but he didn't know enough Italian to question Gia. The sun hardly penetrated this secret little alley at all. Musty smells that seemed to have odors from ages past hanging in them wafted by. It was moist. Some walls seemed almost to sweat. The ancient stones were encrusted with substances that seemed almost alive; some were. Where color was perceptible, umbers, ochres, and slimy shades of green like dark oxides of copper went by. Here and there it was obvious that someone or something had pissed. The further into the alley one went, less and less of the city noises were audible. Also, the alley didn't seem as warm as the rest of the city.

Now they were going through a stretch of the alley where a lot of brick facing was in evidence – darkened shades of siena. Greenish copper flashing punctuated the brick here and there. There were even small windows with bars evident now and then. None of them seem to have any light shining from within. Gia halted. Wally looked to his right: "that looks like a hallway of some kind." Gia nodded in the affirmative. "Come on, Wally. Let's explore." This area was even darker than the alley. Every now and

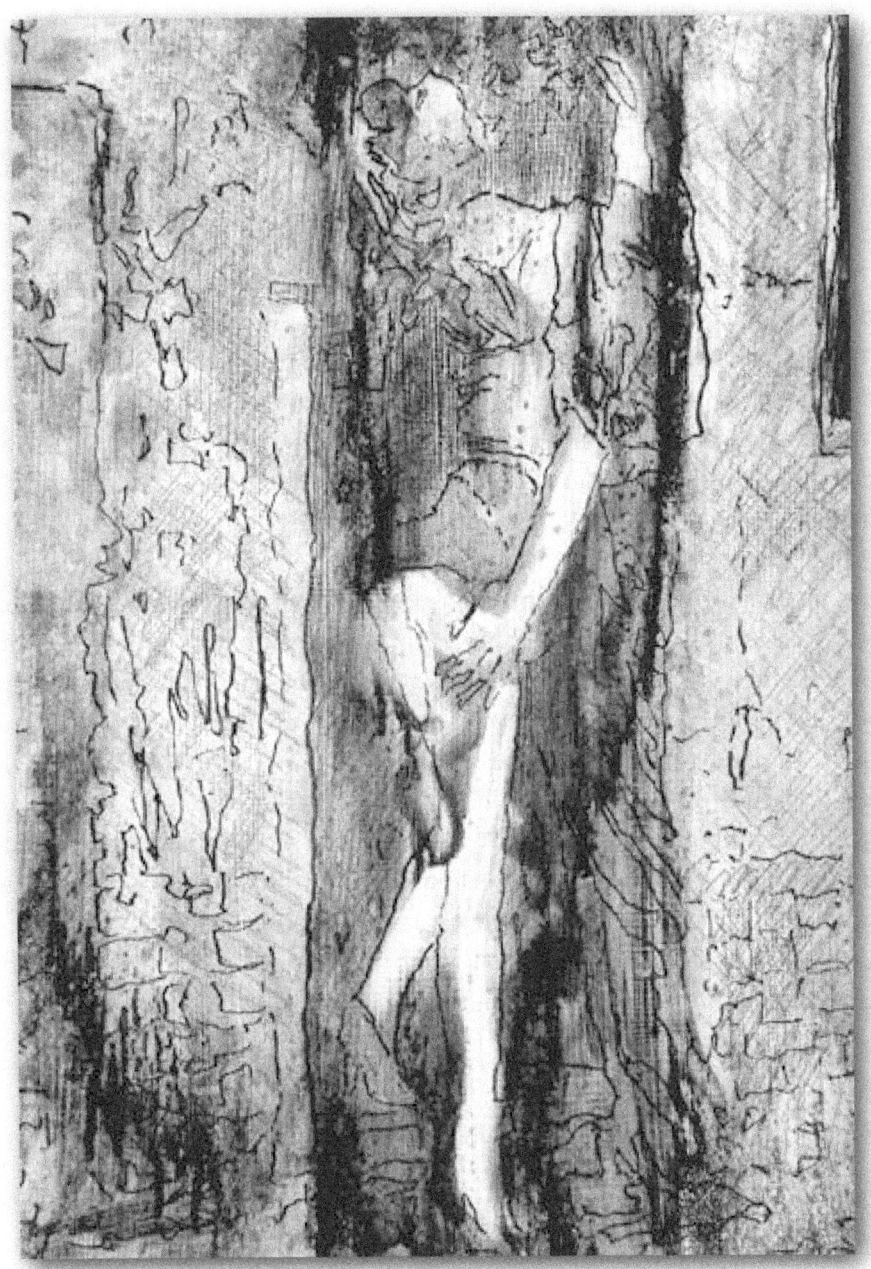

Gia and Wally in an out of the way alley in Venice.

then, what might once have been a door appeared here and there. Nothing in this hallway of sorts gave evidence of any recent use. It had a secret and secluded feel to it. It seemed to be at some great remove from the turmoil of the city. There was a feeling of security here. Gia was not walking now. She just stood in the middle of this space that may once have been a hallway. She was getting a sense of the place. Coming to mind was something Rupert had once talked about, the *genius loci*, or spirit of the place. This place felt like it was under the governance of a benign and protective spirit. As she stood there musing on all this, she became aware of a very physical presence standing behind her. Wally was very close to her, his hands on her hips moving around to her stomach. She became aware of his erect penis pressing against her. None of this in the least troubled her. She was glad she had a short skirt on and wasn't wearing high heels.

In a very quick movement, she turned around and took off her panties. Wally was now massaging her bare buttocks. She undid his belt and pulled his zipper down. Gently stroking his penis, she placed it where she wanted it. They were both breathing very hard now. Once he penetrated her completely, they were in their own world. This hallway, the little alley, and the whole city of Venice were not there anymore. There is no telling just how long they were there. It all came to an end in a pounding, thumping, throbbing conclusion. They both climaxed at almost the same time. They stood there staring at one another gradually becoming aware that there was no door between them and the rest of the world. Gia fumbled in her pocket for her panties. She laughed saying, "let's get out of here." Wally, smiling, said: "that's the closest thing to a zipless fuck I ever had."

Now walking, Gia said: "zipless fuck, Wally – I never hear that." Wally laughed. "I think I picked that up in a book somewhere." Actually, that wasn't quite true. He had been introduced to that phrase by a girl he had known once upon a time.

Back in the dank, dark alley they walked toward an end of it that had strong light showing. Wally commented on the light at the end of the tunnel. "That's another expression I never hear before, Wally." Wally laughed. Coming out into the strong light of a summer day, they both just stood there for a bit soaking up the sun's rays. "Do you think the light in Venice is different, Gia?" She just stood there for a bit thinking about that. "Maybe it is. I can almost hear Rupert saying something about that." Then something off to the right caught her eye. "That bridge Wally – maybe it's the one we started out to find." Arriving at the bridge, they could see a good-sized church on the other side. "I think that's the one on Lucia's map." Walking up the steps to San Giovanni something or the other, Gia said something to Wally almost in a whisper. Wally laughed out loud.

Going into the vestibule, the two of them were immediately drawn to a large painting hanging to their left. It was a battle scene, a naval battle. What looked like Venice was in the background. Further into the church, yet another battle scene presented itself to them. Both paintings portrayed naval battles, and both gave the impression of having been done by the same hand. The painter also was good at capturing that light that seemed to favor Venice and the surrounding territory. In their excursions that afternoon, they came upon yet more battle scenes though there were many other types of subject matter appearing. Much of it was religious. Wally was hoping to see some contemporary works, but this section of the city they were exploring seemed oriented to Venice's past. That in itself was fascinating. There were times when they could stand in a certain section and, looking around, imagine that the last three or four hundred years never happened.

As the day grew long and they grew weary and hungry, they got out the map and plotted their way back to their hotel. "Wally, could you tell if food is served at the hotel? I know Lucia gave us something to eat, but I couldn't tell if guests can eat there regularly. I should have asked." Wally wasn't sure either. "I noticed Lucia mapped a restaurant not far from our hotel. It might be best to try that. I don't want to take advantage of her good nature." By the time they found their way to the restaurant, that golden sunlight of evening had already begun to drench the city with its warm rays.

Going in, they were glad to see the place had just enough people in it to feel comfortable. There was not a crowd, and a table by the window was available. After visiting the restrooms, they sat down and ordered. They sipped wine as they watched passersby and awaited dinner. Most of the conversation in the place seemed to be in Italian. They got the impression that there were few tourists there. Most seemed to be locals. By the time dinner arrived, the long shadows of evening were seen outside. Gia and Wally enjoyed good Italian cooking. "Gia, order as much as you like – wine or food. I have a good bit of money with me that came from my dad's estate. I think this is one of the best uses for the money. I'm really grateful that I have you with me to explore Venice. Not only do you know the language well, but it is really great just to be able to be with you." At that Gia just smiled. She did it in a way that Wally could tell that she too was happy that the two of them could be together.

Dinner was more than sufficient; neither needed dessert. As they made their way to the hotel, shades of twilight were giving the buildings of Venice a different personality. There was just a little of that anxiety of night in the city starting to creep in as they arrived back at the hotel. It was not dark yet, but it would soon be. Lucia came out from the room behind the counter. Gia and Wally noticed almost in the same moment a painting that had not been in the lobby previously. It hung on the wall to their left, or rather, it was propped up there on a stool about two feet high. To their right they also noticed a greasy little man sitting at a table sipping wine. He came across as a bit more inquisitive than necessary. There was also a kind of malevolence about him that was only heightened by the nasty scar on his left cheek. Lucia introduced him as Signore Napolitano, a guest. Gia and

Wally paid no more attention to him as they both had a negative reaction to him. After the introduction to Signore Napolitano, she introduced them to the painting they had noticed. As they stood there looking at it, Lucia commented that she had expected them for dinner. There was then a long exchange in Italian between her and Gia. Wally was guessing that Gia was finding out if they could expect to eat there in the future.

As Wally stood there looking at the painting, he gradually blocked out the babble in Italian. He realized this was one of the paintings Lucia had wanted him to look at. It was yet another naval battle with Venice in the background. He was noticing the facility the painter had in painting water. The artist had probably grown up in Venice and looked at water all of his life. Down in the corner Wally could make out what remained of a signature, R. Mar . . . . The last part of the name had been unfortunately removed by some rotting of the canvas. All now was quiet in the room as Gia and Lucia joined Wally in looking at the painting.

Lucia started to make some comments in Italian and Gia translated for Wally's benefit. "When she and her husband were first married, they received the hotel from his family as a present. An old man lived on the top floor. He was dying when they took over the business. Not long after, he passed away. The painting came to them because doctor bills had consumed all of his money. The painting was the only thing of value he had left." Wally commented that it might be the work of Rocco Marconi, a pupil of Giovanni Bellini. Lucia was curious whether it might have any financial value. Through the agency of Gia again as translator, he did his best to explain that he was not an authority on the pricing of art works – especially in Venice. "But if it is the work of Marconi, it could very well be of value. It would certainly not be on a par with the works of Bellini, but still it would be worthwhile to consult a local expert here in Venice. Marconi usually painted religious subjects. This is a naval battle, and would be a rare find if it is really his."

Lucia seemed very pleased with Wally's comments, then took the painting back upstairs. Signore Napolitano slithered out the front door. Gia and Wally were more comfortable in his absence. With him gone, they felt more at liberty to explore further the large painting and the rest of the very interesting collection of objects in the lobby. These ranged from the bizarre to the curious. Here and there were things that may have been works of art. Gia was inspecting what looked like the bust of a Roman senator when Lucia came back down the stairs. In Italian she asked Gia to thank Wally again for his opinion on the painting. Gia stood between Lucia and Wally, passing information back and forth. Wally told Gia to tell Lucia that in the next few days they would be exploring Venice and may come upon a person who could give a more sure appraisal of the painting. Would Lucia want this person's advice on the painting? Lucia then expressed her willingness to get a more reputable opinion.

Lucia hesitated a bit, then went back to the room behind the counter. She returned with three glasses and a bottle of wine. Putting the glasses on the counter, she poured for the three of them. There was some small talk about the collection of interesting objects in the lobby as they went through a glass of wine. She poured a second glass for all three and then became more serious. She explained a matter to Gia in Italian at some length. Wally could only guess what was going on. Finally Gia came through with a translation: "Lucia says she lied about Signore Napolitano. He is not a guest here. He has for many years pretended to be her brother, but maybe he really is. He tells her he is an illegitimate child of her father. She says it could be true because there is much about her father's life she never knew. Her parents are gone now; she can't ask them about it. Signore Napolitano is retired, but was for many years with the police here in Venice. She invited him over because she thought you might talk about the painting. He has for many years told her the painting is worth money. She thought he would want to know." Wally looked at Lucia and just laughed. They all had a third glass of wine before Gia and Wally went upstairs.

Twelve

The Adventure Continues

Once upstairs in their room, Gia and Wally were glad to relax after what had been a very full day. Wally was glad to see the room had a window looking out on the canal and the buildings opposite. He opened the window. Sitting on the window ledge, he looked up and down the canal to see what could be observed in the dark. The view suggested a painting to him, but with good daytime light. He became distracted by some noise from upstairs. Up to that point, he had wondered if there were other guests in the hotel. There were. He went back to looking out the window. This time he looked at the sky to see what stars could be seen in the Venice night. He had just located the Big Dipper when he heard murmuring coming from behind him.

Turning around Wally looked into the room; he focused on Gia. She sat in a very old rocking chair and had that spaced-out look she got when she started to channel. Once she got into channeling, she became animated in the attempt to express Rupert's ideas. She wasn't in that state yet, though her lips moved intermittently. What was coming from her was mostly noise, but Wally thought that more important stuff might follow. He hopped off of the windowsill and went to his luggage to get pen and tablet. There was an old stuffed, leather-upholstered chair that Wally imagined Mussolini sitting in. Light was not in abundance in the room. Wally slid an old Art Deco floor lamp over beside the Il Duce chair and slumped into it. He waited patiently for something intelligible from Gia – or Rupert. While sitting there he realized he hadn't replaced the screen on the window he had been looking out. Getting up to do this, he heard Gia finally uttering some real words – in Italian. Now with the screen in place, he settled back into the comfy old stuffed chair and listened. Shortly, he became annoyed at the Italian. Wally started repeating: "Italiano, Italiano, Italiano . . . ." Gia suddenly looked over at him. Her face was different now. He couldn't imagine it was the same girl he had been screwing that afternoon in the alley.

I greet my friends once again, this time in the beautiful floating city on the Adriatic. Wally, if I speak too quickly, tell me to slow down so you will be able to take notes. Share your notes with Gia tomorrow. She will want to hear these things. The two of you came upon several matters today that I have a need to talk about. One issue had to do with various battle scenes that you seemed to stumble upon. Remember, you are in the process of creating the life that just seems to happen to you. Also, the light of Venice was another matter that came to your attention today. I have things to say about light. Whether or not it is the light of Venice does not matter – just light.

I speak of battle scenes, paintings on canvas, and war – real war. To introduce the subject I speak again of just how you are situated in what you call your life. You may recall me speaking of All That Is last year, when Gia first started to channel me. This is a pantheistic reference to what appears in your culture as the theistic God. The theistic God is an entity completely apart from and exalted above the world that God created – your world. Now, from a pantheistic point of view, All That Is becomes another way of speaking of what you call God. The significant twist here is that All That Is does not stand apart from what that entity has created. In other words, in a pantheistic world, you and everything in your world are part of All That Is, or God. God in a pantheistic world is not separate from what that God creates. The smallest toad, frog and molecule are part of that God. You are lucky that you live in the 21st century. If you would have written about a pantheistic God in the year 1600, the Holy Office of the Inquisition would have hunted you down, tortured you, and killed you if you would not repent and reject your pantheism. That was done to Giordano Bruno in the year 1600 here in Italy.

From my point of view, from my perspective on the larger scheme of things, your God is that pantheistic All That Is. The creations of that God, including yourselves and your world, share in the creative power of All That Is. You go about creating the world you live in by participating in the creative power of All That Is. The big difference is that you and your fellow humans do not have access to the great and manifold wisdom of All That Is. Your creations are learning experiences, or should be. As artists create scenes of battles, other men create real wars. The artists' scenes on canvas might show their fellow man the horror of war, thus helping them to realize that war is not a good idea. Other men might wage war, hopefully to learn the folly of violence, slaughter, and human waste. Your activities should be a learning experience. You are creating worlds about you, hopefully to learn from what you create. Even when you are creating this senseless violence of war, you are creating. Hopefully you are learning from what you create. Suffering is to be a learning experience for you. You create the sufferings you endure. Hopefully, you learn from your creations how to avoid suffering. The only purpose of suffering is to teach you how to avoid suffering. Those who seek suffering for its own sake are fools.

Here Wally stood up to get Rupert's attention. Rupert then became quiet, looking at Wally through Gia's eyes. Noticing he had Rupert's attention, Wally sat down and asked a question. "Rupert, you said artists paint battle scenes to teach their fellow men the folly and stupidity of war. Are you saying that this is the only reason that artists paint battle scenes? There is another question. The Bruno you mentioned, was he the priest and monk you spoke about last year?"

Bruno, Giordano Bruno, is indeed the priest and monk I spoke of previously. In his own quest for what was holy and good, he arrived at the pantheistic belief. That is the belief that All That Is – or God – is not apart from his creation. I used the pronoun his in keeping with the tradition and custom of your culture. God is a part of what that God has created. That means you and your world. Because of that, and his other beliefs, he was burned at the stake by the Catholic Church. He would not repudiate what his own good sense had taught him. However, in his case the Holy Office of the Inquisition did show mercy. Mercy from their twisted and warped perspective was to tie a bag of gunpowder around his neck. In so doing, Bruno was killed quicker – perhaps by having his head blown off. This was mercy in the eyes of the Inquisition. This stands as a record of history and cannot be contradicted.

In answer to your other question there is a resounding NO. No, I do not mean to say that every artist who paints battle scenes does so to teach his fellow humans the folly and stupidity of war . . . if only that were true. I only said that as a normative statement. I said that to express what should be the artist's intent in doing battle scenes. I realize that the artists' paintings that seem to teach their fellows the folly of war are probably in the minority – sad to say. Many who portray the epics of mass human slaughter do it to glorify the disease of war. Some have been in the pay of the warmongers who perpetrated those monstrosities. Other artists have portrayed battle scenes because they were in the midst of such turmoil and suffering. Depicting the carnage of battle was the only way for them to express the misery of their own life. They were commenting on their own lives. There have been far too many reasons for artists to depict wars.

There have been far too many wars. I finish this diatribe on destruction by saying that we can only hope that man can learn to use his creative abilities better by observing his creations. War and scenes of war are the creative acts of men. War is creative human power gone astray. It is nevertheless the creation of your kind, humankind. I have said as much as I want to for this evening. If Gia does not come out of trance quickly, grab her shoulder and shake her a bit.

Gia sat there staring straight ahead. Wally waited to see what she would do. He was again noticing noise upstairs. That caught his attention for a bit, but he kept looking to see what Gia would do. Finally, Wally saw Gia look over in his direction. He smiled. She gave him a weak smile. He could tell she was back. "Do you remember anything, Gia?" Gia was shaking her head – no. "There were some pictures I remember – almost no words." That made Wally curious. "What kind of pictures?" Gia was making gestures with her hands. "Fighting, battles, the sea, there were lots of people and ships. I almost can see a picture of Rupert talking; maybe he was talking about war – not sure." "Well Gia, that fits right in. Rupert said he was going to talk about battle scenes; we saw a bunch of them today. He also talked about real war. I'd like you to read my notes once I rewrite them. Maybe it will help you remember some stuff. There was something else. Rupert said he was going to talk about light. He brought up how we talked about the light here in Venice, but he said it had to do with light in a more general sense. The funny thing is, he never talked about light." They both sat there pondering that. There was more noise from upstairs, then Gia spoke. "There was more he wanted to say, but now I remember. He says he's not going to go on because we are both tired and had a long day and should get rest. Then it goes black again." Wally settled back into the old stuffed chair. They both seemed relieved, but tired. "Gia, I'm so damn tired I can hardly think. I'm glad Rupert stopped." Saying that, Wally saw a big smile on Gia's face before she spoke. "I think he's going to talk some other time while we're here in Venice. Let's get in bed."

Thursday in Venice dawned with a reddish sky. Wally and Gia were still in bed at sometime around 8:00 AM. Gia heard Wally muttering: "sky red in the morning, sailor's warning." Gia was curious what that meant and asked him. He responded in a groggy, half awake way. "That means it might rain today; we don't have umbrellas." Gia looked out the window. "Might rain, Wally, did you look out the window?" Wally turned his head around toward the window again. "Wow, Lucia was right about boots and umbrellas. Are you hungry, Gia? Do you think we can get breakfast here?" Gia got up and walked over to the window. She stood there for a few minutes looking out at the rain. Wally couldn't help looking at her. She had on one of his white T-shirts – nothing else. She stood in a contraposto position. Her weight was on her left foot. Her right foot was not even on the floor, but held up behind her. Wally was noticing how her spine curved, turning her right shoulder up a bit higher than the left. Then she started to speak: "I'm gonna go downstairs to see if Lucia gets breakfast for us." Wally struggled to get himself out of bed. "I'll be down in a couple minutes."

It was now close to 8:30 in the morning. Gia and Wally were downstairs. They sat at a round table in what might be called the lobby of the old hotel. There were three other tables there. One of them was occupied by three people. They seemed to spend most of their time casting piercing glances at one another while they waited for their breakfast. Gia and Wally were discussing how they were going to explore Venice without an umbrella. Lucia appeared at their table with coffee. Wally sat there quietly as Gia and Lucia exchanged large amounts of Italian. He was getting bored listening to it when Lucia suddenly did an about-face and walked back into the room behind the counter. "Bacon, eggs, and toast are coming. And, Lucia is going to loan us two umbrellas." Wally smiled and put more cream in his coffee. "Do you think we could get her to sit down with us and draw another map? I'd like to explore some parts of the city where we can find some art that is more contemporary. Maybe we could use that map Michelangelo gave us. She could just point out the places."

Wally went upstairs to get Michelangelo's map. When he came back down there was good food on the table, orange juice too. The munching and crunching of breakfast was accompanied by an argument from the other table. Happily, the three left soon after. Gia informed Wally that Lucia was willing to sit down with them and point out where contemporary art could be found. "But, Wally, there is a problem. We might need a boat to get there. I see Michelangelo's number is on his map." Wally sipped some coffee as he looked at Michelangelo's number and map. It wasn't long until Lucia came out to join them carrying two umbrellas. Wally noticed that they were two black, old-fashioned looking umbrellas. He didn't much care. An umbrella was an umbrella. Lucia used Michelangelo's map. She drew X's at the places Wally was looking for. With her finger she pointed to Michelangelo's cell phone number on his map.

Gia wanted to call her mother. While Wally was busy getting in contact with Michelangelo, Gia got through to her home at Borgo. Her sister answered the phone. Gia was happy to find out that her mother was dealing well with her father's passing. His long sickness after the auto accident had prepared her mother for the inevitable. Then Gia got to talk with her mother. She wanted to know when Gia was coming back up to Borgo. Gia's response passed along the fact that the Venturis would be landing at Marco Polo Airport on Saturday. If all went well, Gia, Wally, Secula, and the two Doms would be coming in to Borgo that day. After talking about events relating to the funeral, Gia said goodbye to her mother relieved that things were well with her. Her father's long illness had prepared her for his departure.

Gia sipped some coffee as she listened to Wally talking to Michelangelo on the phone. She wished she were talking to Michelangelo so they could talk in Italian. Wally seemed to be struggling to communicate. Eventually each got across what they wanted to say. When Wally said so long to Michelangelo, Gia poured some more coffee for him. She sat there waiting to hear what had transpired. She looked at Wally, knowing he was trying to formulate what he wanted to say. Being very much a visual person, speech did not always come easily to him. As Wally was trying to formulate what he wanted to say to Gia, Lucia appeared again. She wanted to know if breakfast had been sufficient. Did they want more to eat? Gia and Wally looked at one another. Both nodded their heads in the negative. Lucia walked away looking somewhat disappointed. Wally noticed a slight limp in her step as she walked away. He wondered if it had to do with the weather. It was still raining in Venice. Somehow this jarred him to burp out the words he had been thinking about for Gia. "Ten o'clock – Michelangelo will show up at 10:00. He won't have his gondola. He has a motor boat with a cabin for rainy weather." Gia kept looking at him, still having a question mark on her face. He spoke again: "should there be more?" Gia wasn't sure what to say, but her mouth opened. "This is one of those 'almost Rupert' moments. I can't help thinking there was more."

Wally sat there thinking for a moment; then he finally spoke. "Yeah, there was something about the party Michelangelo talked about. There was a lot of Italian I couldn't understand. I wish you had been talking to him. He didn't have the English words he needed." Gia thought about ten o'clock. "When Michelangelo comes with the boat, I can talk to him. I can find out about the party. Do you want to go?" Again Wally became thoughtful. Gia sat there waiting until Wally registered a response. He sipped a bit of coffee then looked directly at Gia. "I'm wondering who will be at the party – what kind of people. I'm also thinking about the place. We don't have any idea what that island is like. Maybe when Michelangelo shows up, you can ask him about that stuff. That may have been what he was trying to tell me when I couldn't understand his Italian." Gia commented that she would make a mental note to talk to Michelangelo about those things. They got up to look out the front window. They carried their coffee with them. They stood there for a while watching the rain spatter down on Venice.

When ten o'clock came, they still sat at the table in the front room of the hotel. Lucia was sitting with them. Gia and Wally had already gone upstairs to take care of mourning things and fetch articles they wanted with them on the excursion. Lucia was filling Gia in on local variations of Italian that even an Italian might not know. Venice had various idiosyncratic twists to the language that one should know. "The word for house, *casa,* is *ca'* here in Venice. And there is . . . ." The phone was ringing. Lucia got up to answer it. Coming back, she carried a full pot of coffee and some good-looking pastries on a gold-rimmed plate. "Michelangelo is having problems getting the boat started. He says it is a diesel; it always gives him problems. But he likes it because it goes forever when he gets it started." Wally had an idea: "you said there were other paintings around the hotel that you might want us to look at. Do you feel like getting any of them out?" Lucia's face brightened at that. Gia and Wally helped her retrieve three paintings from an empty room on the third floor. Having brought them down to the lobby, they sat and looked at them.

"The one on the left is fairly recent. It looks like it was done by someone who was trying to imitate, or had studied with, Modigliani. It gives the impression that the person was struggling with trying to develop his own style. He had not done that yet. He was still too much slavishly copying his master. It is a pleasant picture with the man holding his guitar and smiling at his girlfriend. It creates a nice feeling, but there is so much struggle there for the artist's own innate self to speak, to visually sing his own song instead of timidly copying a master. The one in the middle is my favorite. It is one of those immediate expressions of the beauty of the Italian countryside. You can tell it was done by someone who instinctively knew how much human effort had been invested into that land to make it productive and beautiful. You can almost smell the soil on that spring morning . . . ."

Wally became quiet; a boat could be heard pulling up out front. Wally went over to the window to look out. "It's Michelangelo. He's tying the boat up and doesn't even have an umbrella." It wasn't long before there were four at the table. Michelangelo was a bit wet, but that didn't seem to bother him. Lucia poured coffee for him. He had one of the pastries on the table and a little coffee, but was concerned because he was running late. Gia mentioned that they had a few things that they wanted to talk to him about. "Would it be better if we talk in the boat, since you are late ?" Michelangelo liked that idea. Wally looked out toward the boat, still running out in front of the hotel.

Lucia was holding the door as the little parade made their way to the boat. Gia and Wally, each having an umbrella, made Michelangelo's trip back to the boat a bit dryer. Gia noted the boat was a bit nicer than she expected. There were a lot of wooden parts above the hull that looked like varnished mahogany. Chrome fittings set off the dark wood. The boat bobbed up and down in the canal as Gia and Wally got down into the boat. Michelangelo untied and jumped in, opening the door to the cabin. The umbrellas were left in the back and the three went into a snug and dry interior. The black upholstered seats looked and felt very much like real leather. The boat was built so it could be controlled from inside the cabin in bad weather. The idling diesel engine was not highly audible, but could be slightly felt by the bit of vibration transmitted throughout the boat. The boat was maybe 25 or 30 feet long and cut a graceful figure as it pulled away from its moorings.

The motor was now working a bit harder. It was a well engineered machine and not noisy. They were able to talk in the cabin without a problem. Wally sat there patiently listening to billowing Italian as Gia and Michelangelo talked about the party and the island. As Michelangelo piloted the boat around a rather treacherous left turn onto another canal, he became silent. Gia took the opportunity to tell Wally that the island was about 40 acres in size and had one owner, the person who was throwing the party. The main house was huge and made of stone.

It dated from the 1600s. There were several other houses on the island occupied by people who worked there taking care of the place and farming. Michelangelo had met the owner in the course of his work ferrying people back and forth. He had known the owner for about 10 years. And, importantly, he always threw good parties. The people would be a mix of the old and young. Sometimes kids would be there too. Sometimes members of the old Italian nobility would show up at parties. There was usually a mix of everything. Michelangelo noted that he had been invited, and he was a boatman. There will probably be artists, intellectuals, businessmen, and everything there. The owner himself is a politician, having access to all strata of society.

They were on a straighter stretch now and Michelangelo started to talk again - in Italian. Gia listened. Wally noted that she was making notes on the tablet she had brought along as Michelangelo talked. Mostly, Wally just enjoyed Venice in the rain as the diesel engine obediently propelled them through the canals. Wally was noticing how the city seemed cleaner in the rain when he noted the boat was slowing down. Michelangelo pulled into a place where there were other boats docked. At this place there were posts in the water and the boats parked perpendicular to the canal. The canal was somewhat wider here. There was a narrow walkway on the right side of the boat. Michelangelo told Wally and Gia to wait a minute. He got out and tied the boat up. Hopping up on the walkway, he disappeared among the buildings along the canal. Gia looked at her notes and started telling Wally what she had just learned about Venice. "Venice has 28 miles of canals. They follow what had been the original watercourses between the 118 islands that had formed Venice. The Grand Canal – the main street of Venice – is about 2 miles long. Along it are some 200 old palaces. Many have been converted into hotels; some are now art galleries. There are about 3000 streets in Venice. Some are only about 3 feet wide. If you add all the streets up, you get about 90 miles of street." Just then they noticed that Michelangelo had jumped back into the boat.

Coming into the cabin, Michelangelo felt he should give a bit of explanation. "I lose a bet and have to pay a friend. I bet it does not rain today. I lose." The motor was still running. Michelangelo slid behind the wheel and backed the boat out into the canal. They were off again. Michelangelo started talking in Italian. Gia again took notes. Wally could tell they were talking about galleries. Wally again watched Venice and the rain, letting the Italian blend with the noise of the engine. This time Michelangelo paused to let Gia translate for Wally: "Giudecca 795 is a gallery we should see. We will be left off close to that one. The Galleria Franchetti is another one to see; it is on the canal . . . ." Michelangelo started talking in Italian again: Gia became quiet. Wally noticed that Michelangelo turned a control that blew a bit of warm air into the cabin. It was a nice, secure feeling to be able to glide over the water and watch this beautiful city in the rain while in the comfort and security of Michelangelo's boat. Gia was again taking notes. The rain seemed to come down harder now.

Michelangelo turned another control. This one made the windshield wipers go faster. He then became quiet. The rain was making it harder for him to see well. Gia started filling Wally in again: "the Galleria Franchetti used to be a palace. On the Piazza San Marco is the Art Moderna Ravagnon-another place to see. And there is Peggy Guggenheim's palace. It is a museum now. We want to see that one." Michelangelo spoke again. This time he spoke in English: "I leave you off at a place where you can go in and get dry. Giudecca 795 is just down from there, three buildings west. Don't give me money now. Pay me tonight. I see you at 6:00 just where I leave you off now. *Ciao*."

Michelangelo was about to exit the cabin when he stopped suddenly. Turning around, he asked Gia for the map she had. Pulling out a pen, he pointed out on the map just where they were so they could find him at 6:00. He then helped Gia and Wally make their way off of the boat. He watched as the two of them under their umbrellas walked to the place he had suggested. Once inside Gia and Wally found a place by a window looking out on the canal. As they sat there sipping coffee, they spotted places on their map that Michelangelo had been talking about during the boat ride.

It was some time before 12:00 when they entered Giudecca 795. Neither Gia nor Wally had ever heard of or seen the place before. They tried to avoid sales personnel; they just wanted to look. They were standing in front of a very large painting. Gia was reading a note on the wall beside the painting. "It says this postmodern art done by some German whose name I can't even pronounce." Wally started laughing. "When I hear postmodern, it always comes into my mind as *post mortem*." Gia laughed too. "Why is it so big, Wally?" Wally chuckled a bit. "Maybe he's taking that old advice that says: 'if you can't sing good, sing loud'". They stood there smiling for a bit and then moved on.

Other rooms provided views of smaller works, which had the ability to hold their attention – some quite good. Abstract figurative painting seemed to be their favorite. Gia comments: "I envy the person who does this. Just a few strokes of the brush. That is all it takes for this person to say what they want about the human body. It looks so easy." Wally was nodding his head. "That person probably worked for years to make it look so easy. It's something like a ballerina. It looks so easy when you watch her on stage. You don't see the years of practice, pain, and discipline that it took to make it look so easy."

In a while they were out under their umbrellas again enjoying Venice in the rain. There were a few times the sun shone through the clouds. "There's that Venice light again, Wally. It makes some of the buildings look almost transparent." That caught Wally's attention. "Maybe Rupert will talk to us about light. He said he would." Gia and Wally wanted to check out the other places Michelangelo had pointed out for them. It involved a good bit of walking, and it rained most of the time. In one of the galleries they visited, there were very colorful paintings that were composed of small areas of color. They both thought that the paintings were outstanding. They were non-objective pieces. The color areas were not large. They were mostly rectangles and around 2 or 3 inches each in the dimension of height.

Gia couldn't help commenting: "the colors in these are so good. Is it special pigments, or something else that makes the colors so good?" Wally stood there a bit with his head bobbing up and down. He then got very close to one of the paintings. He stared at it quite a while before he said anything. Then he turned toward Gia and started to talk. "No, it's not the pigments. These are paints that any artist can buy on the market. It's acrylic paint. What makes the colors so good is that this artist understands the theory of simultaneous contrast." "Simultaneous contrast Wally, is that something new?" Wally was smiling. I'm sure it would be new to a lot of people who call themselves artists, but no; it is old."

"The theory of simultaneous contrast was published in 1839 by a Frenchman named Michel Eugene Chevreul. He was a smart and interesting character who lived to be over 100 years old. He lived through the French Revolution. He was a chemist and became director of a French company that made tapestries. In that job he became aware that there was a problem with some of the colors.

They seemed to lose their intensity in certain tapestries. Upon investigating, he realized there was nothing wrong with the dyes that colored the fabric. The problem arose because of the juxtaposition of certain colors. Investigating further, he realized that if certain colors placed side-by-side could harm one another, other colors could enhance one another when placed side-by-side."

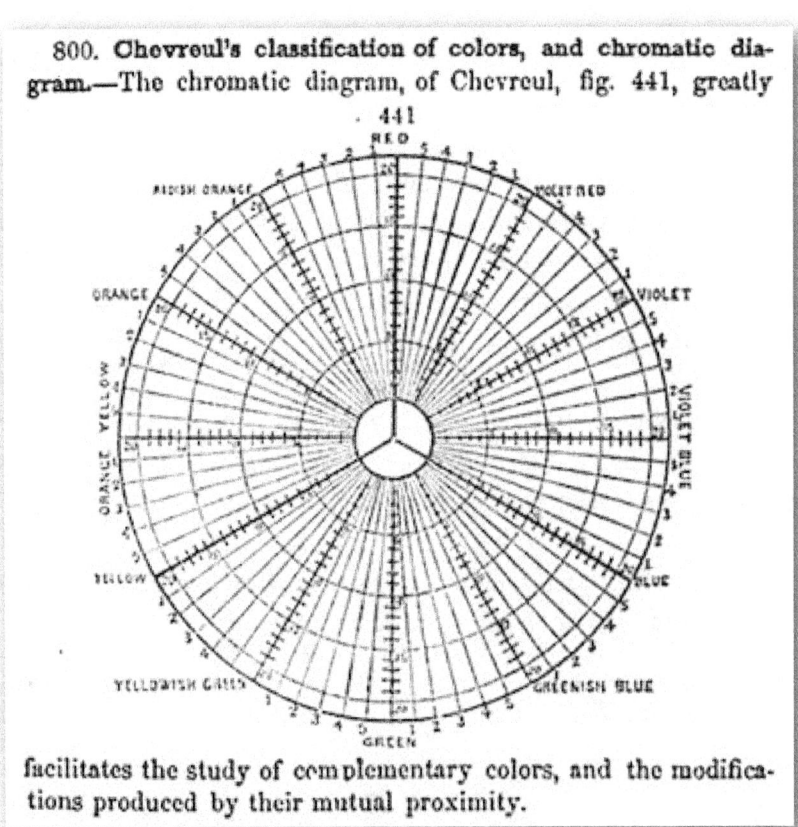

800. **Chevreul's classification of colors, and chromatic diagram.**—The chromatic diagram, of Chevreul, fig. 441, greatly

facilitates the study of complementary colors, and the modifications produced by their mutual proximity.

"Wally, is this why the colors in these paintings look so good?" Wally got a big smile on his face. "That's it, Gia. Although his work is largely forgotten today, there were people, mostly French, who caught on to his ideas and used them with very good results. We call them the Impressionists. Most of those fellows had read, or were conversant with Chevreul's ideas." Gia seemed very surprised. "This is amazing, Wally. How could so much be forgotten – such important stuff?" Wally seemed thoughtful. "I guess some people think that just because something is old, it doesn't matter anymore."

"There is more to the story. One of Chevreul's friends was A.M. Ampere. He is the guy for whom the unit of electrical measurement, the amp, is named. He was a brilliant pioneer in the understanding of electricity. One day Chevreul was explaining to Ampere his discoveries concerning how colors affect one another when placed side-by-side. Ampere was very impressed, but passed along some good advice. 'Chevreul, all your discoveries will be totally useless unless you are able to formulate your discoveries in a law that governs how these colors affect one another when seen by the human eye.' Chevreul followed his friend's advice. The result was the 1839 publication on simultaneous contrast."

"The kernel of the theory tells us that colors opposite one another on the color wheel Chevreul devised are the ones that will make one another look better when placed side-by-side. A good example is the placing of red next to green. Some artists seem to be able to understand this intuitively, without ever having been taught the theory of simultaneous contrast. For others, the lamp of learning must be lit by teaching."

Thirteen

MORE PLACES TO GO

It was sometime between 5:30 and 6:00. Gia and Wally had made their way back to the place where Michelangelo had left them off. They were at the same table they had sat at in the morning and were now sipping wine. Looking out the window at the water, there were still sprinkles coming down. The rain wasn't as hard now, but it still made round patterns as it fell into the water. They had talked about the party Michelangelo had invited them to. They decided they would accept his offer if it still held. They were quiet now. They had covered a lot of territory and were glad to be sitting down. Their travels had involved several rides in a water taxi. The place Michelangelo had left them off was an island. Some of the places they wanted to visit were in the larger area of Venice where San Marco sits. As she sat there quietly, Gia had a thought going through her head. It was about something Wally had said earlier in the day.

"Wally, you say something about the lamp of learning when we look at the paintings with all the nice color. Does that mean anything special? You said it in a way that made me think it mean something to you." Wally looked surprised. "I'm surprised you picked that up. It does mean something to me. Right now, I'm a bit on overload from all the visual input today. Maybe I can explain it a bit. I used that expression, lamp of learning, when I was talking about Chevreul's ideas that aren't much known anymore. That expression, lamp of learning, refers to another idea from long ago that is also sadly forgotten. It's an idea that has been around even longer. It's been around since the days of classical Greek antiquity." Gia stopped Wally for a moment: "do you mean several hundred years B.C.?" "That's it Gia – a long time ago. It's a shame how a person figures something out and then it gets forgotten. It's something the Greeks came to understand about teaching, education. The old saying was: 'education is not filling a vessel; it is lighting a lamp.' The Greeks had learned that filling a person's head with a lot of information does not make a learned individual. Real education is about setting a person on fire with the spirit of inquiry, thus the lamp. Once a person's mind has been awakened, the lamp lit, they can go about teaching them self."

Gia again became thoughtful. "I remember when we were kids. We had tablets at school that had this funny lamp on the cover. It was like Aladdin's lamp." Wally was smiling. "That's to remind us of that idea. I see so much of contemporary education that is just filling the vessel. It's like lighting the lamp has been forgotten. The hysteria over standardized tests is just the latest attempt at vessel filling. Kids don't develop creativity when they are given the impression that everything has been figured out. They are given the impression that all they have to do is load up with all the stuff that's been figured out and they will be educated. That kind of 'education' leaves a huge part of the brain undeveloped. That's why art should not be removed from the curriculum in schools. Art classes, and let's not forget music, are often the only opportunities for students to develop creativity in the information filling stations that are called schools." Just then Wally noticed that Gia was pointing out the window. Michelangelo's boat was slowly pulling in and getting ready for docking.

"Aye, que se diche?" was Michelangelo's greeting as he came in the door. Gia and Wally waved and smiled at him. He went over to the bar, getting

a glass of wine for himself. There was room at the table for a third person, and he joined them. Talk was about the party tomorrow. Then the subject of dinner came up. Michelangelo was for eating right there: "I often stop to eat here when I fly around on the water." Gia was quick to inform him that his aunt expected them for dinner and she did not want to disappoint her again. Michelangelo seemed to understand that, though he was obviously hungry. They decided to finish their wine and move on to what came next. It was not long until they were out the door. It was hardly even sprinkling. Umbrellas were not needed.

Michelangelo did not turn on the windshield wipers this time. Cabin windows were opened on both sides. The sounds of Venice mingled with the obedient growling of the diesel engine. All three in the cabin were somewhat less than energetic. It had been a long day for them all. Not much was said. Michelangelo complained a bit about a fare he had picked up during the day, tourists from former Yugoslavia who: "knew nothing about nothing". It sounded like they were Serbs.

It was sometime between 6:30 and 7:00. Gia and Wally were sitting at a table in the front room of their hotel. They could hear Michelangelo and his aunt in the room behind the counter. They were arguing. Only Gia knew what was going on, and she wished she didn't. The fast and furious Italian was lost on Wally, who could have cared less if he had understood the argument. It was about Francesca, Michelangelo's girlfriend. Lucia was telling him that it was not right that he didn't marry her. Gia also was able to figure out that Lucia had taken care of Michelangelo when he was young. His mother had died when he was just a boy. Lucia had done her best to see he got a good upbringing. She was still working on that project.

Dinner started with Michelangelo bringing out silverware, glasses, and to the surprise of Gia and Wally, lit candles. One other table in the room was occupied. A sad looking old lady sat there eating pasta. Gia thought about inviting her to their table, but good sense stopped her. If the hotel had been hers, Gia would not have hesitated. Being a guest, she knew it would be bad manners. As matters progressed, wine, bread, and butter appeared on the table. Salads arrived. Gia and Wally noticed four salads were placed on the table and guessed Lucia and her nephew would both join them for dinner. Gia and Wally were no longer aware of what o'clock it was when Lucia and Michelangelo emerged from the kitchen together. Both carried trays. It was dinner time. The trays found places on an adjacent table as aunt and nephew shuttled dishes over to the table where Gia and Wally sat. When Lucia and Michelangelo sat down, Gia was surprised that Lucia asked her nephew to say grace. Michelangelo politely said the benediction. Dinner had begun.

Steak, potatoes, and lots of vegetables in a cheese sauce comprised the biggest part of dinner. Gia was surprised that there was no pasta. Conversation was mostly about the next day, Friday. Things were resolved about when Michelangelo would pick them up for the party. Since that wouldn't happen until early evening, Gia and Wally planned to spend the earlier part of the day exploring more parts of the city that they could get to without a boat. They would be places closer to the hotel. Lucia was talking about an old palace that had been converted into an art gallery. She knew the people who ran it. They were distant relatives. Michelangelo explained that they showed local artists. They were people who painted views of Venice, but mostly views of the countryside not far from the city. The gallery liked to show views of the pleasant hillsides with farmhouses, olive gardens, vineyards, and all that one does not see in the city. This appealed to Gia and Wally. They got out their map to make notes. Lucia disappeared and reappeared with dessert. Wally noted that her limp was missing. Michelangelo removed some of the used plates and empty dishes from the table. Dessert was chocolate cake with vanilla ice cream. Gia was thinking that this meal was not quite what she would expect in an Italian restaurant. She wondered if Lucia had put together a meal to please her guests from America.

It was close to 9:00 when Gia and Wally got to their room. They had helped clean up after dinner and had, for the first time, gotten a look at the room behind the counter. It was almost as interesting as the room they had eaten in. Or maybe it was interesting in a different way. It looked like it served both as an office and a kitchen. What made it interesting was the accumulation of clutter from ages past. In this section of the hotel, the clutter was not in any way arranged, or on display. The room and the artifacts therein had seemed to invoke the spirits of individuals who had occupied or used this space. Back in their room, Gia and Wally were still talking about the room behind the counter. Wally was thinking out loud: "I'd like to be in there some day when there's no one else around. I'd just like to be in there and look at the place undistracted . . ." Gia sat down, putting her head back and seemed to be looking at the ceiling. Wally went to the front window, sitting on the windowsill as he had the day before. He still had thoughts about doing a painting out that window when it was daylight. In the very sparse light available at that time of day, he could make out enough of the structural underpinnings of what he saw to compose a kind of visual framework in his mind. He got up to get his sketchbook. He was going to set down a few visual notes, a quick sketch, when he realized Gia was spacing out like she had done the night before. It looked like she might channel again.

Wally did get his sketchbook, but not to sketch in. There were a lot of blank pages in it. He could use these to write down things Gia might say in case she started to channel. Instead of going back to the windowsill, Wally sat in the big chair again with his sketch pad and pen. He sat there waiting. A pigeon came to perch on the windowsill where he had been. It reminded him he had forgotten to replace the window screen. He was trying to encourage the reluctant pigeon to find better real estate when he heard a voice.

The pigeon will go soon Wally. This is Rupert. We are in no rush. I can wait. I keep track of matters through Gia's eyes. In a few more seconds the pigeon took to flight and Wally replaced the screen. He repositioned himself in the big chair with his sketchbook. *I realized the two of you have had a busy and tiring day. I will not keep you beyond your limits. You do recall that I told you I would speak of light. Venice is an especially appropriate place to speak of light – light of any kind. I should mention that Venice is a special place. Perhaps you recall that I spoke to you last year about coordination points. They are places in your world where certain nonphysical planes intersect to enable and facilitate the happening of events. These are events that might not be enabled to take place were these coordination points not intersecting. You might think of the coordination points as catalytic converters enabling the transpiring of desirable happenings in your world. The lovely city of Venice is placed on one of these fault lines where intersect the formative planes that neither the senses of man nor the instruments of the scientists at present are able to register.*

Perhaps it is no accident that the making of glass has for hundreds of years been associated with this city on the waters. The transparent nature of glass says something about the ways that light in this city can at times allow the very stones and bricks seem as though they are themselves transparent. The light here can be of a very special quality. I say 'can be' because those who have been too much infected by the doctrinaire pronouncements of the scientists and churchmen will not allow themselves to believe that such wonderful effects are possible. Belief is everything. This is something I do not tire of repeating. You do create the world you believe in. If you firmly believe that you may only experience the limited scope of reality that science and religion dictate to you, you will only be able to experience that truncated version of reality. It may not be out of place here to recall that medieval theologians did enjoy using the metaphor of light coming through the beautiful colored glass of cathedral windows to explain the nature of God and his goodness.

I began speaking to you of the light that you know and understand in your world to introduce you to a fuller understanding of light. When you think of light, coming to mind is the light you know as coming from the sun. The light from fire or electrical devices may come to your mind also . I want to expand that concept. The light I speak of does not come from the Sun, from fire, or from any electrical device. Indeed, you are not able to perceive this light with any of your physical organs. I should note that the small part of the electromagnetic spectrum that your eyes know as light is only a hint of the fuller reality of light. I want to talk about that fuller reality of light tonight. I realize that those with a scientific bent might be thinking of infrared or ultraviolet light. These too are part of the electromagnetic spectrum, but are not perceived by your eyes. These are not what I speak of tonight. What I introduce is the fact that other spectra exist; they exist as other dimensions of light that neither your eyes nor your instruments can detect. They are not extensions of the electromagnetic spectrum that you know. The spectra that I discuss tonight exist in addition to that.

Perhaps you recall that I spoke to you last year about the inner senses. These are not the senses that you use to perceive sound, the light you know, the sense of touch, etc. The inner senses are used to perceive input of a different kind. There are a number of these inner senses, but to speak of them individually usually does not do justice to the totality of their being. They often function in a more simultaneous manner. That is, when an individual does succeed in experiencing them, they are not normally experienced individually, but together. You might recall that I spoke to you about psychological time, one of the inner senses. It is the inner sense that allows you to experience time as it really is – or as it really isn't.

Time in your world is anchored to the minutes, hours, days, etc. Psychological time allows you to understand that this arbitrary structure is not at all necessary. It allows you to experience the simultaneous nature of reality. It allows you to experience the time behind time. In your dreams you often can experience time this way. This can be one of the reasons you have difficulties recounting your dreams. You try to recount them in a framework of minutes, hours, etc. In your dreams you did not experience events that way. You dealt with a different kind of time there. I spoke to you about other inner senses: inner vibrational touch; disentanglement from camouflage; perception of past – present – future, and more besides. It is not my intention to speak of these tonight. Rather, I introduce inner senses to tell you that it is these that will allow you to perceive the kind of light I introduce to you tonight.

Now, Wally, I want to pause briefly to see if you have any questions about the dictation you are doing. I noticed you looked puzzled several times. For several minutes Wally and Rupert talked back and forth while Wally did a few corrections to the text he was writing. After Wally stopped writing, there was a period of silence during which nothing happened. Then Gia, functioning for Rupert, looked solidly at Wally and started speaking again.

Your minds were formed when you were young. You did show up here as infants with baggage from other physical lives and from other nonphysical adventures of consciousness. However, the culture you were born into accepts none of this. Both the religious and scientific communities see young babies as being born with a clean slate – tabula rasa. The educational processes in your culture assume that children appear in this world unprogrammed, so to speak. If children do show evidence of experiences or knowledge gained elsewhere, strong attempts are made to erase such manifestations. Tampering by the devil or insanity [mental problems] will be blamed. Every attempt is made to force children conform to the prejudices of science and religion. These are strong and potent forces. The process of being incorporated into a certain society, socialization, usually erases any traces of traits that the society does not accept or believe in. We can say that this is the reason why individuals arrive at maturity with no ability to perceive the inner senses. They were taught very early that such nonsense does not exist. If children were not so brainwashed in your culture, their perceptive abilities as adults would be more inclusive; the inner senses would not be forbidden access. It can be instructive to study what your culture calls primitive peoples in this regard. These more often arrive at adulthood with their perceptive abilities intact.

I cover these matters as preface to the subject of the light you do not see. There are times in your dreams when you do perceive this light that in your daytime hours is invisible to you. This light I speak of tonight is a light that illumines even the blackest night. We think of empty space as an area where nothing exists. You might think of the space between your face and its image you see in a mirror as completely empty. This is not the case. A person with some scientific knowledge can tell you that the air that fills that space has existence as atoms and molecules. Just try to compress it. You will see. What the scientists won't tell you is that in addition to the constituent elements of air, there is in that space being of another kind. That being is composed of infinitesimally small units of consciousness. These are primary or beginning stages of what we call matter. Though they are not yet matter at this stage. These are the smallest units of consciousness. Your physical selves are composed of billions of them. Consciousness is really everywhere, though you'd like to pretend it is a quality given only to your kind. Maybe a diminished form of it is grudgingly granted by your kind to the animals.

Below the level of the animals however, nothing in the way of consciousness. So you think. Your kind does not grant consciousness even to other forms of life. The trees, flowers, the grass, none of this has consciousness. To say it does puts one in company with those of diminished mental capacity or madmen. Your whole world – even those spaces where nothing seems to exist – is solidly built of units of consciousness. The twinkling of these units of consciousness is the light I introduce you to tonight. This light is present even when what seems to be the greatest darkness prevails.

The astronomers have peered into what they consider the emptiness of space for hundreds of years. Some have even said that those cold, empty spaces frighten them. You may tell them that those spaces are not empty or dark. Though those spaces may have nothing of or like the air of your atmosphere, they are not empty. They are filled and made of tiny units of consciousness. The light given off by these is the light I speak of tonight. One of the teachers of the nonphysical world I inhabit is known to some in your world as Seth. He has been known to speak of that light in those seemingly empty reaches of space. He mentions that those seemingly empty voids are: ". . . alive with the light with which the very fires of life are lit." Through most of your lives the majority of you never see this light. Sometimes at the point of death, a person will finally see this light that your beliefs have blinded you to. In your dreams you will at times see this light. Religious types will sometimes speak of 'seeing the light'. It is a reference to those times when the veils and blinders of established beliefs are ripped from you. This enables you to see some of the splendor of the universe.

Gia looked around. Wally could tell Rupert was looking through her eyes to see the state of things in the room. He usually did this to get a sense of things before saying good night. Wally watched Gia clutch the arms of her chair. After a spell of just staring at Wally, Rupert spoke. *Thank you, Wally, for taking dictation tonight. Do you have any questions for me before we say good night? If so, now is the time.* Wally shuffled through his sketchbook a bit before saying anything. "No, Rupert, I think we're okay here." *I feel fortunate to have such good friends. I give to the both of you whatever blessing I have the faculty to confer. May the good spirits watch over both of you. For now, good night, and share all this with Gia.*

Gia's head went back in her chair. Whoever was looking through her eyes at this point was looking at the ceiling. Wally sat there waiting. He looked at a clock. It was already the next day, sometime after 12 midnight. He was about to get out of his chair and gently shake Gia when he noticed her looking at him. He could tell this was Gia looking at him and not Rupert. Wally started to smile. Gia spoke: "I'm crawling back to my normal consciousness, Wally. I have the feeling we had a good session tonight. I'm a total blank on what it was about, but I can tell it was good. All I can recall is the pictures. They were pictures of the heavens. It was stars – the blackness of the night and the beautiful light of the stars." She was smiling. "I'm too tired to talk about it, Gia. It was really good though. We'll have to talk about it tomorrow. I'd really like to get you in bed right now."

Morning in Venice was not like the day before. There were birds chirping. The sky was not red. Gia was awake but not out of bed yet. She was totally naked. Through the open windows she heard outside noises. What sky she could see was blue. Wally was still sleeping. Gia didn't want to look at a clock or know what time it was. The day seemed to invite her. She was wishing she had more clothes with her. She and Wally had left most of their baggage in the car at the airport; that was when they were expecting to pick up the Venturis the next day. This was Friday. The latest plans were that she and Wally would pick up the Venturis at the airport tomorrow, Saturday. She wanted to wash a few items out. Getting out of bed, she took her naked self to the bathroom. She did bathroom things, then started to wash out some things in the sink.

There was a small window in the bathroom. Gia opened it and looked out. Although it was a rather drab and depressing scene, it was what she wanted. It didn't look like anyone would be staring at her intimate clothing articles she wanted to hang up to dry. She was positioning two pairs of panties on a clothes hanger she had suspended from the window handle. Just then Wally came stumbling into the bathroom. "Umm, ah, whoops, I didn't know you were in here." Then he spied the panties hanging in the window. He thought a couple seconds. "First thing out of bed, I thought about a painting I wanted to do out the window. Then I remembered we left all the painting stuff in the car." Looking at the panties, he said: "we could use some clothes too. Maybe we could talk Michelangelo into stopping at the airport on the way to the party. I'd feel better with some more stuff to wear." Gia was nodding. "Yeah, me too. You want to take a shower with me?"

Friday morning found Gia and Wally downstairs in the front room of the hotel. They were at table. It was breakfast time; they were having scrambled eggs. Maybe in Italian the eggs would have had a more descriptive and literary term. The eggs included mushrooms and cheese. There was spice in the mix too. Gia and Wally were trying to figure out just what spices made the eggs taste so good. They had asked Lucia. She told them it was a secret. Gia told Wally another secret: "Michelangelo tells me this. The reason that Lucia is so nice to us is that she thinks we are a good influence on him. Lucia worries about him and the people he hangs out with. For some reason I do not know, Lucia has decided we are a good influence." Wally started laughing, almost spitting out some of his eggs. He took a sip of orange juice to calm things down.

Wally was still laughing when Lucia appeared with coffee. "Something funny happens here?" Wally watched the hot coffee fill his cup, then watched it fill Gia's. The aroma of hot coffee hovered about the table. It didn't seem just the aroma of any old coffee. It seemed special. Wally almost asked Lucia what kind of coffee it was. He stopped himself in his tracks thinking she would tell him it was another secret. It did really smell good. A bit of cream, real cream, gave it that complete taste that made coffee in the morning a great idea. Lucia disappeared then reappeared with toast. Gia could tell she wanted to ask a question. Wally watched Gia initiate a conversation with Lucia in Italian that once again excluded him. This went on for some time. Wally took his coffee to the window to see what was happening out on the canal. He then walked out the door to enjoy this beautiful morning in Venice.

Wally couldn't help but notice that the canal had an influx of better water this morning. He thought it had come from the lagoon. Maybe an ocean breeze had blown it in. He didn't care where it had come from. He was just glad for this better water in the canal. There was a lot of activity on the water to pay attention to. Wally had been absorbed by goings-on out front for about 10 minutes when Gia asked him to come back in. He had no problem following Gia into the hotel. He probably would have been willing to follow her into hell.

They sat down at the table again. Lucia was no longer there. They were now the only people in this big room that served as a lobby for the hotel. Gia started talking: "Lucia says a few things for us to know. Most is about Michelangelo. She worries about him like a mother hen. She tries to make us watch over him like she does. We should forget this. He is a big boy now, and a lot better person than she realizes." Wally was not sure how to deal with this and just shook his head. "He came to us like an angel of God and took us on our journey; I think he is the one with moral superiority." Gia smiled at that then spoke again. "You have a good idea there. Hold that idea. Lucia talked a lot about things we can do today. I made notes and a kind of map. It gives us a lot to do before we meet Michelangelo this evening."

The Venice morning saw Gia and Wally exploring more of the old city that so much fascinated them. Some of the back streets with old buildings and shops were as interesting as the galleries and museums they found. Lunch was at a small, out-of-the-way bar and restaurant. It was good that Gia spoke Italian, for no one there knew English. It being Friday, fish was on the menu. There was some mysterious stuff in a very heavy sauce that even the owner could not name. Overall it was a good meal, but somewhat mysterious, and of course there was pasta. The owner kept their wine-glasses full telling them there was no charge for refills. The wine was, for the lack of a better word, powerful. It tasted like it had been made in the basement. When the owner came around, Gia kept asking him about the history of this part of the city. He had a lot to say about fish markets and various kinds of contraband products like whiskey and gunpowder sold on the cheap with no tax. Gia and Wally were tempted to hang out at the bar after they had eaten, but did the smart thing and moved on.

The afternoon got off with a visit to a Venetian Baroque church. They just sat in there for a while soaking up the ambience. Then a sleazy priest began hanging around who seemed interested in Gia. This was their cue to move on. Once on foot again, they began to sense they were moving deeper into a part of the city where 'nice people' did not go. At a certain corner they did an about-face and began to backtrack. They found their way to a museum on the map they had. There Gia talked with some people who told them about a nearby street with a lot of art galleries, shops, and dealers. This proved to be fortunate. They spent the remainder of the afternoon on that street. They even found a dealer who was interested in Lucia's painting of the sea battle.

Upon returning to the hotel Gia and Wally noticed that Lucia was in a very uncharacteristically bright mood. The art dealer had called her. He would be coming next week to see the painting. Dinner was on the light side. There was a party to go to. Michelangelo and his girl, Francesca, arrived during dinner. They sat with Gia and Wally. Wally couldn't help noting how Francesca looked like Secula Venturi. Gia seconded that opinion. She had an office job and was very happy to have two people to practice her English with. Her job involved phone contacts with a good number of English-speaking types. Michelangelo had brought his motor launch and it was not long until all four of them were in it and in motion.

A stop was made on the way. Gia and Wally retrieved some items from their car at the airport parking lot. Back in the boat and in motion again, Gia slipped out of the dress she had been wearing and put on something a bit brighter for the party. Michelangelo pretended not to notice but it was obvious he was very distracted. He almost didn't notice an oncoming water taxi. Francesca asked him if he wanted her to pilot the boat. He was a bit embarrassed at that just shaking his head no. It was a nice ride that gave Gia and Wally a good look at some of the maritime life surrounding Venice. It also gave them a chance to get to know Francesca a bit better. Approaching the island that hosted the party, it appeared that it had its own little port. A good number of guests had already arrived. The various crafts docked there gave the impression of a well-to-do crowd. There were some rather large ones that came across as more status symbol than boat.

The party was an inside-outside affair. There was an outdoor pool. Some people were in the water, a few with their clothes on. Close to the pool was a volleyball court. It seemed to be mostly girls in bikinis playing volleyball. As the sun set most drifted indoors. The huge old stone house made an ideal setting for a party. Festivities moved to another level when a band fired up the party with rock music. Gia and Wally were noticing now why Michelangelo's aunt had concerns about some of his associates. He seemed well acquainted with a coterie of what might be called high Venetian sleaze, or Venetian low life, depending on your point of view. This bunch seemed to be part of what might have been a movable feast that went on for days – maybe weeks. And they did not seem poor.

Gia and Wally met a good cross-section of Venetian society. Even some of the people who tilled the land and kept the vineyards on the island were at the party. And there were those who reeked of money. Wally kept wishing he could be invisible so he could just watch the goings-on without any obligation to get involved in what was becoming an increasingly drunken riot. At a point, Francesca began herding Michelangelo and his guests to the boat. Once in the boat, Michelangelo passed out. Francesca proved to be quite an able pilot. The boat floated over the waters with the starry sky above. It was not certain what time it was when the boat docked at the hotel. The boat was tied up for the night, and all four spent the night at the hotel.

Fourteen

FLORENCE

No one was sure what time Saturday began. It was probably Saturday already when they had arrived from the party the night before. It was morning now. Gia, Wally, and Francesca sat at a table in the lobby. Michelangelo had not appeared yet. A few guests were having breakfast at another table. Lucia seemed in a rather stern and serious mood as she brought out eggs and toast from the kitchen. There was some interchange in Italian between her and Francesca. Conversation was about Michelangelo. Gia and Wally would need his help to get to the airport. The Venturis were to land at Marco Polo Airport on a flight coming in at 6:00 PM. Also, Francesca would need his boat to get back home.

Not much of note transpired until the arrival of Michelangelo. It was getting close to 11:00 when that event took place. Coming down the stairs, he went straight out the front door without saying a word. He appeared to be checking out his boat. When he did come in and sit down with the other three, he seemed much relieved that his boat was all right. He was talking in a mixture of Italian and English. He was saying that the last thing he remembered from last night was a Rolling Stones song the band played, Beast of Burden. Past that he recalled nothing. Gia wanted to talk about the ride to the airport later that day. It was maybe 2 cups of coffee later when Michelangelo got to that subject.

After reassuring Gia that he would get her and Wally to the airport on time, Michelangelo wandered into the kitchen. That did not go well. Even Wally could tell that. Lucia seemed to be in an especially volatile mood that morning. The condition and hour Michelangelo had arrived in last night had a lot to do with that. While Michelangelo fried bacon, he had to listen to Lucia screaming at him about responsibility and proper behavior. When he arrived back at the table with a big plate of bacon for everyone, he seemed to be just treading water in the game of life. It took him a while to start talking again. When he did he spoke of some people he had to pick up in the early afternoon. Francesca offered to come along, or even drive the boat, if that would help. Michelangelo muttered some things about legal responsibility when carrying passengers. Nevertheless, he said she could come along. Gia and Wally felt better about this. They felt their chances of Michelangelo getting them to the airport would be better with Francesca along. Michelangelo did not come across as a paragon of responsibility that morning.

After bacon, toast, and coffee, Michelangelo went out and fell asleep in his boat. When the people at the other table had drifted on, Lucia joined Gia, Wally, and Francesca at table. She was hungry herself and had a bit to eat. Wally was concerned about getting matters financial cleared up with her. He suggested to Gia that she bring that up after Lucia had eaten. Lucia was in no rush to deal with money. Her first priority was to make sure her guests knew how much she was grateful to them for staying at her hotel and befriending her nephew. The rest of the day until evening was something of a blur. It did happen that Michelangelo's boat did arrive later in the day. Gia and Wally did get to the airport. Having made farewells to Michelangelo and Francesca, they went into the terminal to await the American Venturis.

Information on the big board told them that the flight would be delayed close to an hour. They decided to have a light meal at the restaurant there. During the meal, Wally voiced some concerns about Secula Venturi. "She is my girlfriend, my muse, and I've been with you as though she doesn't exist." Gia was thoughtful for a few minutes. When she did speak, it was very slow. She spoke in carefully chosen words. "Secula is my friend too, and my cousin. Maybe you shouldn't worry about this so much. Just be nice to her like she deserves. It was her idea for us to go on this trip together. Maybe she knows what she is doing." Wally got a big grin on his face. "I wish we weren't in here right now. I feel like getting high."

Shades of evening were setting in when the Venturis arrived at Marco Polo Airport. As Gia watched them coming off the plane, she couldn't help recalling the day she had landed at Pittsburgh Airport from Italy. It had been a landmark day for her. These people she had never seen before had given her a reception that made her feel like visiting royalty. She couldn't help feeling twinges of guilt about what she and Wally had been doing. But it had felt so natural and good. She tried to dismiss the guilt feelings as inappropriate. She was turning over in her mind whether she should share with Secula what she and Wally had been doing when Secula walked up to her.

Secula had her own issues. She had been sleeping with Gia's boyfriend, George; Gia did not know this. In addition, she had sent her very attractive cousin on this trip with her boyfriend, Wally. There was a moment of truth just before they embraced. They just looked at one another. Neither said a thing. In that moment there was a nonverbal exchange that seemed to happen when their eyes met. In that meeting of eyes there was a passing back and forth of all that was not said. When that very long moment was over, they both put their arms around one another. It seemed to be laughing and senseless chatter all at once. They were both happy.

The Venturis were hungry. Gia and Wally realized that another trip to the restaurant would delay the trip to Borgo, but went for it anyway. While they were sitting in the restaurant, Gia called her mother. She explained they would be getting in late. She then called Giovanna down the street to tell her that Wally and the Venturis would also be late. She felt better with that arranged. While the Venturis were eating, she and Wally went to the place they had rented the little Fiat and made arrangements for the remainder of the adventure in Italy. By the time they got on the road, darkness had fallen. Gia was glad she had other drivers aboard for the long stretches ahead. She was tired.

It wasn't too long until Gia was able to turn over the driving to Wally. Sitting in the passenger seat in the front, she fell asleep. In the first dream she had, her dad showed up. He wanted to tell her about his teachers. He went on at great length explaining how the spirit meets with those known in life, those who have also made the journey to the world to come. These were not the teachers; these were the ones who had been on Earth like himself. He had been happy to meet his grandmother. He had made peace with his father; the two of them had never gotten along well in this life. He also spoke of those he had known in previous lives. One woman he had been married to in the 1700s especially made him happy when he saw her again. He wanted to know how Gia's mother was doing. He was then talking about other things his teachers had told him. These concerned his next physical life. They told him that when he had been sufficiently prepared, he would begin to meet the people who would be his associates in his next life on Earth. He didn't know who they would be, but he was looking forward to this.

Gia's dream life then progressed through areas she did not understand. There were people she had never seen before, places she did not recognize, and circumstances that left her very confused. What happened next was very memorable. She was on a city street. It seemed she was in Florence, on the outskirts of the city. She was flying, flying with very little effort. In dreams when she had flown before, there was always a struggle to get up in the air and stay there. This time the flying was done with ease. It seemed she was exploring the city of Florence from the air. In a later part of this dream, she was in Florence, on the ground. She was talking with her uncle Alberto, who lived there. She had not seen him since she was a child. There were many more dreams. Most of them Gia could not remember when she got awake. Wakening came with Wally tugging at her shoulder. "Gia, Gia, the turnoff is coming. I don't know the roads there."

Gia was not completely out of dreamland when she took the wheel to pilot the little Fiat in on the home stretch. Wally was glad to be relieved. Driving at night in a strange country was a bit unnerving. It took him a while to calm down. He noticed that most in the backseat were asleep, or not very attentive. The Italian countryside went by with little of note. Lights punctuated the darkness here and there. They reminded Wally of eyes looking out of the houses that when by. Looking at some of the houses, he tried to imagine who lived there, what their lives were like, what their hopes and dreams might be. There were long stretches where there was nothing to relieve the tedium. Wally was still too jangled from driving to fall asleep.

During one of those long stretches, Wally was noticing that the car was getting closer and closer to the protective barrier at the side of the road. It was starting to concern him when in a moment of terror, horror, and fear he realized the car would soon hit a utility pole. What happened next involved no thought at all, only reactions and instincts. Wally looked at Gia. Seeing her head slumped to one side, he grabbed the wheel and jerked it just in time to avoid hitting what looked like a very big power transmission line poll. The sudden jerk woke everyone up in the backseat. Gia then heard Wally screaming at her. "Gia, Gia, are you on cruise control?" Cruise control – Gia was trying to react to that. "Oh, yeah, maybe." Wally quickly said: "hit the brakes, not hard." Gia was slowly comprehending the fact she had fallen asleep while driving. Wally was still steering with his left hand. "Hit the brakes slowly, Gia." Gia touched the brake lightly. The car began to slow down. There was a place up ahead to pull over. Gia brought the little Fiat to a stop in the unlighted area.

Everyone piled out of the car. There was a sense of great relief that something horrible had not happened. Dominic Senior went over in the woods to relieve himself. Gia and Dominic Junior were thanking Wally for what he did. Wally was shaking his head no. "I hardly remember what I did. It was just reactions. Anyhow, I would have been the first person to get whacked by that pole. If anything, it was just self-preservation." Dominic Senior was just then wandering out of the woods. Walking up to the group he said: "look what a beautiful starry night it is." Everyone looked up. It was one of those nights when the stars were so crisp and clear. Looking at them almost took you there, light years away. Then there was conversation about who should drive. Gia mentioned that she was the only one who knew the way. She told everyone to keep her awake. "I'm pretty shook up about what just happened – not likely I'll fall asleep."

The remainder of the trip to Borgo was, fortunately, uneventful. Almost everyone in the car kept a close eye on Gia. Being aware of this, Gia frequently commented on what little there was visible. Periodically she also asked the others in the car if they were awake. It was in the wee hours of the morning when the little mint green Fiat pulled into Borgo. She parked in front of Giovanna's place so the other four in the car could unload their things. Gia reminded them that Giovanna had asked them to come in the back; it would be unlocked. As they were bringing things into the kitchen, Giovanna appeared. She seemed to be in something of a daze, but ambulatory. She insisted on taking them all upstairs to show them their rooms.

Everyone had a room of their own. Giovanna then ushered them back to the kitchen. Wine was poured for everyone. A plate of munchies appeared on the table. Giovanna started talking about how she was related to the Venturi family. Gia was translating. After one glass of wine Gia took off for her mother's place down the street. Dominic Senior tried to continue the conversation with Giovanna. The others listened. His Italian was rusty, but usable. Then Giovanna went into a discussion about how the Venturis were related to others in the town. Secula was interested in this.

She wanted to do some writing about her family in the old country. She got Giovanna to write the names of people and draw pictures showing how they were related. Although most were interested, it had been a very long day. Dominic Senior succeeded in getting this point across to Giovanna. It was not long before all headed upstairs. On the way out of the kitchen, Giovanna told them what time masses would be in the morning. It would be Sunday. Secula and Dominic Junior just looked at one another. Wally seemed heedless. Dominic Senior thanked her in Italian.

Secula's room was right over the kitchen. Some time before 10:00 the next morning, she could hear her dad and Giovanna talking in the kitchen. She assumed they were on their way to church. Dominic Senior had wisely avoided awakening his two children to go to mass. He had a very good idea what their response might be. Secula heard her dad and Giovanna going out the kitchen door and over the back porch. She began thinking about Wally. She lay there in the quiet summer morning for a while. There were birds chirping outside that caught her attention. She was imagining what the birds might look like when she heard Wally's door open. It was just across the hall from hers. She could hear him going down the hall to the bathroom at the end of the hall. Very shortly Secula heard him returning to his room.

As Secula lay there, she found herself wondering what Wally and Gia had been doing together. She was very aware of what she and George had been doing together. Then she heard her brother, Dominic, paying a visit to the bathroom. His room was way down the hall by the bathroom. He wouldn't hear anything if she went over to Wally's room. She decided to ask Wally how things between him and Gia were. She thought she might tell Wally about George, but she hadn't decided about that. Secula got up. She looked out the window. She had on no slippers, her panties, and a Victoria's Secret nightshirt. She felt she was dressed appropriately for the visit she was about to make. She heard her brother return to his room. Without the slightest hesitation, she turned around and went straight for the door.

Wally had not yet fallen back to sleep. He heard the doorknob turn. There was no knock. He figured it was Secula; she entered, looking very much like she was dressed for bed. She was. Wally could not help notice that the sight of Secula dressed for bed was getting something firm between his legs. He smiled at Secula. She closed the door and came over to his bed. After standing there just a few seconds, she sat down beside Wally on his bed. She turned and looked to her right, out Wally's window. She could not help noticing the bulge in the beige bedspread. It told her that Wally was rising to the occasion. No one had as yet said anything. Secula had been formulating a question in her mind. "How have you and Gia been getting along?"

Wally started to lose his erection and got embarrassed. He was close to going into stuttering and stammering mode. After several false starts he got out: "we, we've been getting along really well." Secula's next words came out very quickly: "I should have known better than to send the two of you to Italy together. There is more to the story that I should tell you. Your friend George and I . . . well, things have been happening there too." Much to Wally's surprise, he was getting jealous, jealous of George. He put his hand on Secula's leg. "Do you think I could talk you into getting naked and getting in bed with me?" Fortunately for Wally, it didn't take much talking. He had already said enough. Secula stood up. She took off her panties and threw them on a chair beside the bed. She slipped her Victoria's Secret nightshirt off over her head. Wally was watching. He was rising to the occasion again. Secula slid in between the sheets with him. "My dad and Giovanna are at church now. My brother is down the hall. I don't think he can hear us." That put a great big smile on Wally's face. "So you've been fucking George? I want to fuck you too."

By the time Dominic Senior and Giovanna returned from church, Secula and Wally had showered and were downstairs in the kitchen with Dominic Junior. Coffee was brewing and Secula was making scrambled eggs for Wally, Dominic Junior, and herself. Dominic Junior was making toast. Wally greeted Secula's dad and Francesca when they came in the back door. He tried to assure Francesca that everything was under control. He told her there was no need to get upset about making lunch for her guests. When they sat down to eat, Giovanna got busy getting lunch for Dominic Senior and herself.

It was a nice day in Borgo. Secula, Wally, and Dominic Junior were discussing the possibilities of exploring the town on foot that afternoon. Secula was noticing that her dad seemed interested in their discussion of a tour of the town. "Dad, do you want to go with us if we do a walking tour of Borgo this afternoon?" Dom seemed genuinely interested in Secula's question. He looked at Francesca for a moment, not sure if she knew what they were talking about. He knew that she had her own agenda for that afternoon; there would be no need to ask her to go along. "What time are you going to take off on this grand tour?" Secula looked at Wally and her brother, then at her father. "You tell us. We haven't gotten that far yet." Just then there was a knock at the front door. Wally, seeing Francesca busy at the oven, told her he would answer the door. He started to walk toward the front door wondering what he would say if the person at the door knew no English.

When Wally got to the front door, his concerns about dealing with a non-English speaking person vanished. Through the window of the front door he could see Gia's blonde hair. He opened the door. She stood there facing him. "You're just in time for lunch. Come on in." Gia lost no time stepping in. She quickly said: "I don't stay for lunch. I ate." Once in the kitchen, Gia could see Giovanna busy at the stove. She started talking to her in Italian. After assuring her she needed not trouble yourself cooking anything extra, Gia told Giovanna that she, and all her guests were invited down to her mother's house for dinner. Giovanna explained her plans for the day. This included the fact that she may not be back by dinnertime.

Maria Visconti Francesco had a pleasant group of people for dinner that evening. Even though her husband was no longer in this world, so many friends and relatives in the house put a smile on her face. The American Venturis were an added consolation, distant relatives whom she had never met before. People circulated, drifting around drinking wine and getting acquainted with one another. It was a warm summer evening; some spilled out onto the back porch and yard. Gia was helping with things in the kitchen. Several large birds were roasting in the oven. She chopped vegetables for salads, then helped getting tables set. In the midst of doing that there was a phone call from Florence. It was Gia's sister, Cristina. She had been invited to dinner at her mother's house that evening too, but obligations at work had kept her in Florence. She was calling to again invite Gia and Wally to visit her and her partner, Renata, in Florence. It was a very confusing call for Gia. So much was going on in her mother's house right then. And, Secula Venturi was now in Italy. How could she travel to Florence with Wally now?

In the midst of the phone call came her brother, Vittorio Junior, telling everyone that dinner was ready. Gia explained to Cristina that dinner was on the table and she would be thinking about the invitation. She didn't know what else to say. Gia sat down and Secula Venturi sat next to her, to her right. Wally sat across the table from the two of them. Maria asked her son, Vittorio Junior, to say grace. Wally sat there somewhat mystified by it all. It was in Italian. Dominic Venturi Junior looked as out of place as Wally felt. With formalities over, food and small talk prevailed. There was a large bottle of wine on the table. Wally noticed glasses getting empty and poured more wine for all around him. Toward the bottom of Gia's second glass of wine, she brought up the phone call from Cristina in Florence. As Secula listened to Gia, she made notes on her napkin. She usually had a pen with her. After Gia's comments about Cristina's call, Secula sat there looking as though she were thinking. This continued for quite a while. She sipped her wine but said nothing. Wally made comments about the food; he was enjoying it. Gia's younger sister who still lived at home was sitting to her left. Gia told her about Cristina's phone call, in Italian. Wally felt left out.

Vittorio Junior made a toast to the American Venturis, in Italian. Secula whispered a few words to her brother. Her dad seemed to catch on. Secula smiled gently, then turned to Gia to talk. "I'm thinking I want to stay here in Borgo. I'm trying to learn something about the people I came from. I might be working it into a book. But more than the book, I just want to get to know these people, this place. If you and Wally feel like going to Florence, I'd be happy. If I get done what I want to do here, maybe I'll come to Florence if you're still there." Wally had been listening to all this; it was in English. He had been thinking: "what are you doing Secula? You are sending your totally hot cousin and myself on another trip together." He wasn't sure just what to think. Momentarily he wondered of Secula were trying to get rid of him, but the thought of going to Florence with Gia soon blotted out any unpleasantness. He looked over at Gia. She looked back. Wally could feel that thing between his legs starting to get very happy. He looked over at Secula. She had a questioning look on her face. Wally didn't want to seem too anxious about going to Florence with Gia. "Secula, do you think you might go to Florence too?" Secula just smiled. Wally knew better than to ask any more questions.

It had been some days since dinner at Gia's mother's place. It had been good weather. Wally had been taking advantage of the weather by doing a lot of walking with a sketchbook. On some of those days Secula came along with him. On other days, both Gia and Secula came along. Gia liked to sketch too. As Wally and Gia sketched, Secula sat and looked around. Sometimes she made notes for the book she was working on. One day she was talking. Some of the things she said gave Wally reason to take note of things she said about George. Gia was curious about those comments too. One time she couldn't help looking at Wally. They were both on the same wavelength.

Secula became strangely silent. She realized Wally and Gia were looking at one another. Almost in the same instant, she realized why they were looking at one another. Her somewhat random comments about things she and George had been doing together were adding up to a whole that was much larger than the sum of the parts. All three of them became conscious of an embarrassing moment. Wally was nearly finished with this drawing and said: "I think I'll finish this at Giovanna's place this evening. I like to sit at the dining room table in the evenings and draw." Gia took Wally's cue and closed her drawing tablet. It was not long before the three of them were walking on the Via Liverone.

Days came and went. There was discussion about the trip to Florence. Dominic Junior had a bit of interest in that venture. Wally and Gia did not discourage or encourage him. Dominic Senior was another story. He was of the opinion that his son should stay in Borgo with him and Secula. They were visiting the home of their ancestors; it was an opportunity to be taken advantage of. One should know where one comes from. He prevailed upon his son to stay in Borgo. After all, he was paying for the trip. Since Dominic Junior had no really strong interest in going to Florence, he listened to his father and stayed put.

Dominic Senior also had concerns about Wally going to Florence with Gia. There was probably an element of envy involved here. He liked Gia from the first moment he had seen her at Pittsburgh Airport. Looming larger than this was his concern about his daughter, Secula. He felt she should be married by now. Finally she had found a boyfriend, Wally. But now she was sending her boyfriend off to Florence with her extremely attractive distant cousin, Gia. Both Gia and Wally had heard Dom voice his concerns about this. From that point on, both of them avoided him whenever possible. Dom started to notice that they were avoiding him.

Gia and Wally did not have a lot of opportunities to be together alone to discuss things. They both realized that Dom Senior was making things a bit uncomfortable. There was one afternoon when Dom, Secula, and Dominic Junior went for a visit to one of their long-lost relatives in Borgo. Wally was aware of this. That sunny afternoon he walked down to the

Francesco house hoping to find Gia. She was home that afternoon, her mother upstairs for an afternoon nap. Gia invited him in. He had come to the back door. "Come on in, Wally." Wally was his usual inarticulate fumbling, bumbling self. Gia noticing that he had something on his mind said: "you are thinking about something Wally. Tell me." Wally sat down at the kitchen table. Gia went to the refrigerator and produced a bottle of wine. After sitting it on the table, she got two glasses. She sat one by Wally and grabbed the bottle. After pouring wine for Wally and herself, she sat down.

Wally knew what he wanted to say. "I think it's time to go to Florence. Living in the same house with Dom Senior is getting uncomfortable. We still have the little Fiat. I'm thinking about this weekend. Does that sound okay with you?" Gia got up with her wine glass and went to the back door. She looked out into the backyard. "It's a shame parents always try to control their children even when they grow up. I live in the same house with my mother now. Going to Florence right now is the best thing we can do. I would be okay with going today, but we should be polite about it." Wally was smiling.

Fifteen

MOTION

It was Saturday. The little mint green Fiat was packed and in the driveway at Gia's mother's place. Most of the cast of characters in Gia's life were there to say so long to her and Wally. Conspicuous by his absence was Dom Senior. Gia felt bad about this. She knew it was a sign of disapproval that she and Wally should be traveling to Florence together. Not a lot was spoken. People stood around expecting someone else to say something. Secula was now becoming somewhat concerned about sending her boyfriend to Florence with her very attractive cousin. It was somehow, finally, dawning on her that this might not be the best of ideas. Gia's mother was somewhat curious about it all, but avoided asking questions. People looked at one another, keeping their thoughts to themselves.

There seemed to be a sense of relief when Gia and Wally got in the little car and headed out the driveway. Gia drove. Wally was looking at maps. "Wally, you see the city, Trento, on the map? It is the first big city we come to. We'll go by the East side of it. The priests were always talking about this place. There was a big Catholic Church council there in the 16th century." Wally mumbled something about why a counsel. Gia said nothing. Then she said, "we have to get on E 45 by Trento. Look for that on map." There were little villages. Then came two big Lakes. Time passed. Then came signs for Trento. "You've driven this way before, Gia?"

"I have Wally, but I don't remember everything. What's the map say?" Wally fumbled with the map. "At the roundabout take the third exit. That goes to SP 204." Gia said that didn't sound right. "There are more roundabouts. I want to stop and look at the map." Gia found a place to pull off the road. They had been on the road maybe half an hour. Gia got the map out. "Down here Wally – a bunch of places we have to make turns south of Trento. Watch these for me." Back in the car, the journey proceeded. They did get to the South of Trento, and there were a bunch of turns to negotiate. They succeeded in getting on E 45. It was smoother sailing then. Gia asked Wally if he wanted to drive.

They made a short stop and Wally drove, glancing at the map first. "We'll be coming to Verona. That place always makes me think of Shakespeare, Merchant of Venice and all that." Gia just smiled and said, "I like this part of the trip. I like to look around." Places went by, Roverto, Mari, Ala, Avio. In a while Gia told Wally that she wanted to drive again. "Verona is coming up. You can look around for a while. Map says this trip should take about four hours – not so sure about that." Wally was thinking about that one: "the old Zen saying, Gia, 'to travel well is better than to arrive.' No need to hurry." "I like that one, Wally. Just think about people hundreds of years ago. Their travels were so difficult. We can ride in a nice car and enjoy the trip."

"Wally, I'm gonna pull over at this place up here. I'm getting hungry. How about you?" Wally was nodding his head in the affirmative before he spoke. "It's a good idea to slow the trip down a bit. We should take our time, and we won't be coming into Florence right at lunch time." They were some-where South of Modena when they pulled off. The place where they stopped had a lot of glass windows, probably more than were needed. They found a table that had a panoramic view of the Italian countryside. They talked a bit, and Gia said she would order. Wally was sketching the view out the window as Gia talked to a waitress. Coffee arrived quickly. Wally used a little bit of coffee to do a wash on the drawing he was doing on a placemat.

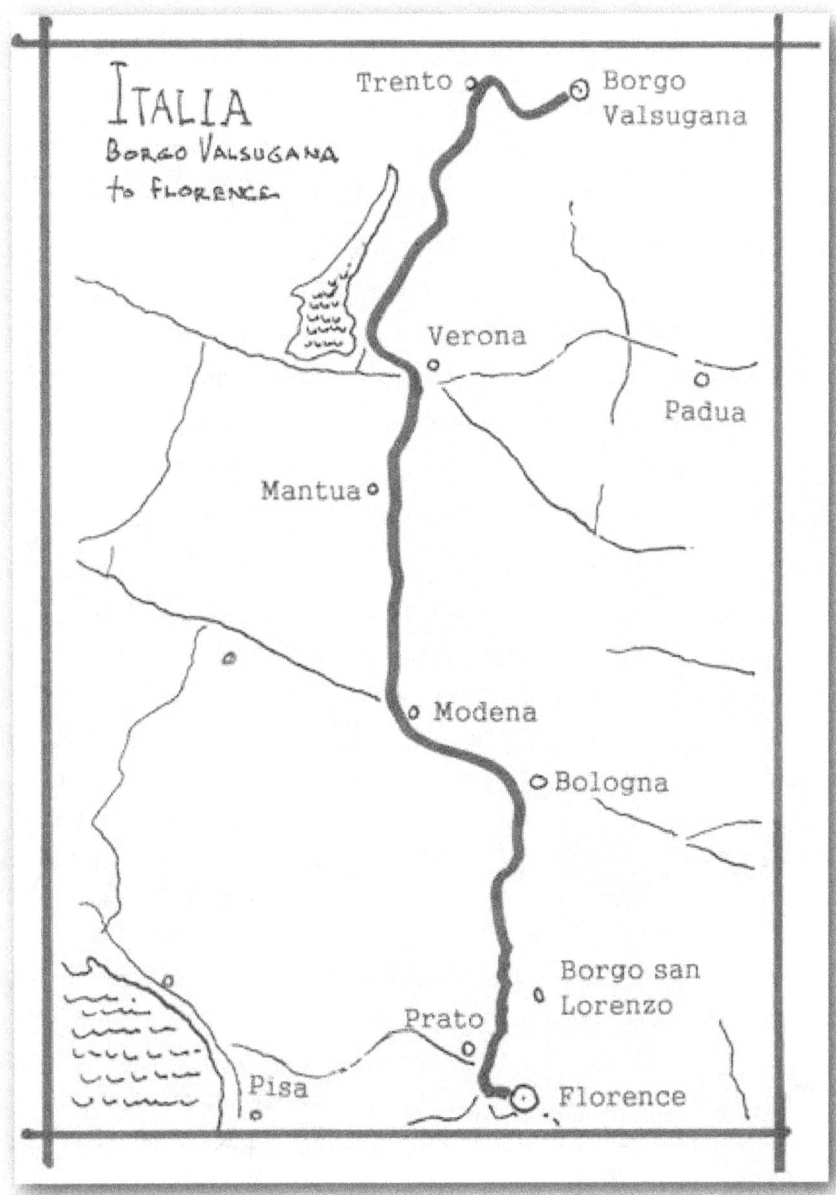

The coffee on Wally's drawing was nearly dry by the time his burger and fries arrived. Gia had been watching him sketch, but the arrival of her angel hair pasta with meat sauce took her attention away from that. Their little meal over, they made restroom stops and headed back to the car. Gia continued driving. It was not long till they had passed Bologna. To pass the time Gia was teaching Wally the little Italian song she sang when she was happy. Wally wrote the words in his sketchbook and they sang together. There were periods of silence when Wally looked around as Gia drove. Wally was trying to get a better view of some rather old farm houses in the distance when he spied a sign for Borgo san Lorenzo. "There is another Borgo, Gia. I guess yours is not the only one." "No, Wally, there are bunches of Borgos. It's just a word that means something like English burg." Wally was glad for the enlightenment. "The turnoff for Prato will be coming up. Florence won't be far then."

It was early afternoon when Gia and Wally found the apartment where Cristina and Renata were staying. Gia had called on her cell phone to let them know they were nearby. Cristina spied them from the apartment window when they pulled in. She and Renata both came down to the street to greet their guests. Renata was an unknown item, so there was some back-and-forth of an introduction. All four of them made several trips to the second floor carrying up baggage from the car. Although Gia and Wally had eaten, there was another sit down with wine, cheese, and other finger food. There was a lot of talk about art; both Cristina and Renata worked at a gallery in Florence. Wally brought out an album of paintings he had done. He was fascinated watching Renata going through the pictures. She was happy to have an opportunity to practice her English. It came in handy at times at the gallery. Wally knew she was lesbian, but couldn't help being attracted to her nevertheless.

Wally fished out some business cards from his wallet, giving them to Cristina and Renata. "These have the link for a page where I have my artwork posted. It will probably look better on your computer." Cristina and Renata spent some time looking at paintings on their computer while Gia and Wally talked about things they wanted to do. Both of them had their cameras out and wanted to spend some time on foot looking around. Cristina heard them talking and commented to Gia in Italian. "We're not far from the river; there are some good views down there. You want to try it?" Wally thought he understood what she was saying but wasn't sure.

It was a half hour later. Gia, Wally, Cristina, and Renata were down by the river. Cristina's and Renata's apartment was not far away. Gia and Wally had their cameras. There was something of a picnic atmosphere though there was no food involved. Wally was taking a picture up the River Arno and mused: "I wonder if Michelangelo ever walked along this river." Cristina heard him and commented: "he was a very thoughtful man. People who think a lot often enjoy being by water." Wally smiled. Gia commented: "Michelangelo never walked by this river. The river constantly changes. As the water flows, is not the same river it was an hour ago." Renata was thinking too. "This is a good philosophical issue – question. Is it ever the same river if it keeps flowing?"

Some people were coming from the other direction. It was a mixed crowd. There were some in their teens – some older. It seemed a rather even mix of males and females, some number around 10 or 12. All in the party sensed a bit of apprehension as they approached. They were not in an area of the city where safety and security were guaranteed. As the two groups encountered one another, there was a momentary standing still. Then there was a bit of chatter in Italian. Wally didn't know what to make of it all. Gia helped fill him in on goings-on. "Cristina and Renata are telling them that they are showing some people around [us] people from America. They are saying you are an artist and this is your first day in the city." Wally could see that a change of plans was in the offing.

There was conversation among both groups. If a bird had been watching from the sky, it could see that there was now only one group. It was heading in the direction that the larger group had been going. A few from the larger group spoke English. They were explaining something to Wally. "All the tourists who come from America – anywhere – see the same things. We can show you the other stuff. You are an artist. You want to see the things that make good pictures. Some here with us study art. They are used to looking for the parts of the city that no one sees, the parts that make good pictures."

Wally could only say: *"Grazie, Grazie mille."* It was obvious that the parts of the city they were headed for were not tourist attractions. Wally was starting to grab his camera. Gia had hers at the ready. In just a few more blocks, they were in old Florence. Some of the structures seemed to be held together by ghosts. Crumbling façades, ancient brick, hand cut stone all worked together to make an architectural medley that had to be recorded, photographed. Gia and Wally did a lot of shooting. Their new friends were pointing out the nooks and crannies that demanded attention. In another block, maybe two, Gia and her friends were being pulled into one of the old drinking spots in this out-of-the-way section of Florence.

It was a group of about 15 people that descended upon this sleepy, little *ristorante.* There was a bar. Gia and Wally gravitated to that centrally lo-cated feature. Cristina and Renata seemed to blend in with the others they had arrived with. Word was passed around that the large number of arriv-als placed heavy demands on the resources of the menu. However, sausage with pasta and sauce would be available for anyone who was hungry. Gia and Wally were checking out the strange little place that circumstances had pulled them into. Hewn ceiling beams protruded from the darkness. They were seen to extend into the notches in the stone walls. Planks on a diago-nal slant were evident on most of the walls. Old engravings, maybe G.B. Piranesi, hung here and there. Knickknacks, memorabilia, sports trophies, and other amorphous nonsense decorated the walls. A kind of dank smoki-ness pervaded the place. As Gia and Wally were soaking all this in, Cristina came up to talk to them.

The hubbub at the bar made it impossible for Wally to hear what Gia and Cristina were talking about. He wouldn't have been able to understand most of it anyhow. They were talking in Italian, but Wally usually listened to try to learn some of that language. Cristina was telling her sister something she had just remembered. It had to do with their uncle, Alberto; he too lived in Florence. "Alberto says he wants to see you when you come to visit me. He wants to give you something. When he was younger, he painted. He did a painting of you and Mama when you were about three. He says he never finished it, but he wants you to have it." Gia looked mystified for a minute before she said anything. "I almost remember that, when Alberto painted us. I know I remember Mama talking about it. I haven't seen him since he moved to Florence. I was only about 12 then."

While Gia and Cristina were talking, Wally got the attention of the man behind the bar. Wally was about to order wine for himself and Gia when he noticed Renata to his left. He asked her if she wanted wine. She did and suggested he get a glass for Cristina also. The man tending bar took a long, hard look at Wally and company and muttered something in Italian. Renata responded; she could tell Wally didn't understand the question. While waiting for wine, Renata introduced some of their new friends to Wally. These were the art students – anxious to meet an artist from America. They knew about as much English as Wally knew Italian. Renata mediated discussions and translated. There was one guy and two girls. Others from the new group hung around and listened – sometimes translating when they could. One of the young artists made a comment about the large state museums being staffed often by people who once had artistic aspirations themselves. They were what she called failed artists. They were people who once wanted to be an artist, but could not make the grade. They either did not have the talent or the ambition to do art themselves. Given this background, they had found positions where they were the judges of what work should be presented to the people as real art.

This comment seemed to evoke something like a seething fury from those listening – not in opposition, but in assent. Renata could not help responding. "I work in a gallery. We do not pass judgment on what is real art. We pass judgment on what might sell. We are trying to make a living. But

I do so much agree with you about the people in the state museums telling people what is real art. How can a failed artist know what art is? What lawyer would allow a group of failed lawyers pass judgment on his work? What physician would allow a group of failed physicians pass judgment on his work? What airline pilot would allow a group of failed airline pilots pass judgment on his work? Do you see what I am saying here?" There was great assent among those listening.

Wally had been listening intently. His voice rose above the silence that followed those remarks. "Airline pilot is a good comparison as far as intelligence goes. I've seen studies that show artists score in the same range as airline pilots in intelligence tests. But there is something else that keeps bothering me here, and I don't bring it up to introduce a red herring." Renata spent some time translating for those who couldn't follow Wally's English. Then there were questions about a red herring. That expression needed some explanation. Wally obliged. "From what I recall, that expression means something thrown out to distract listeners. I was told it came from something that was done to get dogs off of the track of someone they were following. Supposedly, a red herring would be dragged across the path of the person they were to follow. This would get them off the track – distract them."

Things quieted down again, and Wally realized people were looking at him. He went on to get across what was on his mind. "All of the people mentioned were professionals: airline pilots, lawyers, physicians. Now, what I have to say will annoy some people, but please stay tuned." Renata did some translating, a quick summary in Italian. Wally continued: "what I want to say is not an isolated opinion. I've heard it from a good number of people who should know, artists. My point is that artists are not professionals." Renata translated, provoking some quick responses. People were asking why Wally would say this. Even the bartender was paying attention. "I realize this needs some explanation. Professionals are people who have a set methodology to get things done. Doing a root canal requires a fixed way to solve a specific problem. In all the professions, those involved have learned methods to perform specific tasks. My dad was an engineer. I learned a lot about method from him. I don't want to say that artists know nothing about method. In the physical execution of a work, method often comes into play." Renata quieted Wally for a moment to translate.

Some people ordered more wine. A few ordered pasta and sausage with sauce. Wally sat there thinking a bit and continued: "in doing art there comes a point where method does not apply. An artist is bringing newness into the world. There is no method for doing that. Creation is a separate process, apart from method. Creativity is not about method; it often involves the abandonment of method. The methods may help bring about what the inspirations of creativity engendered. Those inspirations were not the result of any method." Gia had been listening intently. "You talked about Michelangelo when we were by the river. That makes me think about what you say. He carved the big statue of David out of marble. He had methods to do that carving. But the inspiration for that form, that was a creation. No one could teach him the methods for that." She delivered that in English, then Italian.

A lot of diffuse conversation followed. Some pasta with sausage and sauce appeared on the bar. The bartender was filling glasses. A question in Italian was heard; Renata translated. "If we don't compare artists with professionals, who will we compare them with?" Wally was noticing a lot of faces with puzzled looks on them. He ventured an answer: "I'm thinking about musicians, writers, some filmmakers and architects might qualify too." A lot of conversation followed that. More wine was poured. As more wine was consumed, the volume of the conversations seemed to increase. Gia was noticing that more heat than light seemed to be generated at that point. In more than an hour, people were exchanging contact information. Those involved in the events of the day were going their separate ways. Gia, Renata, Cristina, and Wally paid, thanked the bartender and departed.

It was morning in Florence, close to 10:00 AM. Around 9:30 a phone call had come in from one of the people they had met down by the river the day before. Several of them were going to the Uffizi on Tuesday. Would anyone want to go along? There was not a lot of discussion. Renata had things to do at the gallery that day. Gia, Wally, and Cristina thought it would be the thing to do. Today it would be sightseeing on foot with Cristina. The gallery where she and Renata worked was within walking distance. That began the tour. After that was everything else. Many galleries were closed on that day, but there was a lot in Florence to see. Brunelleschi's Dome was a highlight of the excursion. Cristina knew where all the good architecture was. There was a wonderful lunch and the excursion continued. There were a few places open where they could see art; they took advantage of these. And there were just so many wonderful things to photograph. By late afternoon Cristina again mentioned that uncle Alberto would be coming over that evening. "We should not be too tired out."

Uncle Alberto arrived sometime around 6:00. He had not seen Gia for close to 20 years. There was much to catch up on. He was now retired. He had brought two packages along. One was the painting he had done of Gia and her mother when Gia was about three. The other package was a big bottle of wine; it looked like it was close to a gallon. They looked at the painting for a while and sipped wine. Wally was interested in the painting. Cristina was mostly busy in the kitchen. While they were talking, Renata came home. Although she had met Alberto before, it had been a while. The painting was set on top of a bookcase, leaning against the wall. Alberto seemed to have a need to talk about it. People were sitting in an arrangement that might resemble a semicircle and looking at the painting.

Alberto was somewhat apologetic. "I struggled so much with the flesh colors – the faces. I never managed to get that right. It looks like you and your mother, but the skin tone is not convincing." Wally was wishing he had some good advice, but he often had similar problems with skin tones. Alberto talked a while about his work as a wine merchant before

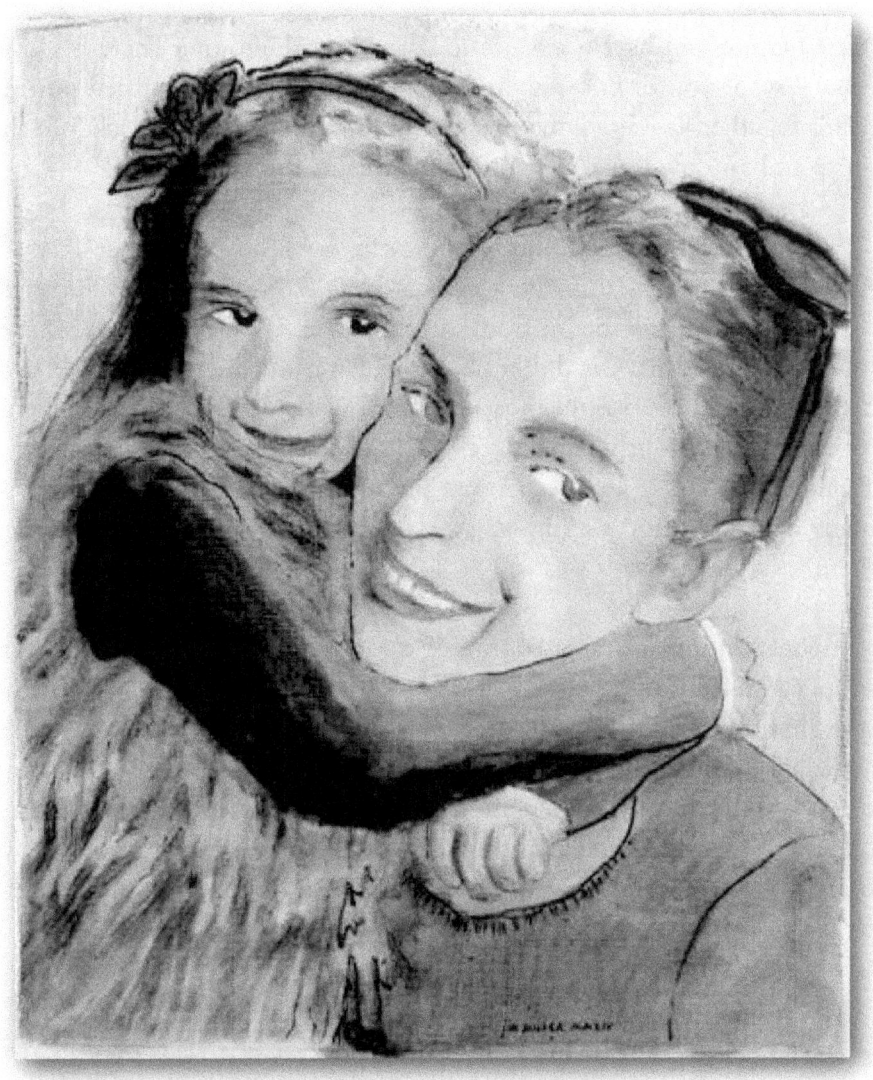

Alberto's painting of Gia and her mother.

he had retired. Then he began trying to get Gia to tell him about her life in America. She talked of her job with the architect, then mentioned her part-time job tending bar. She was again quiet. In her mind she considered telling Alberto and Renata that she had learned she could channel material from the other side while in America. Then she went out to the kitchen.

"Cristina, do you have a minute to come into the room? There is something I want you to know about too." Cristina had just finished putting salads together. It was a good breakpoint for her. They went back into the room and sat down. Alberto poured some wine for Cristina.

Gia got right to the point. "There is something else that I do in America. This is something new. I never dreamed I could do this. I learned that I can speak for someone from the other side." That brought up strange looks and questions. Gia did her best to answer the questions people had. Her sister, Cristina, was the most surprised. Wally volunteered a comment: "I've seen this happen. This is real stuff – not a parlor game." Gia talked about the book she and Secula had produced for Rupert. There were so many questions. In the midst of it all, Cristina, back in the kitchen, called them for dinner.

Conversation at dinner continued to be about Gia's channeling. Wally supplied stories, ones where Rupert gave information on things that no one physical could know. Gia talked about how her cousin, Secula, could actually see Rupert. She told how Secula had met him in a bar, where no one else could see him. When dinner had run its course, and there was talk of dessert, Gia volunteered: "I think I feel Rupert around. It is possible we hear from him tonight." Wally started to look around for something to write on. "Cristina, do you have a tablet and pen I could borrow in case Gia channels?"

They were seated in the other room now, the one that had Alberto's painting propped up against a wall. Gia was noticing that people were looking at her. "There is never any guarantee that I can do this. We should just relax and not think about Rupert so much." Wally, noticing Gia's discomfort, brought up the excursion to the Uffizi planned for the next day. "Does anyone have any suggestions about things to see at the Uffizi tomorrow? It's a big place and I guess a person could spend weeks exploring it." Renata was quick to reply on specific works not to miss. Surprisingly, Alberto had a lot to say. Renata translated for him. There was a long narration about the history of Florentine and northern Italian painting and how a person could better understand the history of the area by studying works there. During his exposition on history and art, Wally was noticing that Gia was spacing out. She was getting that look she had before she started to channel. He grabbed the tablet. When he started to see her lips move, he quietly hushed up the conversation in the room, pointing to Gia.

What started to come out of Gia was mostly in English with some Italian here and there. When there was a need to translate English into Italian, Renata intervened for Alberto, and sometimes for Cristina. *Hello to our new guests: Alberto, Cristina, and Renata. You may call me Rupert. I did not say that my name is Rupert. I said you may call me Rupert.* Alberto blurted out: "Qual e' il suo nome?" *I one-time spoke Italian as my native tongue. There is no need for anyone to translate. Rupert will do here and now as a name. I have had many names and still have quite a few. Where and when I show up in different times and places, I am known by different names. When I suggest that Rupert is not my name, I point out that Rupert is not the name of my whole self, my entity.*

Wally was busy writing down the things Rupert said. Gia, as Rupert, noticing this paused before continuing: *if I go too fast for you Wally, bid me to slow down. There may be some among you who may want to remember a few things that I say. First to Alberto, and anyone else who may want to paint flesh tones . . . portraits in general. In my travels in my worlds, I do interact with many types, artists among them. I am recalling the utterances of a 14th-century Scandinavian. He spoke of flesh tones. What I say might be better understood by someone conversant with the idea of using glazes in painting. Sienas for initial flesh tones . . . do not use the heavy hand here; remember transparency. Then violets lightly, only suggested. A transparent ocher in the layers [glazes].*

On top of it all a broken tone of chrome oxide green. Recall glazing. This final layer is very light and transparent. A person might look at all this in a finished state never realizing that violets and greens were used.

When you paint a person, do not see that person in isolation. Try to see the individual as a part of the larger world that the person connects with. I do not only refer to the physical world here. See the subject of your painting as a member of a spiritual world that does connect with that person. This may include other members of the person's entity – the larger self. Ancestors might be included, counterparts too, the totality of a person's physical and spiritual connected ones. I do not mean for you to actually paint all these others. They are only implied. Show the person as the center of the universe to which that person belongs.

There are many stumbling blocks you must be careful to avoid when doing your creative work. Many approach creative work with a too serious mind. This impedes the freedom you need to allow the larger self, of which you are a part, to participate in the creative process. There are connections that you should be aware of; it may help for me to remind you of these here. You might think about the connection between creative activity and play. You might think about the connection between creative activity and altered states of consciousness. And you might think about the connection between creative activity and spiritual development.

The power of your imagination is something you must come to respect. With sufficient regard for your imagination, you will walk past the pompous seriousness that some usually connect with creative activity. When some think of power, perhaps electrical power comes to mind, or nuclear power. What to bear in mind is that human imagination was the power that conceived those forces and brought them to birth. You must learn to respect the power of your own imagination. It is the power that can bring creative activity to fruition. The name Albert Einstein is much associated with the theoretical work that was the basis for the awesome power of nuclear energy. He made a statement that has *surprised some people. It applies here:* "I am enough of an artist to draw freely upon my imagination. Imagination is more important than knowledge. Knowledge is limited. Imagination encircles the world." *I leave you now, sitting together in this room on your good Earth. Remember what I have told you. Respect your own powers, for they too are awesome.*

Sixteen

Homeward Bound

There had been the trip to the Uffizi. On Wednesday and Thursday more of the gallery world in Florence was explored. It was Thursday evening. Gia, Wally, Cristina and Renata were having dinner at the apartment. Gia's cell phone began ringing just as Cristina was bringing dessert out from the kitchen. Gia began thinking that chocolate cake with vanilla ice cream would have to wait a few minutes. "Hello . . . what's happening Secula?" Gia walked out to the kitchen to talk to Secula. Wally was enjoying his cake and ice cream, but listened to see if he could find out what was happening with Secula. He could pick up fragments of the conversation. At least it was in English. "Yeah, Secula . . . Can you reserve seats for us on the flight?" When Wally heard that he knew something was happening. Cristina and Renata looked at him; they too had heard the word flight.

Wally's dessert had not tasted so good after he had heard the word flight. Italy had agreed with him, and the thought of leaving it was not a happy one. The three at table were silent, waiting for Gia to return from the kitchen. That did not take long. Wally was finishing his chocolate cake when Gia came back to the table. Gia noticed that all were looking at her expectantly. She also noticed that her ice cream was melting. She said a

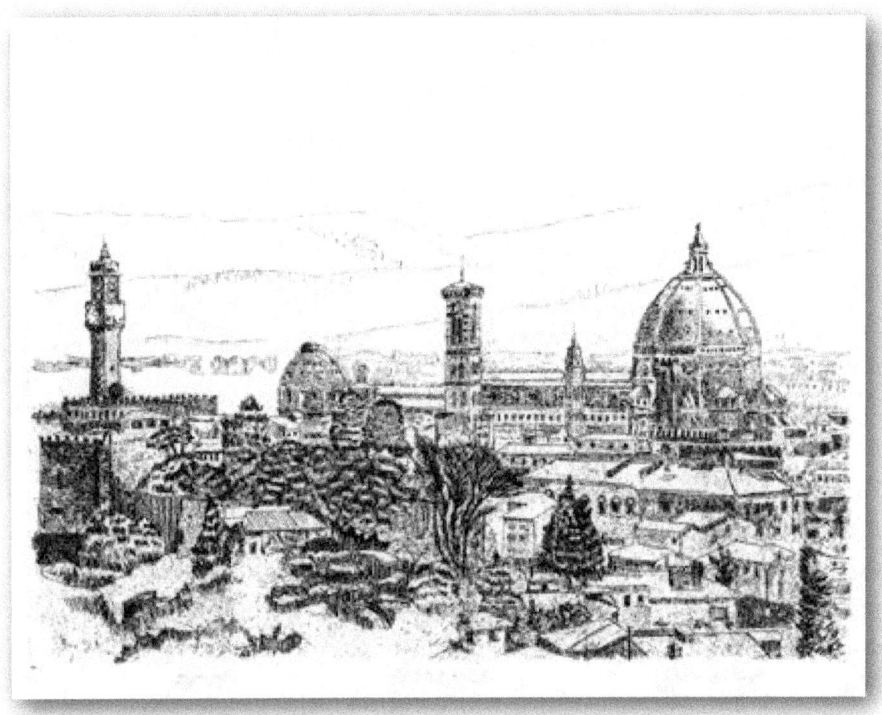

Florence, Italy, the beautiful city they were visiting.

few words in Italian, then had some dessert. Wally didn't have a clue what she said. Renata got up and brought some glasses and white wine from the kitchen. Gia was aware people were waiting for some fill-in on the phone call. She thought she had let the suspense build up sufficiently then smiled. Renata was pouring wine. "Secula thinks we should leave Saturday. Her dad, Dom, is making trouble about everything."

It was quiet for a bit. There was the clinking of china, wine glasses and silverware. Wally was first to say anything. "It is sounding like tomorrow is driving day – back to Borgo. It's hard to leave so soon, and so many nice people." He smiled and looked at Cristina and Renata as he said that. Gia followed up on that. "I feel that way too, but taking all things into consideration, it's probably best that we all go back to Pittsburgh together." Gia then launched into a spate of Italian that left Wally sitting there uncomprehending. Wally guessed she was thanking Cristina and Renata for their hospitality and kindness. Gia was doing that, but there was something more that Wally hadn't guessed.

When Gia finished talking, she got up from the table and moved over to a large stuffed chair nearby. She sat down. Putting her head back, she just stared upward. Wally was watching her and starting to guess what was happening. Cristina filled Wally in: "Gia tells us that she might channel tonight. She said you should get pen and paper in case she does. I'm going to get my recorder." People moved around, getting ready for what might happen next. When Wally came back into the room with his pen and tablet, no one was at the table. Cristina was setting up her recorder. Renata had moved to a more comfortable chair. Wally found a place close to Gia to sit down. Then people just sat, saying nothing. Night noises from outside filtered in from an open window in the front of the building. Now and then voices from an apartment below could be heard; they sounded far away. Wally, Cristina, and Renata tried not to stare at Gia, so as not to make her uncomfortable. They did cast careful, furtive glances in her direction. It was sometime before anything came out of Gia.

Wally sat there hoping Gia would not channel in Italian. When she did say something – finally – it sounded like Italian, but it was garbled and no one was quite sure if it was Italian or English. Slowly and quietly Wally started to mutter: "English, English, English, English . . . ." Gia then got quiet again. When she started to talk the second time, Wally could tell that Rupert was there. *Greetings to my friends again. Greetings and thanks to the two lovely ladies from Florence who give us a place to meet and are so good to my friends from Pittsburgh. I thought, since Gia and Wally will be traveling tomorrow, I will speak tonight. This may be my last chance to speak to you two lovely Florentine ladies. I pass along something tonight that may sound a bit strange to your ears. It is a good thought that is worth consideration. It involves a connection or relationship between your conscious selves and parts of you that seldom come to mind.*

I speak to you of the cell, the humble cell. You don't spend much time thinking of these primary units of your living self. Much less do you attribute any subjectivity to that small organism that is spoken of in biological classes in microscopic terms. I might mention that it has as its basis and center a Unit of Consciousness. That small bit of consciousness will escape the notice of any microscope; it is much too small for that. Having consciousness as its center, the cell does have an awareness that may surprise you. It is aware of its own shape or form, and of shapes nearby – adjacent. To your greater surprise, these humble cells precognate. Their consciousness or awareness takes in not only the present. The consciousness of your cells is aware of the future that has yet to be revealed to your greater awareness. Your cells also possess emphasis toward action, and curiosity – yes, even curiosity.

Now you realize why I told you that some things may seem strange. My concern is to pass along to you – all of you – matters of interest relating to art. I refer to the visual arts here. I told you that this cell has awareness of shapes; its own shape and interior parts, shapes or forms nearby, shapes that may be of interest to it. Now, there is a continuum of consciousness extending from the humble cell to the exalted consciousness your kind is so very proud of – and rightly. Your everyday consciousness has connections with this primary cellular consciousness.

This connection is often most evident in children. Children have not yet been taught that these marvelous connections do not exist. We can see the drawings of children groping to give expression to the forms that their very cells are aware of. Sometimes when people, grown people, close their eyes, these forms can present themselves. I am of course speaking of these cellular forms, forms that the very cells are aware of. You might be surprised if I were to tell you that drawings of cells existed before the existence of cellular structures was discovered by biologists. They were done by people in contact with those primary levels of awareness experienced by cells. Spend some time looking at the drawings of primitive peoples. They – like children – have not been taught what they are and are not allowed to perceive.

Children are not the only ones who may draw upon the wisdom of the humble cell. The understanding that cells have of their own forms of construction – shapes – and of forms adjacent may be appreciated, and understood by mature people doing visual art. If a grown person has not been indoctrinated to believe that no communication from the cells is possible, that person may see the forms of cells and attendant structures. These can show up in dreams. Sometimes when a person closes their eyes, these forms can at times parade before the mind's spectacle in a demonstration of the rudimentary forms of life. We can find art done by some people where these forms appear. Those of an art-critical bent may want to label it abstract, and it very well may be. On the other hand, it may very well be one artist's attempt to demonstrate what is present in the inner reaches of the psyche. It is something that can become present when one is not swayed by the pompous pronouncements of those with a scientific bent. Those types will tell you that such is not possible. To listen to them is to deprive yourselves of much of the true dimensions of your human nature.

I did mention that the humble cell does possess curiosity. That is another trait that artists of whatever kind may receive when in communication with the basic rudiments of their own nature, the simple cellular basis of their own life. This curiosity of artists of whatever kind can sometimes be traced to contact with the deeper reaches of the self. Much of what I give you tonight comes from one of the teachers of the world I inhabit. You might know him as Seth. In his teaching, another idea surfaces that might be of help here. Seth teaches that art is meant by its nature to put each artist of whatever kind into harmony with the universe. The idea here is that the artist draws on the same creative energy that gives birth to stars and children. This energy, when contacted, can produce marvels.

Since I brought up the name and teaching of one from my world, there is more from that source that I shall pass along. From that source comes the distinction between frameworks 1 and 2. Regarding framework 1, there is nothing I need to tell you; it is the physical world you have known since birth. Now, framework 2 is a more difficult subject to discuss. I do want to bring it up because the world of framework 2 is important to the artist – any kind of artist doing any kind of art. It is the nonphysical world I inhabit, a world that the inspirations of any really great art come from. But first I must tell you that there are those in your world who will try to restrict or forbid entrance to the world of framework 2. First in this category are the religious types. These will try to tell you that the nonphysical world is the realm of heaven, hell, death, and judgment. A healthy, sane person will be rightly so repulsed by this rendition of otherworldly existence as to keep a very great distance. For this reason, few will want to hear much about 'the other side', or framework 2.

The others who will try to forbid you entrance to framework 2 are the scientific ones. They will tell you that framework 2 does not exist, thus depriving you of access to the wellspring of your existence. They may try to tell you that a concern with that nonphysical world is a sign of mental problems. In truth, mental problems can come about when a person tries to cut oneself off from the nonphysical world where creativity originates. Those who have studied some philosophy may recall Plato's Ideal World. In Platonic thought it is the nonphysical realm where the original forms or models for the things of our physical world reside. In philosophy, it is an attitude referred to as idealism. I might use this idea to introduce you to framework 2. But caution is needed here. Plato's ideal world was a frozen world of perfection that admitted of no change. Such a world would be a sterile and boring place. Framework 2 is not a static, frozen-in-place world. Constant growth and development happen in this nonphysical realm. Growth is one of the primary laws here. By staying in contact with framework 2, revisions of some of your outdated thinking can happen. Contact with this nonphysical world has allowed inventors to bring newness into your physical world. It has allowed artists, musicians, writers, and people with no grand labels to continue to create updated versions of life.

At this point, I think I would continue only at the risk of boring you all. As the saying goes: 'enough is enough'. I say so long for now, and again, thanks to our hosts.

Gia was not long in coming out of trance. Looking at the recorder she said: "I hope I can hear that. Even though I have a few impressions of what Rupert said, I want to hear the words. It always surprises me when I hear myself talking for Rupert. I always learn something." Wally was smiling. Cristina seemed a bit surprised. She had a question on her face. "I wish Rupert would say more about how we can contact framework 2. It sounds so important, but so far away. I feel like I need help to go there." Gia seemed to understand what her sister was talking about. "I think we all need help to go there. The world we live in does not respect what comes from there. Some of the religious people even say that it comes from the devil. People I know, when they get older, forget their dreams. When a person thinks their dreams are useless, they don't pay attention to them anymore. Rupert says our dreams are very important to help us know and understand about framework 2. He even says that our dreams go on when we are awake. He says that the world of framework 2 goes on even if we pay no attention to it. It is when we start to pay attention to that world . . . when we start to pay attention, we learn the things we need to know."

Wally had been listening. He had a few things on his mind. "I'm glad you said that, Gia. It got me remembering stuff Rupert said. Rupert was always talking about the things we believe, and how the things we believe make our life, our world. This works for framework 2 also. If we believe that this nonphysical world is not available to us, that is what happens to us. Framework 2 becomes a forbidden area for us, or something that doesn't exist. If we change what we believe, the nonphysical world of framework 2 can become a place we can go to learn the mysteries of life and how to live in this physical world." Wally got quiet for a bit. He seemed to be thinking. Renata got up and went to the front room to close a window. Cristina went to the kitchen; she brought back a bottle of wine and filled glasses.

When everyone was sitting again, Wally had more to say. "We look upon more primitive specimens of our kind as being beneath us, or not on the same level with us. This is not a good idea. I'm thinking of the Australian aborigines. They may not be as advanced technologically as we are, but in other ways they surpass us." Cristina found this interesting. "Are you thinking of the dreamtime, Wally?" That's got Wally's attention. "Yeah, that and other stuff. Much of their lives has been changed, and not for the better, by the colonists England has planted in their midst. Many of their old customs have been eroded by attempts to Christianize and modernize them. The ones who are still in touch with their old ways remember, and sometimes practice dreamtime. Dreamtime is something that happens every year. The whole group will go into a state that we, our Western types, can only visit in our sleep. But they live in that dream state for a good number of days. They manage to come close to that area of the psyche that our mechanized Western world alienates us from. They learn things there that are very helpful for their lives. This dream mode carries over into their lives outside of that yearly dreamtime. The conduct of their lives moves on paths and in directions that they have learned from dreamtime. This is sometimes literally true; there are actual roads that they follow that they have learned in dreamtime."

"As an artist I think about this a lot. Real art seems to come from that deeper part of ourselves that the dreams come from. I think of ways to access this undercurrent of our very selves. Our Native Americans, the Indians, have been known to use magic mushrooms for some of this. And they are not the only ones . . . ." Wally could tell the Gia was fidgeting; he thought she wanted to say something and kept quiet. Gia was looking at Wally. She could see he was giving her space to talk if she wanted to. It took Gia a bit to formulate what she was thinking, to put it into words. She began in a somewhat halting manner. "This, this all makes me think about Rupert . . . about things he says . . . about, about that teacher in the world that he, Rupert, is in. The name is Seth, and this Seth person or personality has also spoken in our physical world through a medium, the Roberts lady. That stuff has been published; I've read some of it. The dream world is very important to Seth."

233

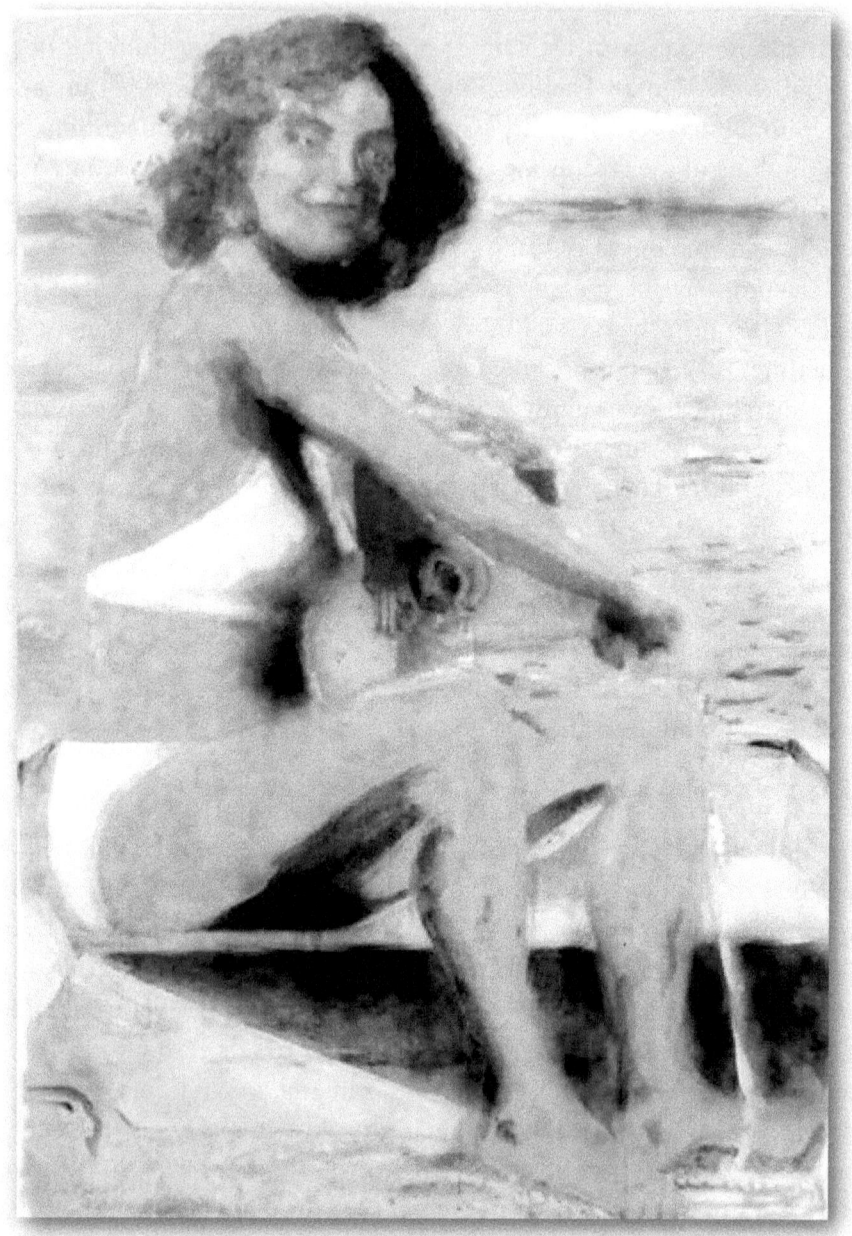

Jane Roberts at about 20, the lady who channeled Seth.

"Seth talks about asking for dreams. The idea is to ask for a dream before going to sleep at night. It is almost like praying. The difference is that we are not asking any god or saint. We're just making request from our greater self. That's the self that life in the so-called rational world makes us keep a great distance from. We sometimes get in touch with that part of ourselves in our dreams."

"Before we go to sleep, we can ask the dream world to help us with our problems and challenges. We can ask for a dream that will give us greater clarity and direction in dealing with challenges life offers us. There is one thing here to pay attention to. Dreams do not speak to us in the everyday language we are used to."

"Dream language is symbolic. We have to learn this symbol system of our dreams. Dream books try to tell us the meaning of the symbols and events in dreams, but don't listen to them. The only person who really knows the meaning of your dream symbols is you. Write your dreams down in the morning. Study them. Patterns will appear after a while. Don't quit or give up. Gradually you will learn the language that your dreams speak to you in. You will be glad that you took the time to pay attention. Dreams are a bit like myths. Myths usually speak to us in symbolic language. Dreams are in a way our own private myths."

Gia took a pause, sipping wine. Wally was having thoughts: "I've been thinking about things Seth said about dream artists." Gia smiled: "I was thinking about that too." Wally continued. "There are people in our world who are dream artists. They are few in number, but this was not always the case. There were cultures in the past where what came from the dream world was greatly respected. Some of this even shows up in the Bible. Today dreaming is mostly dismissed as a kind of psychic overflow, not to be bothered with. That's why you run into a lot of people who tell you they don't dream anymore. Actually they do still dream, but they have developed the habit of not paying attention to their dreams, and they are not noticed any more. But we still have some few people in our world who have made their dreams into a kind of art form. It is an art form that is not at all appreciated by most of our contemporaries."

"These dream artists usually go unnoticed in our world, as mystics often do. They keep track of their dreams by writing them down in the morning. They try to figure out what their dreams are telling them – understanding their own private symbolism. They try to correlate their dreams with the things that happen in their waking world the following day. They talk to other people about their dreams and are often interesting people. In addition to recording and studying your dreams, there are other things you can do to become better at this art form. Seth talks about bringing your normal waking consciousness into the dream state. You can set this as a goal before you go to bed at night. And don't get discouraged if it does not happen the first time you try. Keep trying. Another thought here, you can take dream snapshots that you may bring back to your waking life in the morning. You can try to set this as a project before going to sleep. During the dream you can pick a certain tableau or scene from a dream; this can be brought back in the morning to you."

When Wally stopped talking, Gia had something on her mind. "All this talk about sleeping and dreaming reminds me that tomorrow is travel day for me and Wally. We have to drive back up to Borgo. It's getting late and we should get some sleep." Cristina made a comment about some new artwork that would be coming into the gallery the next day. Everyone took things out to the kitchen and said good night there.

When Gia got awake the next morning, she noticed Wally was twitching the way people do when they are in the middle of a dream. She was remembering that she could often remember a dream better if something or someone got her awake in the middle of that dream. She took hold of Wally's arm and gently shook him until he was awake. Wally was staring at her, both of them naked in bed. He said nothing; he was still in that no man's land between sleep and awake. Gia was realizing she should say something: "you were dreaming, Wally. What are you dreaming about?" Wally was still very much in stuttering and stammering mode. "Uh, well, yeah, uum, yeah right . . . it was a dream." She was smiling at him. Wally couldn't resist reaching out and putting his hand on her hip. He liked feeling her. She always felt good. Gia tried again: "what were you dreaming about?"

Wally stretched and looked up at the ceiling. He was trying to get a coherent sentence together. Finally he became verbal: "it was my dad; I was talking to my dad. I met him in this dream, telling him I knew he was dead. He died some years ago now. I was asking him about where he was. I wanted to know something about how things were where he was." Gia became interested: "what were you asking him about?" Wally started to fumble again: "I, I don't have any good English word for what I was asking him about. In the dream it all made good sense, but now, when I am awake, I can't find the word. The, the word I said in the dream meant something like a very important teacher, or a god, that's what I was asking him about. I asked him if, in the place he is in now, if there was one or many of these that I don't have a word for. Was there one or many of these [teachers? gods?]? He answered me very quickly: "thousands, there are thousands." Wally seemed content now that he had gotten that out. Gia thanked him.

It wasn't long before everyone was in the kitchen again. It was still rather early. Gia and Wally only wanted coffee and toast. Cristina and Renata had a bigger breakfast. It was going to be a big day at the gallery. There was not a lot of conversation. Gia and Wally thanked their hosts, letting them know how much they appreciated the visit. Everyone walked down to the street together were the little mint green Fiat sat. Cristina and Renata helped with baggage. There were goodbyes at the sidewalk, then Gia and Wally were on their way.

Seventeen

The Return

Another road trip had begun. Gia and Wally were heading north. Once on the open road, Gia let Wally drive and got on her cell phone. She was talking to her mother, telling her that she and Wally would be coming in that afternoon or evening, depending upon how the trip went. Gia asked her mother to call Giovanna, Wally's landlady. She asked her mother to pass along the information. The trip was uneventful. They stopped for lunch, after which Gia drove. By the time they came to the turnarounds by Trento, Gia was still driving. She easily negotiated getting on the road to Borgo. Wally wanted to stop at the lake they had passed on their way down to Florence. He and Gia seemed both to enjoy being by a body of water. They took some photos. Wally did a bit of sketching. While that was going on they talked about what it would be like traveling with Secula's father, Dom. They realized he had not been a happy camper of late. Both wondered if their traveling together was the cause of Dom's upset.

Somewhere around three or four in the afternoon they pulled into Borgo. It was a summer afternoon. Bees were visiting the flowers in the backyard of the house Gia had grown up in. Her mother had been waiting for her. Coming into the kitchen by the back door, Gia and Wally were greeted with billowing greetings in Italian, none of which Wally understood. Maria Visconti Francesco was happy to see her daughter. A big bottle of red wine was planted solidly in the middle of the kitchen table. Glasses followed. Wally sat patiently sipping wine as he listened to Gia and her mother talk.

Wally tried to pick up a word or two here and there. He could understand that they were talking about Dominic Venturi Sr. However, the full impact of the conversation escaped him. At some point Gia noticed that Wally was being left out of the conversation. She shifted to English and began filling Wally in. Wally's mother got up and got things out of the refrigerator. While she was puttering around the stove, Wally listened to Gia: "Dom, Secula's dad, isn't upset so much about us. Maybe he was a little bit at first, when we left for Florence. The two Doms and Secula were going around visiting their relatives in Borgo. Young Dom met a distant relative; they got along very well, too well. This boy and young Dom wanted to spend time together. Young Dom didn't come home one night. Big Dom has been getting very upset. That's when Secula called us."

There was a noise on the back porch. Gia's mother said, "Vittorio". Vittorio sauntered into the kitchen, dragging his feet. There was a polite, Hi, to his sister, Gia, and Wally. He kept walking and went upstairs. Gia noted that he seemed preoccupied. She asked her mother how things were with Vittorio. Maria mumbled something about girls, girls. That part of the conversation Wally understood. He smiled. It didn't take Maria long to get something on the table. Gia helped wherever she could, mostly setting the table. Maria called for Vittorio to come down, but he stayed upstairs.

Maria sat down and said grace. It was in Italian and Wally couldn't pick out all the words. He said amen with Gia and her mother. Conversation went to the people down the street, the two Doms and Secula. Maria commented that Giovanna had told her that Dom Senior was grumpy most of the time. Gia and Wally looked at one another. "Wally, do you think we

Jim Miller

should go tomorrow?" Wally finished chewing some salad. "Didn't Secula make reservations already?" Gia just nodded her head and asked her mother where her younger sister was. Wally listened to Gia and her mother talk in Italian. There was a kind of strudel with ice cream for dessert. Wally was thinking about going down the street. Unpacking and packing was on his mind; they were leaving tomorrow. He wanted to get input from Secula on things. He was, however, in no rush to run into Dom Senior. He talked with Gia a bit on the back porch. Gia watched the little mint green Fiat back out of the driveway.

Wally walked into the house where he was staying. He could hear an argument going on upstairs. He didn't want to go up there. He went out to the kitchen. Giovanna was in the kitchen, just sitting at the table. Her English was not good and Wally's Italian was not good. Despite their difficulties, Giovanna managed to explain to Wally that things in her house were not good. Since he and Gia had gone to Florence, Dominic Senior had become one serious pain in the ass. Of course, Giovanna used a more polite expression. Nevertheless, Wally got the complete meaning of what she said. This despite the limited linguistic abilities of them both. During their struggle to communicate with one another, Secula appeared in the kitchen. Wally smiled at her, aware that he had been having a very pleasant time with her cousin. Secula seemed not to mind. She was more concerned with matters upstairs. The two Dominics, her father and brother, were engaged in some very unpleasant conversation about Dominic Junior's decision to spend his last night in Italy elsewhere in town.

As Secula was trying to explain the particulars of the situation, Dominic Junior appeared in the kitchen. He quickly said hello to Wally. He then exited by the back door. The screen door banged as he stomped across the porch. Secula, Wally, and Giovanna just looked at one another. Giovanna made a beeline for the refrigerator. A bottle of good red Italian wine and glasses appeared on the table. She went to some trouble to explain that there would be no cooked meal. Secula and Wally told her that they did

240

not mind that at all. It was a warm day. After Giovanna's second glass of wine, things appeared on the table from the refrigerator that resembled a picnic lunch. Secula disappeared upstairs after explaining she was going to ask her dad to come down and eat. Her feet were quickly heard coming back down the stairs. As she reentered the kitchen, she mentioned that her dad was not hungry. Wally mumbled something about Americans having lost the art of eating.

Saturday arrived early and bright. Gia was awake early that morning without an alarm clock. She knew it was another traveling day and wanted to be ready to go. She wandered downstairs. While she was making coffee her mother appeared in the kitchen. Marie insisted on making breakfast for the two of them. Gia went back upstairs to collect the few remaining items. In not many more minutes, she reappeared in the kitchen with luggage she took out to the back porch. She was hoping Wally would bring the little Fiat up the driveway so she could put things on board there.

Gia had just poured her second cup of coffee when her cell phone rang. It was Secula. Dominic Junior had called, and he was not going back on the plane with them. He had decided to stay in Italy with his newfound friend and distant relative. Dominic Senior was in a state bordering on rage. He was talking about going over to the relatives' place and making his son come back with them. Secula told Gia that it would be best if they left for the airport as soon as possible. The quick exit would not leave time for Dom to fume about his son's decision to stay in Italy. Before Gia realized what was happening, Wally was talking to her on Secula's phone: "we have to go quick. I think it's the only way to keep Dom from doing something really stupid. Down here we're ready to go. How soon can you go?"

Gia's mother was putting breakfast on the table when Gia told Wally to give her 15 minutes then to bring the little Fiat down to collect her and her baggage. Gia explained things to her mother as they ate. Her brother and younger sister somehow appeared in the kitchen. As they had coffee they were filled in on relevant matters and seemed unhappy that their sister was leaving so soon. In not more than 10 minutes they were all on the back porch. Vittorio sat on the steps sipping coffee. Gia's mother and sister were on the swing trying to decide what time to go grocery shopping. Gia was standing in the driveway beside her luggage.

The little mint green Fiat appeared as Gia had her left foot on top of her large suitcase and was retying a shoestring. She was not too sure how to respond to a car with a very angry man aboard. She walked up to the porch to say goodbye to her family. Wally had been driving and got out to load Gia's baggage. As Wally was closing the trunk, Gia, her mother, sister, and brother came down from the porch. Wally handed the car keys to Gia, who said nothing and just nodded. She held hands with her mother as they walked to the driver's side and Gia got in. Vittorio was pounding on the roof and yelling stuff in Italian. Gia was smiling and yelled back to him through the open window. The little Fiat obediently backed out onto the street.

Gia was feeling the pain of separation as she drove through the town she had grown up in. She had not been away from home so long that all of her ties were broken here. Secula and Dom were in the backseat saying nothing. Wally wished someone back there would say something. There were times when the silence was almost audible. Wally started to blurt out something about Dominic Junior. Almost at the same time, he realized this would likely make matters worse. He cut himself off in midsentence. Secula, usually quick to pick up things, asked Wally if he had said something. Wally mumbled something about thinking out loud. Gia could tell he had made a false start on something, but thought it best to let the matter slide.

Dom was in the backseat somewhat puzzled about what was happening. He had just begun to look at the scenery outside his window to get his mind off of his son. He decided to ask Gia a question: "did we come into

Borgo this way? I don't recall all this." This somewhat lessened the tension in the car. Gia was glad to fill Dom in. "No, I just want to see a little more of the town before we go back to Pittsburgh. It is a different way, not the one we came in." Shortly they pulled onto the large artery heading south. Wally was asking Gia questions about nearby buildings that looked like farms. Then they started talking about when to switch drivers. This seemed to appeal to Dom. "I don't think I'll mess up too bad on an open highway like this."

They were rolling along easier now. Things in the car felt better. When they began getting hungry for lunch, Dom was driving. Gia had gotten in the backseat with Secula, who was commenting on the relatives they had met during their stay. She carefully avoided talking about the house were Dom Junior had met his friend and relative. Wally was listening to it all, but he was distracted looking for a place to eat. He was hungry. Dom was hungry too. Dom's good eyes were the first to spy a place to eat. He didn't say anything to anyone. He just pulled over. Before anyone got out of the car, he declared: "I'm buying for everyone. Don't argue. It's something I want to do." Secula knew what was going on. Her dad was feeling bad about the grump he had been earlier. He was trying to make it up. Lunch was adequate if not exotic. Surprisingly, there was a good number of Chinese items on the menu, but only the normal Italian fare. All took advantage of the Chinese dishes. While they waited for lunch, the three Americans took in the rolling Italian countryside outside the window by their table. Gia called her mother. Then they sipped tea for a bit. Secula's phone punctured the quiet of sipping tea. It became obvious that it was her brother, Dominic Junior, calling. Dominic Senior got up and went somewhere.

"Dominic says hi to you two." Gia and Wally shouted hellos to Dominic. Soon Dominic Senior was spotted approaching. Secula's phone was away before Dom sat down. "Your son says hello. He hopes you both can get past the way things ended here." Dominic had a glass of wine with him. Saying nothing, he sipped wine quietly. Arrangements for were made for Wally to drive after lunch. Gia said she would take over before they got too close to the airport. Hot food arrived.

Maybe it was the phase of the moon, or the conjunction of Jupiter and Saturn. Maybe it was the way the wind was blowing that day, or the kind of star dust falling to earth. Whatever the heavenly influences, things at Marco Polo airport all came off without a hitch. The four were airborne with what seemed no trouble at all. Gia was hoping she could fall asleep on this trip as she had on the flight to Italy. She told herself not to try to go to sleep; she thought she would have a better chance of sleeping, and thus dreaming. At some unknown elevation and over what may have been northern France the noise of the jet and the company of the other earthlings went away.

At first Gia was aware only of grayness. From somewhere came the sound of what might have been wind blowing. After a long while of this seeming emptiness, the gray was punctured now and then with a shaft of light. This light was very clear and white; it was in no way annoying or intrusive. The light seemed friendly. There were times when there was no light, only grayness. Gia looked forward to seeing the light again. In her dream she felt herself to be moving forward. After a boring stretch of the grayness, she thought she could see light ahead in the distance. She was traveling in that direction, though she was in no airplane in her dream.

In Gia's mind in the dream, memories were coming to her. They were memories of things she had read when she was awake. It was about near-death experiences people had gone through. There was this thing about going toward a light. Gia started to wonder in her dream if she had died. She thought that, even if she had died, things weren't all that bad. She kept approaching the light. The sound of wind blowing had stopped. It was total silence now. There was a steady movement toward the light, or lights, in the distance. She was getting closer. There were what looked like shadowy human forms in that light she could see now. She recalled the dream on the trip to Italy, when she had met her father and relatives. She was hoping it would be like that this time too. The earlier dream had been a really good experience.

Time and sequence of events never seemed an issue in Gia's dreams. Now she was among the people seen in the light up ahead. They were all around her, but she did not know any of them. The light was present and no longer in the distance. It provided an environment like a room or building where Gia and those unknown people were. Gia kept looking for someone she knew. Suddenly, to her right was a person talking to her: "he has been expecting you. I think he is here. Look over that way."

Gia looked over toward her left. Toward the outer edge of this gathering of people was a very short creature. He was wearing an overcoat. She was expecting it to be Rupert. Walking in that direction, she came close enough to smile at him. It was Rupert. He seemed to know the others around him. He was in front of her now. She had an impulse to kneel down to talk to him since he was so much shorter. Feeling this would be inappropriate, she remained standing. Maybe Rupert also noticed this difference of stature. He spoke to her now from what seemed an equal height. Maybe he was floating, without his feet touching the floor.

Rupert began speaking about the group assembled all about. In this dream he explained to Gia that many of them – depending upon probabilities – would somehow be involved in her life. He encouraged her to make initial contacts with ones he was about to introduce to her. He further explained that we often make contact in dreams with those people who will be important in our lives. We also might make these dream contacts with individuals who play lesser parts in our lives. During these dreams we can make arrangements as to what kind of interactions we will have with them when physical. We can make agreements as to whether we might be casual acquaintances, close friends, lovers, relatives, etc. Gia interrupted to ask Rupert whether we make arrangements with others in dreams to be enemies. Rupert seemed annoyed by this.

He explained that we become enemies with a person when things go wrong. It is like an automobile accident; one does not arrange to have an auto accident with someone. He explained further that we might meet old enemies in dreams, enemies we made in physical life. In these dreams the two people can agree to meet again in physical life to try to have a better outcome, to try to resolve their difficulties.

By this time Gia was no longer noticing whether Rupert was touching the floor in this dreamland. He told her to follow him. He introduced her to a good number of individuals, one at a time. There were two of them she felt she had met before. Rupert had cautioned her not to follow up on these feelings as a subject of conversation. The conversations were all pleasant. They all seemed to involve an exchange of information. In one of them a man asked her if she would marry him. Gia only smiled. Now Rupert was leading her to yet another group of people he wanted her to meet. Suddenly she became aware of being shaken sideways – then up-and-down. She felt a hand clutching her arm. Everything was changing; a voice was saying something about turbulence. Wally was telling her something about her seatbelt. She was awake.

Not totally awake yet, Gia looked out the window. Things were mostly gray out there. She noticed Wally had two books on his seat. She noticed that one was a book Rupert had mentioned. It was a Seth book: "The Nature of Personal Reality". Gia asked Wally if she could look at it. She opened it to the table of contents. She wanted to find something about dreams. Secula said something about being over the Atlantic Ocean. Wally said he was guessing it would be another half hour before they were over land. Gia started wondering how things would be between Wally and Secula once they were back in Pittsburgh. She wasn't aware how things had developed between Secula and the guy who lived in the apartment on the first floor. She found some stuff about dreams in the book. Seth was talking about dreams as a connector between the physical world where we live and the nonphysical dimension of existence where Seth and those like him had their being. Seth spoke of those two dimensions of being as framework one and framework two, one physical and one nonphysical.

There was a bit more turbulence, fortunately not as strong as previously. It interrupted Gia's reading. She had been reading about things Seth had to say about the whole dimension of our existence. He was talking about our entity. That is a word Seth liked to use instead of the word, soul. He didn't like to use that word, soul, because of the ways religious people have used it in an attempt to threaten people, and control people. They often threaten people with losing their soul. Seth says that the soul cannot be lost; it is what we are. He likes to use the word, entity, because it does not have the threatening overtones that priests and preachers have attached to the word soul. Seth in the book spoke of the word entity as comprehending the complete dimensions of our existence. This includes the physical self we are at present. That is what most of us think of as comprising our entire self. The entity also includes the selves we have been incorporated in as individuals in past lives. Time being simultaneous, it includes the selves we shall be in future physical lives. We must not leave out here the nonphysical existences we participate in. These existences spring from probable selves. And the possibility of probable physical selves also exists.

Seth commented that the culture we have been born into exalts only physical existence. Those dimensions of our entity which are not physical are seen by most of our present culture as non-existent. Sadly, those who might contact the nonphysical dimensions are looked on with suspicion or seen as mentally ill. The only ones who are allowed at all to contact the nonphysical dimensions are the religious types. Seth sees this is unfortunate; they often use this only as a way of gaining status. In addition, they often present bogus versions of what nonphysical existence is all about.

We have grown up in a science-dominated culture that would forbid entrance to the nonphysical dimensions of our entity, our very selves. Seth tells us that our dreams are still there to help us make contact with those total and complete versions of ourselves. With that contact can come abilities we never had hope of having access to. An artist might feel a need to have the abilities of an engineer at times. Perhaps some part of that artist's entity has the skills of an engineer. Our dreams can help us contact those distant parts of our entity. Those dreams can help us believe in powers that are ours by right, powers that our own self-definition has kept us apart from. Much of that self-definition comes from the culture we live in. Much of that self-definition is not helpful. Seth is working on expanding that definition of who and what we are, an expanded anthropology.

Our dreams are still there to allow us to prowl at will among what might seem lost parts of our very selves. Seth affirmed emphatically the need to know our complete selves. If we are allowed to be in contact with the totality of what we are, we will be able to be the complete selves we dream of. Our dreams can help us become that complete person we want to be. Our dreams can also serve more useful functions. For an artist, it can be seeing in a dream the advice needed to complete an in-progress work. It can also be in a dream that an artist is given a good idea for a new work that will bear fruit in a finished work of merit. For an artist in the midst of a quandary about a work that he/she he is struggling with, ask the dream world for help before going to sleep. This also helps with problems/questions that have nothing to do with art. But a warning comes from Seth: we must pay attention to our dreams. As people get older, many claim they no longer have dreams. They still have dreams, but are no longer aware of them. This comes from a lifetime of ignoring their dreams, paying no attention. We must not neglect to acknowledge what the dream world tells us. Recall your dreams in some way: write them down, speak them into a recorder, talk to someone about them. Whatever means you use, do not neglect them. It can come about that you are no longer aware of them if you neglect them.

Eighteen

Fast Forward

I t had been some years since the little group coming back from Italy had landed at Pittsburgh Airport. Things in Pittsburgh had changed. Things in the country had changed. An administration of greedy dimwits held sway in Washington. It made Gia want to go back to Italy at times. When she heard the evening news, she often thought of something her grandmother had often said: "stupid people always destroy what smart people create."

But things in Gia's little world were not so bad. George no longer lived in the building. His business was increasing; he took on helpers and needed more shop space. He was still in the Strip District, but in another building closer to downtown. He came around at times to visit. He was often seen at Secula's place. Gia often saw him when he stopped in. Wally had moved into the first floor with its shop and garage. His antique Stewart truck was still there. Gia had moved into Wally's apartment on the second floor and had access to his shop and Secula's backyard. The shop was good for building supports for paintings. She still worked for the architect; the shop was helpful when she built models for him.

Donnie Diangelo had bought George Willis' share in the building. He was living in the third floor apartment that Gia had lived in. He had become a junior partner in an architectural firm in town. He too used the shop on the first floor at times. In addition to his painting and illustration, Wally had begun to do videos. He had a camera and was teaching himself to do video editing. He was using the old antique Stewart truck in a video he was working on; he had it running. He enlisted Gia, Secula, Donnie, and anyone else he could convince of their acting ability in his ongoing video creations. Since the truck wasn't licensed yet, they stuck to the back alleys when shooting was done. The plot of the video had something to do with Pittsburgh in the 30s and the bootleg business. Dominic Senior had lived briefly at Secula's place when they had returned from Italy. His wife had threatened him not to return home, and he didn't. As time went on, Dom's wife relented, and he was now at home with her. Dominic Junior was still in Italy. Secula and Dom heard from him now and again. His comments were often about life for him being better in Italy.

The really big news was the acquisition of new real estate. For some years Wally had a dream of developing a community of artists, a group of people that would allow the work of cultural facilitation to happen. The idea was that a group of creative people would be able to keep one another alive creatively. Rupert had commented that a person does their best work when surrounded by good people. He meant decent individuals well-versed in their arts. Wally had been careful in choosing people. A nonprofit corporation had been set up as the owner of the new buildings. Donnie's dad had been the major factor in finance for the new project. He was still involved as attorney and on the board of directors. Secula's uncle Louie had, once again, come to the rescue in dealing with City Hall for matters of code compliance.

The new real estate consisted of two large buildings and a garage. One four-story building sat beside the building that Gia, Wally, and Donnie lived in. Besides that was the garage. The garage was a one-story affair that could be used for shop space in good weather or for studio space for large projects. Another building of four stories sat back-to-back with the other buildings and fronted on Penn Avenue. It had a large space on the first floor just off of the street; that area was in the process of being converted to gallery space that could also be used as performance space. There was living space for maybe about 20 people or more in the new buildings. There was no problem finding people who wanted to live there. Wally sifted carefully through the applicants to find ones who would be able to contribute to a creative venture and be able to pay the minimal rent. Not all of the space had been let out yet. There was still more room, but improvements had yet to be made.

In the two new buildings there were five painters. There were three artists working in video. Sculpture and allied arts numbered four people. There was someone doing fabric arts, another worked in neon, and there was a photographer. Five of the people living there managed to support themselves with their art. The others had jobs that helped keep life going. When there was money available, Wally would hire those willing to do work on the buildings that remained to be done. There were times when he would accept work on the buildings in exchange for rent payments.

It was a Sunday afternoon. Gia, Secula, and Wally were sitting around the table in Secula's kitchen. Although there had been some days of tension and strife for these three when they came back from Italy, a lot of water had gone under the bridge since then. Other matters were afoot today. The three of them comprised one third of the board of directors of the artists' space project. There were meetings of the artist-residents of the project on a bimonthly basis. Most of the people in that project had, one way or another, heard about Gia's activities channeling Rupert. At one of the bimonthly meetings, the question came up whether Gia could come to a meeting and talk about channeling Rupert. In particular, the question focused on whether Gia could talk about things Rupert had to say about art and creativity.

This Sunday afternoon get-together was a result of that question. Wally had been present for nearly all of the channeling sessions. Secula had, in the past, been able to see Rupert. She recorded many of his utterances during those sessions. After Gia had moved to Pittsburgh, it came about that she began to have the ability to go into a trance and channel utterances from Rupert. Either Secula or Wally would record or write down whatever Rupert had to say. Gia thought it best to get the three of them together in an attempt to pull together what Rupert had passed along that the artist-residents might be interested in.

For the last half-hour they had been listening to tapes that had been recorded at the Rupert sessions. Secula got up to get three glasses out of the cupboard. After placing them on the table, she went to the basement and brought up a bottle of wine. She opened it and set it on the table, letting everyone pour their own. She then got some cheese out of the refrigerator. She put it on a cheese board with a knife and sat down after putting that on the table. The tape had come to an end. Things were very quiet in the kitchen. Secula was looking at Wally and could tell he had something on his mind. She could tell he was trying to get something out. "What are you thinking, Wally?"

Wally momentarily went into stuttering and stammering mode. It wasn't too long before something coherent emerged. "There is an idea that's been rattling around in my head for some time. I'm not sure if Rupert ever talked about this or not. But I think it's a good idea. It's the idea that art flourishes in ambiguity. When things get too specific, that's what drives the music away." That caught Gia's attention. "Wally, do you mean this about visual stuff, music, how do you mean this?" "I'm not being that specific myself here. When I talk about driving the music away, that could apply to visual art, literature, or any kind of creative expression. My dad was an engineer. The stuff that he did was a good example of places where ambiguity is not helpful. In engineering and the sciences, the attempt is to eliminate ambiguity. However, I've found that in dealing with art, being too specific

is often not helpful. Art that has some ambiguity to it allows more partici-
pation by those who experience it."

Gia had been listening intently: "I'm thinking about things Rupert
said about blueprints for reality. It brings up ideas of that dichotomy between art and science. The whole root idea of science, the word science,
comes from the Latin word that means to know, *scire*. Maybe people
forget that artists, creative people, are in the business of trying to know
also. They too are trying to find out what this thing called reality is all
about. They too are searching for where the roots of meaning are found.
The artists and the scientists have very different ways of going about their
quest to know. The scientists limit themselves in their knowing to the
physical world. Number, measure, weight . . . cut chop and slice smaller
and smaller, but the blueprint for reality will not be found in the physical
world. Rupert's idea is that these blueprints will only ever be found when
we explore the deep places of human consciousness. This is something
that the artist has to remember. The scientist has set himself apart from
what he studies in order to know it; this is what his method requires. This
is not the kind of knowing that the artist should get caught up in. The
artist becomes one with the reality that is studied. This going beyond the
surface cannot be done with scientific instruments. Human consciousness is the tool we need here."

This really caught Secula's attention: "when I hear someone talking
about reality, reality . . . . I can't help thinking it must be a philosopher
speaking. Then I say to myself: 'why should we let philosophers have reality
all to themselves?' After all, I'm a writer. I'm trying to understand what is
real also. I don't express myself as a philosopher does. Life – reality is the
basic material we all deal with. A painter in his or her own way is trying
to come to some understanding of what it is all about. A person who does
videos is often doing the same thing. We are all trying to come to some
understanding of this thing we call life. Call the understanding art, philosophy, science, or what you want to call it. I didn't say much about the

sciences did I? That must be because they so much restrict themselves to that very thin skin of reality we call physical reality."

Wally grabbed the bottle of wine and poured for anyone who wanted a refill. Everyone did. Listening to Secula got him thinking again. "Philosophy . . . philosophers and reality . . . It reminds me so much of the French painter, Jean Dubuffet. He talked so much about philosophy never being anything but clumsy poetry. But what to a painter might be clumsy poetry might to a writer be a great and penetrating insight into the nature of things. Secula, you are writer. I'm passing the ball into your court. Do you have any comment here?"

This caught Secula completely by surprise. It was one of those rare moments when she had not a ready rejoinder or turn of phrase. "I wasn't looking Wally; that was not fair. Only maybe I have something to say. This creative community you are working on, this brings up a new idea that maybe you have not thought about. So, you have all these creative types grouping here now: painters, sculptors, video artists, and representatives of just about every branch of creative activity available. What's wrong with making room for philosophers in your creative endeavor? Just because they express themselves in words like I do, is that a reason to exclude them? And, maybe you shouldn't forget that there are a few philosophers who get their ideas out by doing video. Maybe, Wally, it is your concepts that need examination."

Wally could tell that Secula was not entirely happy with him. Human feelings are simply what they are. Wally was thinking that Secula had no real reason to be unhappy that he was no longer with her the way he was with Gia now. After all, she had sent him off to Italy alone with her cousin, Gia. Silently pondering all this, he came to the conclusion that feelings have nothing to do with reason. Wally noticed that Gia was looking at him. She seemed to be expecting him to say something, but he said nothing.

Realizing that Wally was not about to make any response, Gia decided to bring up something she recalled from Rupert.

"About this community of creative types, I remember Rupert saying something that might be worth talking about. He says it is important to think about the kind of people you surround yourself with. He talks about being around good people . . . ." Wally finally said something: "yeah, I recall some of that. But he wasn't meaning it as morally good people. It wasn't about any kind of moral qualities people had. It was about those who are good at what they do, about the kinds of creative activity people get involved in. Painters might want to think about trying to be around the better painters in their environment. A writer might try to keep company with the better writers, and so on." Wally noticed Secula was not in entire agreement with what was said. He got silent for a bit, giving her space in case she wanted to talk. She did.

"I'm not sure Rupert meant that it is so important for a painter to be around good painters, a writer to be around good writers and all that. My recall on what he said was that one should try to be around the better creative types in general. It isn't necessary to be around those in your specific discipline. That's what the idea of a creative community is all about. I think it is about allowing input from all types and kinds of individuals to have an impact on you. I see people getting stuck in a creative rut just from always hanging out with their own kind. There are writers I try to avoid because they are too noisy and self-involved. I'm glad to be able to be around people using their creative energy to do other stuff. And yeah, you can find noisy and self-involved people in other pursuits than writing, but there is a lot of other good energy to be found in many places."

Gia was smiling at this. Looking at Secula she said: "sometimes I try to get ideas out by writing. I usually end up by convincing myself I'm not a writer. Could you say something about writing ? Are there any thoughts or words of advice?" Secula got up and filled wine glasses. She sat back down and stared out the window on the back door. Clouds she could see were gently moving from west to east. Heaving a sigh, she got out just two words: "creative distance. Humm, how can I say this without giving the wrong impression? I'm trying to say something about not always being completely involved in the game of life."

"It is about standing back at times. It's almost like creating an alternate self, a self who is only an observer of the life going on about one. This is where I don't want to be misunderstood. Psychotics develop alternate selves also, but that's not what I'm talking about. They are not in control of this shift to another personality. The other self I refer to is one you may or may not inhabit; it is your choice. It is certainly possible to write without doing this. And, you will find writers and other creative types who have become a victim of what you might call an occupational hazard. These are cases in which they are no longer in control of which self they inhabit. I mean they begin to occupy a personality that is not sufficiently connected with the world they actually live in. When all is said and done, to be a writer a person has to write. This sounds simpleminded, but it is something like going to the gym to do exercise. There is just no other way; you just have to do it, write. A certain creative distance in the process of life can help you have something to write about when the pen hits the paper or your fingers hit the keyboard. It's also probably a good idea to talk to other writers and ask them what you asked me."

Wally was quick to pick up what Secula said about "just have to do it". "You know, Secula, what you say about writing -you just have to do it- really applies to the stuff I do too. No matter how much I try to figure out a painting in my head, I have to do it in real stuff, real paint on a surface, in order to make it work. Contrary to old Dr. Hegel, the real is not rational. What happens in the real world of physical stuff can go above and beyond whatever I can do in my head. What happens in your head can only go so far. I find that most of the time it is not far enough. I usually have to take it the rest of the way into the world of actual stuff."

Wally got quiet and seemed to be thinking. What he had said got Gia's mind going. "Another thought, Wally. For some reason, what you said got me thinking about another way that I get my creative mind going. It was what you said about doing something. When I make myself do something boring it often happens. I remember scraping the floor in my bedroom before I painted it. Doing something so boring got my mind to figure out a design thing I've been trying to solve. It has to be something really mindless that occupies your body but lets your mind free to roam. Doing dishes can do it too; that's boring enough. What I say, I know contradicts what you just said about actually doing the creative project. What you say is true enough, but these creative projects are often born in the mind. We then take them from the mind and make them real in physical stuff. It is taking them from the mind and into the world of things that is often the real challenge. Like the philosophers say, matter matters."

Secula caught that ball very quickly. "You got that right, Gia. That is the real challenge. To take an idea out of your head and get it made into something physical, that's what stops people so often. Have you noticed that kids are often so much better at this than grown-ups? As people get older, they often become afraid of actually getting their ideas out where others can see them. So much of this fear comes from adverse, and often undeserved, criticism. I think of how much damaging criticism I've seen in the educational system as I grew up. So many so-called educators are out there quashing young peoples' hopes and dreams by totally irresponsible criticism. Whatever it takes to get past the fear of getting ideas out of your head and made into physical stuff, whether you are doing writing, painting, video, architecture . . . ."

Both Gia and Wally noticed that Secula was again looking at the door. She quickly bounded out of her chair and headed in that direction.

"George, I didn't expect to see you this afternoon." "Am I interrupting something important?" Secula explained to George what was going on, and got a wine glass out for him. George sat down, said hi to Gia and Wally, and got a pack of papers out. He ripped one off and commenced to roll a joint. Wally was carefully watching George roll the joint. George's craftsmanship in that department always impressed him. "What have you and your guys been up to, George?" After George fired up his handiwork, he went on to detail the specifics of a project his gang was working on. The joint got passed around several times and all was quiet for a while.

Out of the quiet a question from Wally surfaced: "George, maybe you have some thoughts on what we've been talking about. You've been around a number of times when Gia channeled Rupert. You have any thoughts or memories about Rupert's comments on creativity?" George exhaled, blowing out a big puff of smoke. He didn't say anything right away. He tapped the fingers of his left hand while staring vacantly out into space. No one was sure if he would say anything. It took quite a while for George to get something out, but he eventually became verbal again.

"Yeah, I'm glad you asked me. I always felt kind of privileged to be able to be there when Gia channeled Rupert. Not everyone gets to be a part of something like that. And I know Gia well enough to know she wasn't fakin' it. Yeah, something Rupert said was very important to me. That one thing was that your creativity doesn't always have to be used just for things that can be called art. Don't get me wrong. I like art. But, like Rupert said, so many people who do creative stuff think creativity can only be applied to stuff called art and the like. Rupert insisted that people use their creativity in their lives , , , use their creativity so that they can have a decent life. I mean, use that creativity to have a decent place to live, enough to eat, not have to live in perpetual anxiety about money. That's what I remember from Rupert."

Secula commented, that was the best thing she heard all afternoon. Gia and Wally nodded and mumbled assent to that. It made them happy to hear that again. All of a sudden from Gia: "oh my God! The roast, I put in a roast before I come over here this afternoon. I hope I didn't burn it." Without saying anything resembling a goodbye, she was up and out the door and across the porch. Wally was mumbling something about the drywall he had to put up as he took leave of Secula and George. Going in the door of their building, Gia turned to Wally. "You want to come up for dinner?" That put a big smile on Wally's face. He just nodded yes. Then Gia said: "you don't have to go home tonight if you don't want to."

www.ingramcontent.com/pod-product-compliance
Lightning Source LLC
Chambersburg PA
CBHW051634170526
45167CB00001B/190